"Recent popes have called upon Catholics to get to know, understand, and respect Islam. All this in order to be better Catholics and partners in the future. Abbot Timothy received a commission from the Abbot President of all Benedictines to bring together people who were already in dialogue and friendship. This book amplifies his journey and the providential spiritual and cultural baggage he brought with him. It is a fascinating trip.

"The book is based on his doctoral thesis about a new way of transcending the apparent chasm between those seeking God by contrasting paths. He proposes a community founded for a dialogue of spiritualties—Muslim and Christian. He kindly breaks his proposal out into thirty-six chapters, with clear titles, and thus the reader can pick and choose between the practical steps and the deeper contemplative traditions in each tradition.

"The challenges to a peaceful future in our world are obvious. Abbot Timothy has essayed an imaginative step forward, based on his own experience and extensive contacts with unobtrusive dialogue groups in both hemispheres."

—Fr. Finbarr Dowling, OSB
Pastor
Marthasville, Missouri

MONASTIC INTERRELIGIOUS DIALOGUE SERIES

No Peace without Prayer

Encouraging Muslims and Christians to Pray Together

A Benedictine Approach

Timothy Wright, OSB

LITURGICAL PRESS

Collegeville, Minnesota

www.litpress.org

Cover design by Ann Blattner.

Scripture texts in this work are taken from the *New Revised Standard Version Bible* © 1989, Division of Christian Education of the National Council of the Churches of Christ in the United States of America. Used with permission. All rights reserved.

Excerpts from the Qurʾan are taken from *The Qurʾan*, translated by M. A. S. Abdel Haleem © 2004 (Oxford University Press). Used with permission.

1	2	3	4	5	6	7	8

Library of Congress Control Number: 2013937791

ISBN: 978-0-8146-3822-4
ISBN: 978-0-8146-3847-7 (ebook)

To my parents who died within an hour and a half of each other in 1968.
To my novice master, Fr. Bruno Donovan, OSB,
who one Rule Class came out with this limerick:

There was a young novice called Wright
Who argued from morning to night
Rebuked one day
He was heard to say
Even if wrong I'm (w)right!

They say I am like my mother in that respect, but I adored my father.

To my two long-suffering elder brothers
Stephen Wright, OSB, at Ampleforth Abbey, UK, and
Ralph Wright, OSB, at St. Louis Abbey, USA,
and our youngest brother Miles, who died in 2012.

And to my Brethren at Ampleforth,
whose patience and good humor I have pushed to the limit.
And to the many others, in all parts of the world,
who have supported me in this work.

Contents

PART 7 Seeking Inspiration and Encouragement: Can Anyone Inspire?

Acknowledgments

Excerpts from the *Catechism of the Catholic Church* © Libreria Editrice Vaticana (London: Geoffrey Chapman, 1994), are used with permission.

Excerpts from *Encyclopaedia of the Qurʾan* (Leiden: Brill, 2008), CD-ROM version, are used with permission.

Excerpts from *In Quest of God: Maneri's Second Collection of 150 Letters* by Sharafuddin Maneri (Gujarat, KT: Mathew SJ Gujarat Sahitya Prakash, 2004), are used with permission.

Excerpts from *Interreligious Dialogue: The Official Teaching of the Catholic Church from the Second Vatican Council to John Paul II*, edited by Francesco Gioia, ©Libreria Editrice Vaticana (Boston: Pauline Books & Media, 2006), are used with permission.

Excerpts from *The Monks of Tibhirine: Faith, Love, and Terror in Algeria* by John W. Kiser (New York: St. Martin's Griffin, 2003), are used with permission.

Excerpts from the Qurʾan are taken from *The Qurʾan*, trans. M. A. S. Abdel Haleem (Oxford: Oxford University Press, 2004), and are used with permission.

Excerpts from *Sharafuddin Maneri* from The Classics of Western Spirituality Series, translated and introduced by Paul Jackson, SJ, Copyright © 1980 by The Missionary Society of St. Paul the Apostle in the State of New York. Paulist Press, Inc., New York/Mahwah, N.J. Used with permission of Paulist Press. www.paulistpress.com

"Every true prayer is prompted by the Holy Spirit,
who is mysteriously present in every human heart."

—John Paul II, *Redemptoris Missio*, 29

"I have a vocation to unite myself to Christ through the one
who lifts up every prayer and who offers to the Father, mysteriously,
this prayer of Islam along with the prayer of every upright heart."

—Christian de Chergé, *A Theology of Hope*, 185

Part 1

The Path to Dialogue: Why Walk It?

1

Introduction

This book presents a small seed, vulnerable and almost invisible, but once sown could bring about real change. The context is our contemporary world, in which billions of our brothers and sisters struggle to survive due to the competitive violence endemic in our social, economic, political, and religious societies. I elaborate with six points:

1. The voices of the world's religions are discordant. Some speak peace, while supporting violence at least tacitly. This is particularly true of those who commit to the revelation of the One God, whether in Sinai, Bethlehem, or Mecca. Rarely do they unite in protest and with little effect when they do. Their spiritual experiences have limited influence, usually only in particular communities, a situation that spells *competition* rather than *collaboration*. Alongside this, the penetration into regions beyond our planetary system has opened up astonishing dimensions, challenging their belief in a Creating God.

2. The human story in all continents is increasingly the story of rivalry, competition, and violence, partly because of the

ever-widening gap between the rich few and the poor majority. Exploitation of the latter by the former is so ingrained that the voice of religion is ignored. Some go further and think religion is a cause. Rarely in human history have people of different races or religions settled down to live peacefully. They have lacked the skills to affirm difference, appreciate goodness, and acknowledge the uniqueness of every human life.

3. Advances in the scientific understanding of how our planet works, from its smallest unit to the incredible dimensions of the universe, have both empowered and disempowered human beings. At the same time, the advances in technology have improved the quality of life for many but pushed a significant percentage of the world into a deprivation made all the worse by the omnipresent, "signs" of affluence, which create an unattainable dream for billions of our fellow human beings and provide a launch pad for violence. The human world has come closer together, more crowded and yet more divided.

4. Advances in medical science have enabled those better off to have greater control over their own health, some considerably more than others, affecting birth rates, increasing life expectation, and limiting the spread of disease. They are able to make more informed decisions about their lives. Serious moral issues have been raised without worldwide agreement about their respective values. At the same time, the poorest billion live from day to day with little hope and less security.

5. Nationalism remains an important element in human identity; fewer dictatorships are able to survive without the consent of their people. Democracies are scrutinized to ensure minorities are respected and local needs satisfied. It often results in less concern for what happens to the impoverished neighbor, whose only voice comes from the humiliating images of deprivation.

6. But the greater materialism in the lifestyle of the rich minority has eroded their idealism by which they gave the needs of the destitute a higher priority. One result is more focus on their own family and friends and less concern for those in greatest need. This is fertile ground for "fundamentalist thinking," which breeds intolerance sometimes manifested in violence.

Taken together, these six points provide a global view—in detail both more complex and more demanding. Technology may unite but cultures separate, people differ in attitudes and personality but are one in their humanity. The deeper the divisions, the greater the risk for the whole. Armed force does not solve problems; it pushes them underground. Exploitation, if not corrected, builds ever greater resentment.

Diversity will remain: religions are an important part of that diversity. They have a tendency to focus on their security in doctrine rather than reach out to each other with the hand of love, cooperation, and mutual affirmation. The world community needs them to start working as partners in the promotion of a spiritual dimension under a threat led by the rich minority. Sadly, many religious people are deeply implicated in the lives of the rich minority.

In this book I present an idea, a seed, infinitesimally small and extremely vulnerable, but from it might grow communities based on greater mutual respect between the world's two largest religions, Islam and Christianity. The seed has, in fact, already been planted. Christians give unique value to their revealed scriptures as the Word of God. Muslims speak of the Qurʾan as God speaking to them.

In the pages that follow I present the case for developing this faith in the Word of God to establish groups of Christians and Muslims dedicated to sharing their respective Divine Word in ways that will enhance the other. This is emphatically not a tussle for converts but a way into greater mutual understanding, under the eye of the God who communicates this Word uniquely to each. This opens up the possibility of creating a new shared memory of that Word. Such can only be a work of prayer—a prayer that can lead to lasting peace, the gift of the One God.

The key phrase is "partnership of trust," arising from a shared belief in the One God, creator of the universe, communicating with revelation to the humans who can read and absorb it, while extending mercy to the repentant. As partners, each acknowledges the other's obligations: first, the right to spread the Word; second, to respect the Word of the other; and third, to open opportunities to develop a sustained dialogue between the Word of God revealed to each, enabling the other to affirm what is consistent and identify what is different. Such dialogue conducted in the presence of the One God is a rich form of prayer. It is not a dialogue for an agreed statement, but a dialogue leading to an ever-deeper understanding of the mystery of God revealed in the inspired Word. This prayer will build mutual respect and be the foundation of a new culture of peace.

This book is an adaptation of a doctoral thesis dedicated to showing the close relationship between the spirituality of the Rule of Benedict and that of Islam. It accounts for the subtitle: *A Benedictine Approach.*

The emphasis on the Word of God opens this presentation to the Christians of every denomination, encouraging them to consider a way to dialogue with their Muslim neighbors. By building trust and respect at the local level, a foundation for a new culture of peace will emerge, showing the wider world that peace is more effective if founded on spirituality.

The case is presented through seven phases, each focusing on a question:

1. Why do it?

2. Will they do it?

3. Can they do it?

4. How far can they get?

5. Is this enough encouragement to do it?

6. How useful is this experience for others?

7. What further inspiration is available?

This quotation is particularly apt:

> The task of leadership is to create an alignment of strengths in ways that make a system's weaknesses irrelevant.[1]

The strength of Islam and Christianity lie in their commitment to God through prayer. Praying together will bring greater strength; what follows is a justification for this optimism.

---

[1] Diana Whitney and Amanda Trosten-Bloom, *The Power of Appreciative Inquiry* (San Francisco: Barrett-Koehler, 2003), Kindle location 215.20, from the foreword by David L. Cooperrider.

Chapter 2

The Author's Journey

The author, a Benedictine monk since 1962, spent twenty-five years teaching and eight years as abbot before being asked by the Benedictine abbot primate, Abbot Notker Wolf,[1] to examine the relationship between followers of the Rule of Benedict and Islam, wherever they live in close proximity. The original thesis would never have materialized but for a number of key moments over the last six years.

The first was a meeting, while he was still abbot, with a young Iranian theologian, Mohammad Ali Shomali,[2] studying for his doctorate at Manchester University. Arising from that meeting

---

[1] Notker Wolf, b. 1940, Bavaria Germany, monk of St. Ottilien, elected Archabbot of St. Ottilien 1977, elected Abbot Primate 2000, reelected 2004 and 2008.

[2] Mohammad Ali Shomali, graduate of the Islamic Seminaries of Qum, has a BA and MA in Western philosophy from the University of Tehran, and a PhD in moral philosophy from the University of Manchester. Publications include _Self-Knowledge_ (1996, 2000), _Ethical Relativism_ (2001), _Shi'a Islam_ (2003), and _Islam Doctrines and Morals_ (2007). He is a cofounder of the Catholic and Shi'a in Dialogue in 2003, 2005, 2007, and 2011.

was an invitation to speak to the monks about Shi'a spirituality and, later, came five conferences titled "Catholics and Shi'a in Dialogue." The papers of three have been published.[3] The first three conferences, sponsored jointly by Ampleforth Abbey and Heythrop College, London University, began with a Heythrop open day and were followed by a three-day conference, the first two at Ampleforth and the third at Worth Abbey.[4] Between the conferences there were visits to Qum, Iran, to continue the dialogue in the Imam Khomeini Institute for Education and Research. Much was learned; friendships were formed: a tangible sign is a carpet in the Ampleforth cloister with the inscription, "To the monks of Ampleforth Abbey from the Imam Khomeini Institute for Education and Research, Qum in prayer and thanksgiving to the God who is Love." The series restarted in September 2011. This time sponsored by Monastic Interreligious Dialogue[5] and taking place at the Benedictine Pontifical College

---

[3] Anthony O'Mahony, Wulstan Peterburs, and Mohammad Ali Shomali, eds., *Catholics and Shi'a in Dialogue: Studies in Theology and Spirituality* (London: Melisende, 2004); Anthony O'Mahony, Wulstan Peterburs, and Mohammad Ali Shomali, eds., *A Catholic-Shi'a Engagement: Faith and Reason in Theory and Practice* (London: Melisende, 2006). Anthony O'Mahony, Timothy Wright, and Mohammad Ali Shomali, eds., *A Catholic-Shi'a Dialogue: Ethics in Today's Society* (London: Melisende, 2008). All reprinted in paperback in 2011.

[4] Ampleforth Abbey, Yorkshire, and Worth Abbey, Sussex, belong to the English Benedictine Congregation, one of the family of Benedictine communities. Their work is mainly pastoral and education.

[5] The organization, founded in 1977, exists to coordinate dialogue between Benedictine communities of men and women and other world religions. Each region has a coordinating committee. The secretary general's task is to encourage, organize, and promote the activities of different communities in different regions, reporting them on the DIM/MID website and arranging publication of relevant books. Fr. William Skudlarek, its current secretary general, is a monk of Saint John's Abbey, Collegeville, Minnesota. In addition to teaching homiletics and liturgy at the School of Theology / Seminary of Saint John's University, he served as an associate of the Maryknoll Mission society in Brazil for five years and later was a member of the Saint John's Abbey's priory in Japan for seven.

of Sant'Anselmo in Rome, it was smaller and more monastic.[6] In September 2012 a fifth conference took place, this time in The International Institute for Islamic Studies, Qum, on the theme of friendship,[7] a follow-up from that of the previous year.

The second moment was the invitation in 2005 from the president of the Pontifical Council for Interreligious Dialogue, Archbishop Michael Fitzgerald,[8] to work for two years with him. While waiting for Vatican approval, the author was asked to research the development of interreligious dialogue since the Second Vatican Council and came to appreciate the huge influence that Pope John Paul II[9] a had on its development, especially with Islam.

The third moment came from the abbot primate, when he, realizing the Vatican role was shorter than anticipated, asked the author to specifically research the Benedictine-Muslim dialogue, a task that required travel.

The fourth moment was an invitation from Mgr. Roderick Strange, rector of the Pontifical Beda College in Rome, to become a spiritual director, carrying with it a modest salary and free board and lodging. The Beda was, at that time, linked to the University

[6] The report is available on DIM/MID web site. Its papers will be published shortly.

[7] The papers of this conference have yet to be published.

[8] Michael Fitzgerald, MAfr (b. 1937). Secretary of the Pontifical Council for Interreligious Dialogue 1992–2002, president 2002–2006, papal nuncio to Egypt 2006–2012, when he retired on reaching his 75th birthday.

[9] Pope John Paul II (1920–2005), b. in Wadowice, Poland, youngest of three children (his sister Olga died before he was born); his mother died when he was nine, his elder brother died in 1932 and his father in 1941, when he was twenty-one. University studies interrupted by WWII, when he worked for four years in a quarry, later in a chemical factory, at same time studying privately for priesthood, ordained in 1946. Doctorate in Rome completed in 1948; 1948 worked in parishes and with university students in Krakow, 1958 auxiliary bishop of Krakow, succeeded in 1964 and made cardinal in 1967. Took part in Second Vatican Council and elected pope in 1978, 264th Successor of St. Peter, lasted twenty-seven years (one of the longest reigns). Particularly noted for his energy in promoting dialogue, not least with Islam. Died in Rome in 2005.

of Lampeter for its degrees in theology. It became the natural academic "home" for his research. Alongside that research, the author taught the Islam course for the students as part of their BD/BTh degree.

The fifth moment was a meeting of the European Committee for Monastic Interreligious Dialogue in the Trappist Monastery of Midelt, Morocco. There, the two surviving monks from the community of Tibhirine, Algeria, spoke about their experiences, providing an insight into how monastic life can be lived in a Muslim country. It led him to the writings of Christian de Chergé[10] and visits, first in 2008 to Tibhirine and a second in 2011 to its motherhouse, Notre Dame d'Aiguebelle, near Montélimar, France, where he had useful meetings with members of the community, some of whom had once been part of the Tibhirine community.

The sixth moment comprised a series of travels to Benedictine/Trappist communities of men and women living alongside Muslim communities, large and small, representative enough of their diversity, difficulties, and opportunities. It also included visits to Coptic monasteries in Egypt and Antonine monasteries in Lebanon arranged through mutual friends. Other, equally valuable trips were made to monasteries in different parts of the world—in Asia: Indonesia, Philippines, Bangladesh, and India—in Africa: Senegal, Burkina Faso, Ghana, Nigeria, Togo, Cameroon, Kenya, and Tanzania. The picture was completed by visits to monasteries in Europe, USA, Canada, Chile, and Australia.

---

[10] Christian de Chergé (1937–96). From 1939 he spent his early years in Algeria, which inspired a love for the country, later reinforced during his National Service in the French army during Algeria's War of Independence. After completing his studies in the Séminaire des Carmes in Paris, he was ordained priest in 1964, served as chaplain to the school of Sacré-Coeur de Montmartre. In 1969 he joined the Trappist community of Tibhirine and made his novitiate at Aiguebelle. After completing his studies at the Pontifical Institute for the Study of Arabic and Islam in Rome, he returned to Tibhirine. He was elected prior in 1984 and reelected in 1990.

The seventh moment was the positive effect of five visits to Singapore, where meetings with senior members of Muslim communities resulted in ever deeper friendship and appreciation, kindly organized by Dominic Davies, an alumnus of Ampleforth. Their welcome has been particularly warm. Muslim scholars and Imams, alongside Catholic priests, religious sisters, and laypeople, provided many opportunities for dialogue—both challenging and informative. Over the years I have been particularly grateful for the help of the Islamic Religious Council of Singapore and three Muslim friends, Imam Syed Hassan Bin Mohamed Alattas of the Ba'alwi Mosque, Amurali Jumabhoy, and Syed Farid Alatas, Head of Malay Studies at the National University of Singapore.

The eighth moment was an invitation from the former Archbishop of Canterbury Rowan Williams[11] to attend two of his Building Bridges Seminars, one in Rome (2009) and the other in Qatar (2011). Friendships formed in these meetings have endured; they provided fine examples of best practice in dialogue with Islam.

The ninth moment has been the friendship, for over thirty years, with José-Manuel Eguirgurn, the founder of the Manquehue Apostolic Movement in Chile, a community of lay Benedictine Oblates, whose spirituality is founded on *lectio divina*, the Divine Office, and the Rule of Benedict. His community has opened up new ways of being Benedictine.

The tenth moment, in 2006, was the visit to the new Benedictine community in Rostrevor, Ireland—a community dedicated specifically to dialogue between Protestants and Catholics.

---

[11] Rowan Williams (1950–), b. Swansea, Clare College Cambridge, BA (1971), MA (1975), DPhil Oxford 1975, deacon 1977, priest 1978. From 1977 to 1980, Tutor Westcott House, Cambridge. From 1980 to 1983 Honorary Curate, Chesterton St. George, Ely, 1980–86 Lecturer in Divinity, Cambridge, 1984–86, Chaplain, Clare College, Cambridge. From 1986 to 1992 Canon Residentiary, Christ Church, Oxford, 1986–92 Lady Margaret Professor of Divinity, Oxford, 1989 DD, 1990 Fellow, British Academy. From 1992 to 2000, bishop of Monmouth, 1999–2000, archbishop of Wales, 2000–2002, 2002–2013 archbishop of Canterbury.

The eleventh moment, in 2009, was a visit to Chicago where Dr. Scott Alexander provided an inspiring few days with his Muslim contacts and spoke about his work in the Catholic Theological Union.

The twelfth moment came on that same trip, when he visited Benedictine University, Lisle, IL, where 25 percent of the student body is Muslim. On that occasion, President Dr. William Carroll shared his vision. This developed with the particular help of Abbot President Hugh Anderson and Abbot Austin Murphy into an appointment to the faculty beginning in August of 2013.

The thirteenth moment, in 2011, was a session of shared *lectio divina* with a few monks of the Trappist Abbey of Notre Dame de Kotaba, Cameroon, with local Muslim theologians.

The fourteenth moment came in 2008 when the author was invited to lead a workshop at the Congress of Abbots in Rome on Islam. Fourteen of the 250 participants attended; this minimal response was repeated in 2010 when a questionnaire from the primate's office to the many hundreds of male and female communities following the Rule of Benedict yielded a mere seventy replies. Interestingly, less than ten had a member of the community with a qualification in Islam. Few had any dialogue of spirituality with members of their local Muslim communities; clearly it is still a low priority for the majority of male Benedictine communities. At the 2012 Congress of Abbots an even smaller number attended the workshop on Islam, but those who did were clearly interested in the project.

The fifteenth moment came with the projection that within a few decades Islam would overtake Christianity as the world's largest religious group. This may not sound alarm bells in many Benedictine cloisters, but a more marked presence of Islam in those places where an aggressive Muslim cell already exists will bring new challenges to Christians.

The sixteenth moment was the challenge of the abbot general of the Trappists, Bernardo Olivera, at the funeral of the Tibhirine monks, when he said, "they showed that we must enter into the world of others, be that 'other' a Christian or a

Muslim. If 'the other' does not exist there can be no love of 'the other.' "[12]

The seventeenth moment was the submission of the thesis for a PhD in March 2012. The author is particularly grateful to Fr. Kevin Alban, OCarm; Fr. Finbarr Dowling, OSB; Sr. Gertrude Feick, OSB (who also checked the draft of this book); Mohammad Ali Shomali; Asma Asfaruddin; and Fr. Bonaventure Knollys, OSB, for their comments on drafts prior to submission and particularly to the author's supervisor, Dr. Augustine Casiday, for his support prior to submission and through the viva process that followed. The PhD was awarded by the University of Wales in September 2012, with encouragement to seek publication.

The eighteenth moment brought a new direction from the abbot primate: to find ways of presenting the results of the thesis to Benedictine communities of men and women. Early discussions with Benedictine women in communities at Queen of Angels Monastery, Mount Angel, Oregon, and Saint Benedict's Monastery, St. Joseph, Minnesota (where Sr. Hélène Mercier was particularly helpful in arranging meetings), showed great enthusiasm.

The nineteenth moment came when Liturgical Press, Collegeville, MN, agreed to accept an edited version of the thesis for publication as part of their Series on Monastic Interreligious Dialogue. Hans Christoffersen and his team have been particularly supportive in the transformation of the text for publication.

These nineteen moments provide the background for this book. There are important questions still to be answered: Is it possible to create such a dialogue? Would there be support from authorities, Muslim and Christian? This book is more a journey into whether it is possible, not a blueprint to follow. Widespread traveling in the Muslim world has shown the great diversity in their communities, just as there is among Christians. This proposed dialogue is but a framework, adaptable to the widely

---

[12] John W. Kiser, *The Monks of Tibhirine: Faith, Love, and Terror in Algeria* (New York: St. Martin's Griffin, 2003), 4, quoting from his address at the funeral of the seven monks.

differing situations in which Muslims and Christians live side by side.

Once begun, members of such communities would soon realize they shared not just a similar understanding of their Inspired Scriptures but with careful listening will be enriched by the insights of the other. In this way, many will be strengthened in their desire to live each moment of every day in the presence of God, the source of true peace.

Chapter **3**

A Brief Outline of Muslim and Benedictine Spiritualities

Introduction

A short summary of the two spiritualities will help readers to orientate themselves in relation to the other in this dialogue of spirituality. I have chosen the Benedictine way as representative of a Christian spirituality because it relates to all areas of daily life, as the Muslim spirituality does. This similarity is important for development of a dialogue of spirituality.

In the narrow sense, the word "spirituality" refers to the content and style of prayer practiced and lived by believers, Christian or Muslim.

Within the Christian world there is diversity: each of the families has its distinctive approach, with many elements shared. The Benedictine tradition is particularly suited because its spirituality is largely based on the "word of God," the most commonly shared element across the different denominations. This they inherited from the earliest monks living in the Arabian desert. Benedict's Rule was written some 130 years before the first version of the Qurʾan, making them almost contemporaneous, an important aid for comparison.

A Christian Spirituality of the Word: The Benedictine Experience[1]

Although there is one Rule of Benedict, there are many ways of living it, as shown by the many "styles" of Benedictine spirituality, whether as a committed Benedictine male or female or as a layperson using it as a guide. Today the Rule is translated into many languages including several English versions, of which two are used here.[2]

---

[1] Benedict of Nursia lived in Rome in the late fifth and early sixth centuries CE, before the time of the Prophet. Initially his influence on the monastic movement was minimal. He used common sense, followed the monastic norm of the time, and wrote a rule for his community at Monte Cassino, south of Rome, who had asked him to be their superior on the evidence of his holiness in a cave at Subiaco, some fifty miles away, whence he had come having abandoned study in corrupt Rome. Four centuries later, this Rule was officially made normative in the European lands under the then emperor. Thus was born the movement of the Black Monks of Benedict, black because of the color of the monastic habit, later modified by a twelfth-century reform group known as Cistercians (centuries later a group broke away from them and became known as Trappists—after La Trappe, the place where they began). While the Benedictine tradition has male and female communities both of apostolic work (such as parishes, schools, universities, hospitals, and retreat centers) and cloistered or contemplative work (such as writing, printing, and farming within the cloister), the Cistercian tradition normally has only the latter. The Rule was composed by Benedict when abbot, borrowing much from existing monastic rules, as shown by the patchwork of quotations in his Rule.

[2] The two translations used in this book are RB 1980, *Rule of Saint Benedict 1980*, ed. Timothy Fry (Collegeville, MN: Liturgical Press, 1981), and NPB, *Saint Benedict's Rule*, trans. Abbot Patrick Barry (York: Ampleforth Abbey Press, 1997). Translations will be noted with either RB 1980 or NPB.

Two quotations illustrate this: one affirms that the Benedictine community's "most evident characteristic is that it is a family,"[3] quoting the Rule's advice to the novice to live "the directions that come from your loving Father" (RB Prol. 1),[4] while the other asks whether the Benedictine Rule has a "spiritual node."[5] For many, the language of family is more attractive, recognizing the uniqueness of each Benedictine community. A "spiritual node" suggests a single reality that distinguishes Benedictines from everyone else and is a more difficult concept to define.

Within the context of family, the aspirant, whether committed by vow or attached as oblate, male or female, comes to learn from the older Benedictines, and, as Basil Hume[6] put it, "everything you do and everything that happens to you must be seen as an opportunity to deepen your love of God; that everything you do and everything that happens to you is to be enjoyed, or suffered, whichever it may be, with and through Christ."[7]

Benedictine life focuses on Christ; not Christ "out there" but Christ as the Benedictine model for living. It requires a great change of attitude. The self-confident candidate enthusiastically knocking at the door has to learn to become the humble novice, aware he or she has little to give and much to absorb, especially learning to accept whatever the Superior asks, seen not just as

[3] Abbot Herbert Byrne, "Saint Benedict and His Spirit" in *Ampleforth and Its Origins*, ed. Justin McCann and Columba Cary-Elwes (London: Burns Oates and Washbourne, 1952), 1–16, here at 8 .

[4] All subsequent quotations from the Rule will be from *Saint Benedict's Rule*, trans. Patrick Barry (York: Ampleforth Abbey, 1997).

[5] Terence Kardong, "Benedictine Spirituality," in *The New SCM Dictionary of Christian Spirituality*, ed. Philip Sheldrake (London: SCM, 2005), 148–50, here at 148.

[6] Cardinal Basil Hume, OSB (1923–99), History MA, Oxford, STL Fribourg. Housemaster, games coach, head of the language department at Ampleforth College. Abbot 1963–76. In 1976 he was nominated archbishop of Westminster and became a cardinal later that same year. *Searching for God* was a compilation of his conferences to the community given while he was abbot. Subsequently he wrote several books.

[7] Basil Hume, *Searching for God* (London: Hodder and Stoughton, 1977), 26.

the will of an individual, but the will of Christ expressed through the Superior. Through the disciplines of self-denial Christ is discovered more as a loving parent, enabling each to understand that "to be a son or daughter of God is to be reborn again and again."[8] To achieve this "high standard in monastic life we all depend on mutual encouragement and example."[9]

At the heart of monastic life is the daily rhythm of formal prayer. The Rule devotes thirteen chapters (RB 8–20) to outlining its structure, organization, and priority. Eight times the community comes to pray the Divine Office. They gather once during the hours of darkness (called vigils if celebrated before midnight or Matins if celebrated after midnight) and seven times during the day—Lauds (at dawn) followed by four "Little Hours": Prime, Terce, Sext, and None (called *little* because they are short and may be celebrated while at work). At the Second Vatican Council, Prime was suppressed, as it was an unnecessary duplication of the office at daybreak. The others are celebrated at 0900, 1200, and 1500 hours. At dusk, Vespers is celebrated and later the final Office of Compline before all retire to bed. These offices are largely composed of psalms and readings taken from the Inspired Scriptures. Benedict is firm: "Any monastic community which chants less than the full psalter with the usual canticles each week shows clearly that it is too indolent in the devotion of its service to God. After all, we read that our predecessors had the energy to fulfill in one single day what we in our lukewarm devotion only aspire to complete in a whole week" (RB 18.6). By constant repetition the psalms are learned by heart and become the agent for "a constant and reverent sense of the presence of God."[10] Enveloping the Benedictine is the silence of recollection, whose "ultimate aim is interior silence, when we find a deep centre within ourselves which is always open to God."[11]

---

[8] Ibid.

[9] Ibid., 24.

[10] Abbot Herbert Byrne, "Saint Benedict and His Spirit," 13.

[11] Cyprian Smith, *The Path of Life* (York: Ampleforth Abbey Press, 1995), 72. Cyprian Smith, after a degree in French language and literature at Manchester

An essential feature of Benedictine life is daily *lectio divina*, "when we work with God's word so that it may work inside us, transforming our behavior, our ideas, our life."[12] Benedict urges all to spend several hours a day pondering the Word of God, read by one who has "the ability to fulfill this role in a way which is helpful to others" (RB 47.3). Living before printed books, Benedict intended the Word of God to be memorized and repeated, especially during manual labor; no one should escape from the challenge and affirmation from the Word of God. Today with printing and universal literacy, communities normally allow three periods of about thirty minutes each, for, respectively, *lectio divina*, contemplative prayer, and the reading of spiritual books.

The Benedictine monastery is bounded by an enclosure, the private space where each can undertake manual work, be recollected, take exercise, read, or relax. Some Benedictine communities find all their needs within an enclosure; others are involved in work that takes them out of the enclosure to parishes, schools, hospitals, and other works.

A priority for the community is care for the elderly, sick, infirm, and others with special needs. Visitors are treated with great respect. Benedict writes: "the care of those who are sick in the community is an absolute priority which must rank before every other requirement, so that there may be no doubt that it is Christ who is truly served in them. . . . Any guest who happens to arrive at the monastery should be received just as we would receive Christ himself" (RB 36.1; 53.1). The community is also of service to its local community, where it can sell its goods at a price "somewhat lower than the price demanded by other workshops" (RB 57.2), provide employment, and be a center of prayer.

At its heart, Benedictine life is confirmed by vows taken after a period of formation, for three years at the end of the novitiate,

---

University, lecturing on French poetry at Hull University, and five years teaching English in Brazil, became a monk at Ampleforth Abbey. He has written on Meister Echkart. *The Path of Life* is the fruit of six years as a novice master.

[12] Denis Huerre, *Letters to My Brothers and Sisters* (Collegeville, MN: Liturgical Press, 1994), 19. See also the Rule, chapters 47–49.

and for life after that. Benedictine vows differ from those taken by other Christian religious men and women: not poverty, chastity, and obedience, but obedience, conversion of life, and stability. On obedience, Cyprian Smith writes, "the essence of obedience is putting others before myself. This means that we obey everyone,"[13] but also those in authority, "because obedience given to superiors is an offering to God" (RB 5.4). Willing acceptance of a command requires an inner freedom, empowering the subject to find God even in the most unlikely request. The vow of stability is, in Columba Stewart's words,[14] "about shared history and affections: it is inherently particular . . . the life does not work unless one feels at home in a particular community";[15] the members of the community become in a real sense one's family. The third vow, conversion of life, includes chastity and poverty but goes further, because at its heart is the special Benedictine gift, as Basil Hume expressed it, of discovering "whether our heart is set on God or whether we are preoccupied with self."[16] The application to take vows is put to vote in the community chapter. Once the junior has taken solemn vows, he or she becomes a member of the chapter. Transfer to another community is possible only in exceptional circumstances.

Benedictine life, though simple in style, now requires skills for which formal training may be needed. Farming, retreat centers, hospitality, shops, food, schools, colleges, seminaries, art, crafts, music, hospitals, clinics, and specialist training schools all require appropriate professional skills. But there is another point: the Benedictine is not defined by the work done but by the life lived. The work is a means by which the community can

[13] Cyprian Smith, *The Path of Life*, 43.

[14] Columba Stewart, Benedictine monk of Saint John's Abbey, Collegeville, MN, who teaches monastic studies at Saint John's University. Publications include *World of the Desert Fathers*, *Working the Earth of the Heart*, and *Cassian the Monk*.

[15] Columba Stewart, *Prayer and Community: The Benedictine Tradition* (London: Darton, Longman & Todd, 1998), 72.

[16] Basil Hume, *Searching for God*, 87.

support itself financially. More important is the family spirit, dedication to God, and commitment to the Rule.

Many Benedictines live on the hinge between the cloister of separation and involvement through work in the world. None are so detached as to be uninformed about events outside, but they are careful not to be so preoccupied with worldly issues as to be distracted from their main focus: an ever-deeper union in love with God.

Apart from their formal duties, the community has time for recreation, sharing with each other the issues of the day, building mutual support, and enjoying some relaxed entertainment, usually after meals.

Benedict's legislation for the Eucharist assumed a Sunday celebration and perhaps occasionally during the week. Since his time this has changed: for the last millennium Benedictines usually have a daily Eucharist. Not all male Benedictines become priests; in recent years greater emphasis has been put on Divine Office, *lectio divina*, and private prayer.

Benedictine spirituality arises from a life lived in one place. In its enclosure Benedict aimed to establish "a school for the Lord's service. In the guidance we lay down to achieve this, we hope to impose nothing harsh or burdensome" (RB Prol. 8). At this school the members will be transformed into Christ, not without some challenge, failure, and pain—all necessary for growth into intimacy with God. Alongside this each community continues to serve its local community, Christian and other, in ways appropriate to its monastic life and their needs. It is significant that today there are twice as many oblate laymen and -women attached to a Benedictine community and living the spirituality of the Rule in their daily life, mainly in families, as there are men and women vowed in the sense that Benedict outlined in his Rule.

Muslim Spirituality

It is significant that the word "spirituality" is hardly used in Muslim literature—an indication both of the distinctiveness of their approach to the relationship with God, described by Reza Shah-Kazemi,[17] "in principle, remembrance is understood as the consciousness of the divine reality. . . . Remembrance is also an activity, an all-embracing contemplative practice."[18]

In contrast to Benedictine spirituality, Muslim spirituality is a growing relationship with God achieved by living this central obligation of Islam "to remember God," openly, every day, allowing it to provide the framework in which to deal with unpredictability, challenge, and temptation. It is not without significance that one commentator has called Islam a monastic spirituality lived in the ordinary community of daily life.

The first and fundamental element in Muslim spirituality is the confession of faith in Allah, the One God. From that faith stems the whole meaning of life: God is Creator, Sustainer, the One who forgives, and the One who punishes the unrepentant. God lives to love and, in that way, invites a relationship of obedience, acceptance, and hope for the future. As one writer has put it, "to remember God is to have God in one's heart in such a way that one never forgets Him."[19] Hence, Allah is revered as only God can be, and significantly is remembered day and night, every moment of conscious life. The relationship matures through the repetition of one of the Names, not only at the times of prayer but in the recollection "if God wills," which accompanies every utterance. At the heart of Muslim faith is "God

[17] Reza Shah-Kazemi studied international relations and politics at Sussex and Exeter Universities before obtaining his PhD in comparative religion from the University of Kent in 1994. He has authored several works, including *Spiritual Quest: Reflections on Qur'anic Prayer According to the Teachings of Imam 'Ali* (London: I. B. Tauris, 2011); formerly a consultant to the Institute for Policy Research in Kuala Lumpur, Malaysia, now attached to the Institute of Ismaili Studies, London.

[18] Reza Shah-Kazemi, "The Principle and the Practice of the Remembrance of God: An Islamic Perspective," in *Spiritual Message of Islam*, ed. Mohammad Ali Shomali (London: Institute of Islamic Studies, 2010), 73–90, here at 73.

[19] Mohammad Fanaei Eshkevari, "Reflections of Prayer: A Muslim Perspective," in *Spiritual Message of Islam*, ed. Mohammad Ali Shomali, 103–12, here at 103.

knows everything you do openly and everything you conceal" (Qurʾan 24:29).[20]

Muslim prayer has four aspects: first, "praise of the beauty and magnificence of God"[21] by recalling blessings received and honoring the magnificence of God; second, thanksgiving for all that has been received from God, a role that can never been fully achieved; third, prayer for forgiveness, saying, "I ask forgiveness from God and turn repentant to Him";[22] and, fourth, the prayer of petition, a typical formula, "Our Lord, give us good in this world and in the Hereafter, and protect us from the torment of the Fire" (Qurʾan 2:201).

The key figure in Muslim spiritual life is the Prophet Muhammad, to whom God revealed the teachings, later enshrined in the Qurʾan, uniquely holy in its Arabic form, and in the Hadith Qudsī, which are words of God recorded by the Prophet but not included in the Qurʾan. These revelations provide instruction on the priority and methods of prayer.

Formal prayer is announced by the call of the muezzin five times a day (dawn, noon, afternoon, evening, and night) from the minaret of the mosque. Many then make their way to the mosque, while others pray at home or at work. Wherever prayer is said, the ritual gestures are the same, accompanied by words learned by heart, especially the first Surah of the Qurʾan, sometimes called "the Muslim Our Father": "In the name of God, the Lord of Mercy, the Giver of mercy! Praise belongs to God, Lord of the Worlds, the Lord of Mercy, the Giver of Mercy, Master of the Day of Judgment. It is You we worship; it is You we ask for help. Guide us to the straight path; the path of those You have blessed, those who incur no anger and who have not gone astray" (Qurʾan 1:1-7).

---

[20] *The Qurʾan*, trans. M. A. S. Abdel Haleem (Oxford: Oxford University Press, 2008). All subsequent quotations from the Qurʾan are from this edition.

[21] Mohammad Fanaei Eshkevari, "Reflections of Prayer: A Muslim Perspective," in *Spiritual Message of Islam*, ed. Mohammad Ali Shomali, 104.

[22] Ibid., 105.

Before formal prayers each has to be purified: facilities are provided at each mosque. The daily rhythm of ritual prayer is a reminder to believers of the central role of God in their lives; it should never be forgotten: "If My servants ask you about Me, I am near. I respond to those who call Me, so let them respond to Me, and believe in Me" (Qur'an 2:186).

This prayer is organized in such a way that "sincerity, monotheism, submission and worshipping God would be exhibited and witnessed."[23] One hadith states, "Whenever a servant [of God] performs a congregational prayer and then asks God for a favor, God is embarrassed to let him leave that place without his request being granted."[24]

The Friday noon prayer is also the moment the community meets. The prayer is supplemented with longer readings from the Qur'an, a sermon from the Imam, and ends with a greeting of peace. Members usually stay to talk, share experiences, and offer support to charities.

Private prayer is encouraged to strengthen the relationship with God, and the advice given is that "the more this relation is kept away from the eyes of others the purer his intentions can become."[25]

The Muslim year follows the lunar calendar, resulting in the annual cycle of festivals occurring eleven days earlier each year. There are five important feasts. First, the first day of the first month recalling the Hijra, when Muhammad and his companions left Mecca for Medina in 622 CE; second, the twelfth day of the third month commemorating the birth of Muhammad; third, the ninth month, Ramadan, "You who believe, fasting is prescribed for you, as it was prescribed for those before you, so that you may be mindful of God" (Qur'an 2:183–185). So, during this month, all fast

---

[23] Mahnaz Heydarpoor, "A Shi'ite Perspective on Public Prayer," *Monks and Muslims: Monastic and Shi'a Spirituality in Dialogue*, eds. Mohammad Ali Shomali and William Skudlarek (Collegeville MN: Liturgical Press, 2012), 96–106.

[24] Ibid.

[25] Ibid.

from the moment of first light until sunset to commemorate the time when the Qurʾan was revealed. At the same time it reminds all of the importance of charitable giving. Fourth, the festival of breaking the fast, "Id al-Fitr," marking the end of the fast on the first day of the tenth month; and fifth, the tenth day of the twelfth month, "Dhu-l-Hijja," the month of pilgrimage, celebrating the sacrifice of the sheep and other animals at Mina, outside Mecca, commemorating Abraham's sacrifice of the ram in place of his son.

Many fulfill this alongside their "once-in-a-lifetime obligation" (if at all practical) to go to Mecca on pilgrimage. Once there, all wear ritual clothing and start their pilgrimage with prayer while walking round the Ka'ba seven times and then running seven times between the two sacred pillars of Safa and Marwa while remembering Hagar's desperate search for water, going to seek forgiveness of sins at the rocky heights in the center of the Plain of Arafat, and returning to repeat the prayer round the Ka'ba before, finally, throwing stones at a pillar in Mina, symbolizing their rejection of the devil's temptations. Finally, if practical, pilgrims will go to pray at the tomb of Muhammad in Medina.

In addition to these spiritual activities, Muslims are required to pay *zakat*, a tithe, encouraged in the Qurʾan: "If you give charity openly, it is good, but if you keep it secret and give to the needy in private, that is better for you, and it will atone for some of your bad deeds" (Qurʾan 2:271). And later the Qurʾan quotes the righteous saying, "We feed you for the sake of God alone: We seek neither recompense nor thanks from you. We fear the Day of our Lord" (Qurʾan 76:9-10).

Alongside these personal and communal obligations, all Muslims know their obligation to welcome each visitor to their house as the arrival of God: all are ready to offer generous hospitality, "be good . . . to the needy, to neighbors near and far, to travelers in need, and to your slaves" (Qurʾan 4:36).

This framework of prayer, faith-filled living, and generosity to the visitor, is based not just on reading the Qurʾan or the teachings of the Imams, it is a way of life that penetrates to the heart of the family, where the faith is born and nurtured. This tribute of one to her mother, expresses it well:

From my mother I learned a love of Allah or God . . . my moth-er's relationship with God was all heart. She prayed regularly and with six children, the ritual was also one of deep love. I watched her bend to God in humility. She taught me also that our heart is a gift given to serve others. She gave us the reality that praying is the foundation, and that serving others is our duty as a Muslim, the branches that emanate from our faith. I saw her take in one homeless person after another, build a shelter for women.[26]

This shows one of the attractive features of Islam: simplicity, both in its spirituality and in its way of life, both of which are easily passed from generation to generation.

Final Comment

Both Muslim and Christian share a deep awareness of God present in all aspects of daily life. By faith they build trust in God revealed through Inspired Scriptures, made present through recited prayers, obliging selfless service to family and visitors, sensitive to the needs of others, each guiding to the divine will in moments of trial. Not one second of daily living for Muslim or Christian will count as virtue unless it is fully lived in the presence of God, with a love that is a gift from God and di-rected toward others. Both Muslim and Christian depend on disciplined formation in prayer, enabling each to value truth, honesty, courage, faith, generosity, common sense, and humor as essential in daily life, inspired with a vision of a future, fulfilled in God, Giver of Risen Life. Taken together, Christian and Mus-lim spiritualities seem well suited to a dialogue of spirituality.

[26] Professor Najeeba Syeed-Miller, JD, teaches interreligious education at Claremont School of Theology. She has extensive experience in mediat-ing conflicts among communities of ethnic and religious diversity and has won awards for her peacemaking and public interest work. See http://muslimvoices.org/author/nsyeed.

4

The Healing of Negative Memories

Introduction

Before this presentation begins there is one important point the reader has to acknowledge: the majority of Christians and Muslims will have negative memories of the other. This is partly a historic legacy and partly a contemporary reality. These refer either to stories handed down from one generation to another or to current opinions—some accurate and others the product of misrepresentation, prejudice, or ignorance.

This means a process of healing is essential if a dialogue of spirituality is to take place. Even when participants approach with positive intentions, some may still carry, recognized or not, negative memories. So before dialogue, these negative memories should be identified and a process of healing established. This process can be then used in the future when other issues arise, allowing the process of healing to be effective, strengthening the community. In serious matters this process may need professional advice.

Role of the Word

One element of the healing process will be engaging with the Word of God, the spiritual healer for people of faith. M. Robert Mulholland recognizes the living Word as both alive in the memory and able to discern "the thoughts and intentions of our hearts and addresses us at the points of our brokenness."[1] Such encouragement invites honesty and perhaps recognition that memories are not only from personal experience but also inherited from family, society, or religion. In such cases only God can bring "our lives into the wholeness of that new mode of being,"[2] because it is through faith that each finds conversion and healing, achieved by sharing Inspired Scriptures, which, as Charles Elliott explains, describe the role of God as healer of "the destructive memories that are incorporated or instantiated in the oppressive structures of our world."[3] The healing process requires an admission of guilt and assurance of forgiveness in the sure understanding that the One God is a God of mercy and forgiveness. Once forgiveness has happened, quoting Paul Ricoeur,[4] "memory is liberated for great projects. Forgiveness gives memory a future,"[5] words that

---

[1] M. Robert Mulholland, *Shaped by the Word: The Power of Scripture in Spiritual Formation* (Nashville: Upper Room Books, 2001), 45. M. Robert Mulholland Jr. (ThD, Harvard) is professor of New Testament at Asbury Theological Seminary in Wilmore, Kentucky. He is the author of several books, including *Shaped by the Word* (Upper Room), *Revelation* (Zondervan), and the landmark spiritual formation book *Invitation to a Journey* (IVP).

[2] Ibid.

[3] Charles Elliott, *Memory and Salvation* (London: Darton, Longman & Todd, 1995), 47. Charles Elliott, dean of Trinity Hall, Cambridge, author of several books, including *Praying the Kingdom* (DLT) and *Memory and Salvation* (DLT). Winner of the 1985 Collins Religious Book Award.

[4] Paul Ricoeur (1913–2005), philosopher: BA 1933, University of Rennes; 1948–56 Strasbourg University; 1956–65 Sorbonne University; 1965–70 University of Paris, Nanterre; 1970–85 University of Chicago.

[5] Paul Ricoeur, "Memory—History—Forgetting," in *The Collective Memory Reader*, ed. Jeffrey Olick, Vered Vinitzky-Seroussi, and Daniel Levy (Oxford: Oxford University Press, 2011), 474–80, here at 480.

open the way, in a spirit of humility before the Inspired Word, for participants to find healing.

The Healing Process

Healing processes require time and take place within an agreed framework. Given the healing power of the Word of God, participants will engage actively until, in Mulholland's words, "our word is shaped by the Word in our inner being (memory); our life in the world will be shaped according to that same Word. Our word will become the Word God speaks us forth to be *in the lives of others*."[6] Each will learn to trust the healing power of the Word, and the community will grow stronger from that healing process.

Victims of abuse, misrepresentation, injustice, and prejudice may need access to specialists. One element of the healing process will be for all to listen to the victim's account of the abuse. All come to know the story, all can share the pain and become part of the healing process. They come to realize, as Elliott puts it, "Memories—real life memories—are not emotionally flat or homogeneous: each has its own affect and that helps determine the role it plays in our inner world."[7]

Miroslav Volf describes three demanding steps "toward redeeming memories of wrongs suffered—'remember truthfully!', 'remember therapeutically!' and 'learn from the past!'"[8] As a victim himself, he admits this only goes so far; it does not guarantee lasting healing.

---

[6] M. Robert Mulholland, *Shaped by the Word*, 46. Author's italics.

[7] Charles Elliott, *Memory and Salvation*, 113.

[8] Miroslav Volf, *The End of Memory: Remembering Rightly in a Violent World* (Grand Rapids, MI: Eerdmans, 2006), Kindle edition, location 1017. Miroslav Volf (b. 1956 in Croatia) attended Osijek Evangelical-Theological Faculty (BA); Fuller Theological Seminary, Pasadena, California (MA); and Tübingen University (PhD). Currently Henry B. Wright Professor of Theology at Yale University. Publications include: *Exclusion and Embrace* (1996), *The End of Memory* (2006), and *Allah: A Christian Perspective* (2011).

If the victim can, "discover a freedom from the past and its memories, and an openness to the future and its possibilities,"[9] then there is a possibility of finding forgiveness and reconciliation, because, as Gerald May puts it, all must "try to be open to it [God's presence], but we cannot control it."[10] Within a context of strong mutual love, forgiveness becomes possible and negative memories may enjoy some healing.

But that may not be so for those whose memories are particularly painful. It is not clear how such a wounded memory can sufficiently overcome the trauma, to face a new future, in which the wrongs suffered play a reduced role. Even after a process of reconciliation, the memory may still be alive with what happened, for "every act of reconciliation, incomplete as it mostly is in this world, stretches itself toward completion."[11] Victims may never forget the wound, but they can learn to "remember wrongs rightly when memory serves reconciliation."[12] This is unlikely to be successful, however, if the memory is full of pain.

On the spiritual level, Christians and Muslims will be successful in mutual reconciliation when God is active in their hearts, especially those with negative memories of the other. The divine gift of healing works best when it is accompanied by a community committed to the task, though sometimes it takes longer.

On another level, Miroslav Volf[13] writes of the negative memory arising from the violence of one religion against another; the battles between Muslim and Christian have left deep scars, as do memories of forced conversion. The Qur'an and the Bible encourage faith as a free commitment: all have the right to adopt or abandon or change faith, but not all respect it, either today or in the past. Its absence is not a block to dialogue, but a community focused on healing memory will recognize the inconsistency.

---

[9] Charles Elliott, *Memory and Salvation*, 243.

[10] Gerald May, *Addiction and Grace* (New York: HarperOne, 2007), Kindle edition, location 327–36.

[11] Miroslav Volf, *The End of Memory*, Kindle edition, location 1618.

[12] Ibid., location 1620.

[13] Ibid.

Within this context access to Inspired Scriptures will act as a reminder that God is both healer and forgiver.

If some participants are unsympathetic to this process, then it might be that they are, as Gerald May puts it, addicted to a religious system, which, "like addiction to anything else, brings slavery, not freedom."[14] Such persons are unlikely to be suitable for a community in dialogue.

Why Walk It?

There is a desire for peace from every quarter of the globe. That is what people want. It is possible for Muslims and Christians to engage at the level of their most cherished desires, their relationship with God, from whom alone the gift of lasting peace can come.

---

[14] Gerald May, *Addiction and Grace*, 1532–39.

Part 2

Finding a Way through Disputed Issues: Will They Do It?

5

Christians and Muslims in a Dialogue of Spirituality

In a preliterate world, the majority of the early followers of the Rule of Benedict were required to learn, as Columba Cary-Elwes[1] states, "by heart those parts [of Scripture] that had struck home. These parts . . . [were] garnered in the storehouse of the memory to provide the food for the spirit during the rest of the day."[2] Their memories were filled with the events and sayings of the Bible, which was their guide and inspiration. Regular repetition lies at the heart of this spirituality and leads

---

[1] Columba Cary-Elwes (1903–94), monk of Ampleforth, prior at the Abbey, founding prior of St. Louis Priory (now Abbey), St. Louis, Missouri, 1955–67. Later helped in the foundation of the Benedictine community at Ewu, Nigeria. Author of several books: *Law: Liberty and Love* (1943), *The Sheepfold and the Shepherd* (1956), *China and the Cross* (1957), and *Monastic Renewal* (1967). His long correspondence with Arnold Toynbee was published as *An Historian's Conscience* (1987).

[2] Columba Cary-Elwes, *Work and Prayer: The Rule of St Benedict for Lay People* (Tunbridge Wells: Burns and Oates, 1992), 125.

to an ever-deeper understanding of the One Revealing God. Benedict's Rule legislates for this journey with time to ponder, appreciate, and be enhanced by the richness of the Word.

It was the same with Islam. The revelations to the Prophet were remembered and retold to his friends who also remembered. Their memories became full of these different revelations, or, in Daniel Madigan's words, "the Qur'an comes as a Word not to be interrogated and analysed but to be received, believed and obeyed. It speaks for itself. . . . it must be listened to since it claims to be a divine Word."[3] These quotations show not only the priority given to the Word by each but the opportunity to learn from each other in dialogue.

Even today many Muslims learn the Qur'an by heart. It is prized as a way of ensuring a life lived entirely in the presence of God as well as an opportunity to go ever deeper into the mystery of the Uncreated Divine Word, spoken in Arabic. Such Muslims not only learned the riches of their Divine Revelation but also committed themselves to live by it. Only a few decades after the Prophet's death, these sayings were edited to form the Arabic Qur'an as memorized and prayed today.

Significantly, the early monks, also largely illiterate, would learn their Scriptures by heart, memorize them, and be able to repeat them while about their work during the day. Benedict's advice was that the 150 psalms should be said each week, embedding them, too, in the memory, at the same time reminding his community that the earliest monks would say the whole psalter each day.

---

[3] Daniel Madigan, "Jesus and Muhammad: The Sufficiency of Prophecy," in *Bearing the Word: Prophecy in Biblical and Qur'anic Perspective*, ed. Michael Ipgrave (London: Church House Publishing, 2005), 90–99, here at 95–96. Daniel Madigan, SJ, Monash University, Melbourne (1974–77 history BA), Melbourne College of Divinity 1980–83 (BD); Columbia University, NY, MPhil (1993) and PhD (1997). Assistant professor of Islamic and Interreligious Dialogue, Pontifical Gregorian University, Rome, 2000–2007; Woodstock Theological Centre, Washington, DC, 2007–8; Georgetown University, Department of Theology, associate professor, 2008 to present.

From this it is clear that both monk and Muslim lived in a culture that encouraged memorization of the Inspired Scripture, enabling recall at any moment during the day—a clear reminder of the presence of God.

Today, in an age of universal literacy, techniques of prayer have changed, but the underlying obligation of both the Muslim and Christian is the constant remembrance of God without distraction. This shows how appropriate it is for Christians, dedicated to their Revealed Word, to enter a dialogue of the Word with Islam. Both focus on this truth: God reveals in Word; each of us can listen, appreciate, and be inspired by this Word, even when spoken to the "other." It is the One God Who Reveals.

It is the purpose of this book to show how this might be possible: there are many Christian communities living alongside or within the neighborhood of Muslim communities. Of course, not every Christian or Muslim community would find this appropriate. My intention is to open up the opportunity. Such a dialogue should be seen as a gift from one to another. Once established it forms a stronger foundation for other Christian-Muslim dialogues dealing with issues of peace, freedom of religious practice, and freedom to convert.

But it will be a long road; both Christian and Muslim have fundamentalists who would do anything to prevent such an initiative. For those with the courage to engage it will be the beginning of a friendship, deeper than language or social position, reaching to the very heart of the One God, revealed uniquely in each, inviting to faith in the One God, Merciful and Forgiving.

To achieve this will require a journey into dialogue: it involves emptying oneself of one's own framework of spirituality (some would use the Greek word *kenosis*), enabling one to hear and understand the other as the speaker intends to be heard and understood. It is a demanding skill but essential for anyone trying to understand accurately what the other is saying.

In a dialogue of spirituality, there are two extreme reactions to hearing the Word of the "other." Either there is an *echo*, affirming the comment as in accord with one's own faith, or there is a *counter-echo*, an indication of difference from which, through greater clarification, a dividing line can be drawn, indicating the boundary more clearly between the beliefs of speaker and listener. The echo might indicate a truth articulated by one indicating similarity or agreement with the other; the louder the echo the stronger the agreement. This may be a revelation of a truth shared or of ideas that correspond to those of the listener, or of an insight into the meaning of a text that touches the heart of the listener. The counter-echo, whether arising from content or experience, signals difference, even contradicting the beliefs or teachings of the "other." These may be words, spoken with love, that carry no affirmation of truth. In dialogue there will be moments of both. Working with these ideas in honesty, openness, and careful listening brings the prospect of greater mutual understanding.

An essential element in the dialogue is *difference*. It is not a threatening concept but an important element in the dialogue with the spiritual world of the "other." The listener, though aware of the counter-echo, can still be enriched by the insights offered, which will help to define more clearly the boundary between the two.

Participants are expected to express their insights with clarity and care, making it as easy as possible for the other to both understand and appreciate the message and be clear where the difference lies. On occasion there will be misunderstandings: they should be clarified immediately. In this way, differences come to be seen, as an opportunity to appreciate the teachings of the other more clearly.

In this process the role of memory becomes important. Both Muslims and followers of the Rule of Benedict emphasize the role of memory—the skill by which key moments of divine guidance are retained, meditated, and applied. Insights arising from personal meditation on the Inspired Scriptures provide one way to start creating the spiritual memory.

In a dialogue of spirituality, these insights should be recorded and then worked into a shared memory as will be described later. In this way progress can be recorded allowing mutual respect to increase and the conviction to strengthen belief that

God is truly "alive" in the hearts and minds of the participants. From this author's research, a new initiative of this type would do much to open up a new way of building friendship between Muslims and Christians.

For followers of the Benedictine Rule, whether as vowed men and women or oblates, a dialogue of spirituality with Islam opens up a new dimension. It is also a model available to all Christians seeking a way of dialogue with the spirituality of Islam.

One question that might be asked is whether any Muslims would be interested. This author's experience suggests there are communities ready and willing. But there are places where the culture is not yet sympathetic. So progress will be slow and will require much sensitivity of one to the "other." In this way each community will find its own way. What follows is not a blueprint, nor even an exemplar, but a framework to encourage those interested to move forward.

What the Second Vatican Council Said: Interpreting *Nostra Aetate*

The document *Nostra Aetate* affirms six important elements that provide the theological foundation for this dialogue of spirituality. After a preamble it clearly affirms that toward Muslims "the Church looks with esteem,"[1] making clear that the era of rivalry and fighting should be over. A new attitude is needed; the document requires it of Catholics.

Next the document gives the reasons for this change of heart. First, "they [the Muslims] adore one God, living and enduring, merciful and all-powerful, Maker of heaven and earth and Speaker to men" (NA 3). That is of huge significance: accepting that God, Omnipotent and Transcendent, believed by Muslims and Christians, is One. There are other aspects of God with which there are important differences. But the One God, acknowledged by Muslim and Christian as the Creator of heaven

---

[1] Walter M. Abbott, *The Documents of Vatican II*, trans. Joseph Gallagher (London: Geoffrey Chapman, 1966), no. 3. Unless otherwise noted, all subsequent references to Vatican II documents are from this edition.

and earth, shows that without such a God nothing would exist outside of God. This God is not distant but intimate with each, holding all things in being. As divine Speaker to human beings, this One God communicates with each of them, in that way opening up the opportunity for greater friendship and understanding between Christians and Muslims. From that intimacy arises a clearer understanding of what is considered appropriate and inappropriate behavior of one to the other, while at the same time affirming that forgiveness and mercy are available to repentant sinners. The God of the Muslim and Christian is intimate, always offering encouragement to believers.

The second statement: "they [the Muslims] strive to submit wholeheartedly even to [God's] inscrutable decrees, just as did Abraham, with whom the Islamic faith is pleased to associate itself" (NA 3). The example of Abraham's obedience refers to that moment when God asked him to sacrifice his only son, his heir to God's promises, recalled at length in the book of Genesis, and repeated albeit in a single sentence in the Qurʾan. *Nostra Aetate* is pointing to the fact that both Christians and Muslims live in a relationship of faith with a God who urges them to obey. Abraham's unquestioning obedience to that impossible command provides Christians and Muslims with an example of how God expects them to respond.

The third statement has it that Islam does "not acknowledge Jesus as God, [but] they revere Him as a prophet" (NA 3). For those unfamiliar with Islam, their title "prophet" has a significantly different meaning from that used by Christians, especially with regard to their moral status: the Muslim prophets are sinless, either they never sinned or they repented and were forgiven. Being acknowledged as sinless before God gives them a higher status than the prophets named in the Christian Scriptures.

The fourth statement: "they also honor Mary, His virgin mother; at times they call on her, too, with devotion" (NA 3). Indeed, Mary has more coverage in the Qurʾan than in the New Testament, but again there are significant differences. In Islam she is not "Mother of God," but Muslims affirm the virgin birth and honor her in prayer.

The fifth statement: Muslims, like Christians, "await the day of judgment when God will give each man his due after raising him up" (NA 3). The framework for growth in faith is the same: each is born at the will of God, each lives his or her life according to faith in the God of Mercy, and each will die with the promise of resurrection.

Given that shared framework, *Nostra Aetate* in its sixth point, states approvingly that Muslims "prize the moral life, and give worship to God especially through prayer, almsgiving, and fasting" (NA 3) disciplines of daily life, which confirm for them as for Christians their commitment in faith. Both firmly agree that the neighbor, of whatever race or color or religion, is "God" for *me*, as Jesus famously said in the New Testament, "Just as you did it to one of the least of these who are members of my family, you did it to me" (Matt 25:40).

Given these elements of similarity a dialogue focusing on the divine Word revealed in Inspired Scriptures becomes not just a possibility but an obligation: believers are obliged to acknowledge God's gifts.

The chapters that follow build on this "obligation" developing the possibility of a dialogue of spirituality, undertaken by Christians dedicated to the Word of God, provided of course that they are willing to learn from the "other."

If we accept that God speaks through the Word, whether the Hebrew Scriptures, the Christian New Testament, or the Muslim Qur'an, we can look for echoes from the other that inspire us. The purpose of the dialogue is not simply clarifying what is obscure but recognizing the value of positive echoes of the "other," which will enhance one's own faith. That has been this author's experience in reading not only the Qur'an but also the Muslim spiritual writers, as will be seen later.

This journey requires courage, offers challenges, and needs preparation. Participants need to be strong in their own faith before beginning it. For only the solidity of faith, tested, lived, and loved, can form the foundation for a dialogue of spirituality. Anything less will cause difficulties.

Chapter 7

Chapter

Issues of Yesterday and Today

The Patriarch and the Caliph

In the eighth century CE, the Nestorian patriarch Timothy started a discussion with the third Abbasid Caliph al-Mahdi[1] (d. 785). When asked what he thought of Muhammad, the patriarch replied, "It is clear that Muhammad walked in the path of the prophets."[2] He went on to give evidence for this judgment—namely, "Muhammad's preaching of monotheism, his strictures against idol worship and polytheism, his institution of authentic worship, and his ethical teaching and leadership."[3] By naming these four qualities, Timothy focused attention on key

---

[1] Patriarch Timothy (d. 823 CE), Nestorian Patriarch of the Church of the East, best known for his dialogue with the third Abbasid Caliph al-Mahdi (d. 785 CE), which has survived (available on the web, in English, thanks to Roger Pearse, Ipswich, UK, 2008). Patriarch Timothy is also known for his encouragement of missionary work toward the East, even to China.

[2] Daniel Madigan, "Jesus and Muhammad" in *Bearing the Word*, ed. Michael Ipgrave, 90–99, here at 91.

[3] Ibid.

elements shared by both Christians and Muslims; by believing in One God he dismissed the claims of traditional idols of that society; by emphasizing the truth of divine worship he showed the One God is the God who communicates with, and is accessible to, believers; by teaching doctrine he shows there are truths that need to be taught and explained; by emphasizing ethical values he underlined the link between faith and behavior; by stressing the role of leadership he showed that particular people are chosen to lead because of their closeness to God.

Sadly, the history of the centuries that followed showed this brave attempt at dialogue was not enough to secure peace. Growing mutual suspicion, the descent into caricature, and the desire for power became priorities. Dialogue about the revelation of God was forgotten; armed conflict took its place. Only in recent years has the importance of dialogue been better appreciated, as much by secular authorities in multireligious communities as by the leaders of religions. Even after this emphasis on dialogue one or the other faith is subject to abuse, misrepresentation, and violence in many places.

The patriarch went as far as he could. To have stated plainly that Muhammad was a prophet would have been misunderstood; this would have sounded too like the Muslim formula of faith. The patriarch, aware of that potential misunderstanding, was careful with his words.

But the patriarch's remarks opened up a way to dialogue, a path, which, as Madigan put it, "by and large was not and still is not taken."[4] Elaborating, he continues, "Timothy's response showed us what a Christian response should be: collaborative rather than competitive, seeking out and welcoming the undoubted resonances in the diverse Muslim images of Muhammad, and the familiar echoes in the Qurʾan of a revelation already heard."[5] Many Christians, since the patriarch and down to the present, dismiss such resonances as examples of the Islamic edi-

---

[4] Daniel Madigan, "Jesus and Muhammad," in *Bearing the Word*, ed. Michael Ipgrave, 90–99, here at 93.

[5] Ibid.

tors, borrowing or copying elements from the Christian Inspired Scriptures. To them, the opposite view, that these resonances are doorways by which each, in dialogue, can come to a better understanding of the "other," was dangerous and liable to both syncretism and relativism. Today most Christians accept that the faith of Islam is evidence that the One God speaks to the human family in different ways, through different situations, starting with the divine Word spoken at the moment of Creation.

Patriarch Timothy's statement opened up an opportunity, which was taken up largely by theologians but never took root among ordinary believers. Madigan explains that Muslims understand the Qurʾan to be the very Word of God spoken in language; it cannot be altered. It is words to be pondered, prayed, and obeyed. Christians see Jesus as God made man, beyond definition, for Jesus is experienced by Christians too "as the divine Word. He is believed in neither as one word among many, nor as one prophet among many."[6] Dialogue, then, should start by accepting the integrity of each position and continue with the intention of understanding more clearly the dimensions of this central revelation, both remembering the Word of God is a Word of Love, penetrating and enlarging the heart.

The troubled history of dialogue is not a safe guide to a new initiative. The pressing need for the world's two largest religious families to enter a serious dialogue of spirituality is self-evident; only deeper understanding of the One God will bring hostilities to an end—a view echoed by Bediuzzaman Said Nursi,[7] who quoted

[6] Ibid., 96.

[7] Bediuzzaman Said Nursi (1878–1960), "*Bediuzzaman*," or, "the wonder of the age," author of '*Risale-i Nur Collection*. Born in Nurs, Eastern Anatolia, Turkey, he was educated by local scholars. He is the inspiration behind the Nur Movement, which shun political ambition and focuses on reviving personal faith through study, self-reform, and service of others. Nursi lived through the period when Turkey became a secular republic. He mastered modern Western philosophical and scientific ideas from which he was able to address the challenges Muslims faced. The *Risale-i Nur* is seen as an interpretation of the Qurʾan for contemporary life. Many have been inspired by his writings.

a hadith of the Prophet, "at the end of time, the truly pious among the Christians will unite with the People of the Qur'an and fight their common foe, irreligion. At this time, too, the people of religion and truth need to unite sincerely not only with their own brothers and fellow believers, but also with the truly pious and spiritual Christians."[8]

This dialogue is more urgent today. Participants can take some encouragement from the continual thread—sometimes thicker, sometimes thinner—of this dialogue in different parts of the world where Christians and Muslims have found themselves side by side. In the past this dialogue has included theologians and philosophers, Christians and Muslims, in Arabic-speaking countries of the Middle East and North Africa, and Andalusian Spain.[9]

The Charter of Privileges

This important text, currently in the archives of the monastery of St. Catherine at the foot of Mt. Sinai, was granted in 628 CE to the monks by the Prophet Muhammad after a delegation of monks had visited him and demanded a guarantee for the security and peace of Christians. Presenting it on their web site, the monks describe it as "covering all aspects of human rights

---

[8] Thomas Michel, SJ, *Muslim-Christian Dialogue and Cooperation in the Thought of Bediuzzaman Said Nursi*, in Three Papers from the Fourth International Symposium on Bediuzzaman Said Nursi (Istanbul, 1998). Paper titled "Muslim-Christian Dialogue and Cooperation in the Thought of Bediuzzaman Said Nursi," 11. Thomas Michel (b. 1941), St. Louis, MO; 1967 ordained diocesan priest for St. Louis; 1971 joined Jesuits in Indonesian Province; 1978 PhD Chicago, after studies in Cairo and Beirut; 1978–81 taught at Sanata Dharma University of Yogyakarta; 1981–94 Pontifical Council for Interreligious Dialogue, Vatican; 1994–96 Bangkok, Ecumenical and Interreligious Affairs for the Asian Bishop's Conference; 1996 Interreligious Dialogue in Jesuit Secretariat, Rome.

[9] See Sidney H. Griffith, *The Church in the Shadow of the Mosque: Christians and Muslims in the World of Islam* (Princeton: Princeton University Press, 2008).

including such topics as protection of Christians, freedom of worship and movement, freedom to appoint their own judges and to own and maintain their own property, exemption from military service and the right to protection in war."[10]

Given the rivalry and fighting that subsequently took place between Christians and Muslims, the document ends with the sentence, "This charter of privileges has been honored and faithfully applied by Muslims throughout the centuries in all lands they ruled." Here is the full text:

> This is a message from Muhammad ibn Abdullah, as a covenant to those who adopt Christianity, near and far, we are with them.
>
> Verily I, the servants, the helpers, and my followers defend them, because Christians are my citizens; and by Allah! I hold out against anything that displeases them.
>
> No compulsion is to be on them.
>
> Neither are their judges to be removed from their jobs nor their monks from their monasteries.
>
> No one is to destroy a house of their religion, to damage it, or to carry anything from it to the Muslims' houses.
>
> Should anyone take any of these, he would spoil God's covenant and disobey His Prophet. Verily, they are my allies and have my secure charter against all that they hate.
>
> No one is to force them to travel or to oblige them to fight.
>
> The Muslims are to fight for them.
>
> If a female Christian is married to a Muslim, it is not to take place without her approval. She is not to be prevented from visiting her church to pray.
>
> Their churches are to be respected. They are neither to be prevented from repairing them nor the sacredness of their covenants.
>
> No one of the nation (Muslims) is to disobey the covenant till the Last Day (end of the world).[11]

[10] Dr. A. Zahoor and Dr. Z. Haq, "Prophet Muhammad's Charter of Privileges to Christians: Letter to the Monks of St. Catherine Monastery" (2007), http://www.cyberistan.org/islamic/charter1.html.

[11] Ibid.

The importance of this document is self-evident. Dr. Khan[12] writes, "These rights are inalienable. Muhammed [*sic*] declared Christians, all of them, as his allies and he equated ill treatment of Christians with violating God's covenant." He continues, "The first and the final sentence of the charter are critical. They make the promise eternal and universal. Muhammad asserts that Muslims are with Christians near and far straight away rejecting any future attempts to limit the promises to St Catherine's alone."[13] He comments that the only qualification needed is that they are truly Christians. The Prophet was giving them privileges as a result of their faith, to encourage them to live it.

Given this document, Christians should have no difficulty establishing a dialogue of spirituality in Muslim lands. Sadly, that may not be universally true, not because Muhammad's words have been revoked but because of suspicion about Christian motives. To succeed they would have to make it clear their aim was to enrich, not to evangelize.

Mohammad and Bahira

In the early years of Islam there is evidence of a positive relationship with Christians. First, "the biographical traditions concerned with Muhammad's early years mention several encounters between monks and the young prophet-to-be, most famously his encounter with the monk, Bahīra, who reportedly recognized the sign of prophecy on his body."[14] This positive

[12] Dr. Muqtedar Khan (b. 1966), 2000, PhD international relations, political philosophy and Islamic political thought, Georgetown. Currently associate professor in the Department of Political Science, University of Delaware. He is a Sufi.

[13] Dr. Muqtedar Khan, "The Prophet Muhammad's Promise to Christians," *Middle East Online* (December 28, 2009), http://www.middle-east-online.com/english/?id=36388.

[14] Sidney Griffith, "Monasticism and Monks" in *Encyclopaedia of the Qurʾan*, para. 3. CD-ROM (Leiden: Brill, 2008).

assessment is confirmed by Muhammad's Charter of Privileges and by his decision to exempt monks from the tax (*jizya*).

In those times early monks studied Islam, learned Arabic, and saw in it a spirituality of the same genre as their own. These communities were renowned for hospitality, and the earliest dialogues took place within their walls.[15] Only lifelong celibacy was rejected.[16] Early Islam had no fundamental objection to dialogue with faithful monks, and indeed, the Sufi movement owed much to the Christian contemplative life.[17] Such friendship could be renewed today if Christians were inspired to form communities dedicated to a dialogue of spirituality.

Early Muslim-Christian Dialogue

A little after the Charter of Privileges, in 630 CE, a Christian delegation of sixty men was given a friendly reception by the Prophet, with whom it engaged in a vigorous theological discussion at the end of which, as Asma Afsaruddin[18] writes, "both sides

[15] "In a number of places, such as the monastery of St. Euthymius in the Judean desert, the monks actively fostered the growth and development of Christianity among the neighboring Arab tribes, who then had the monastery as the centre of their religious life." Sidney Griffith, "Monasticism and Monks," para. 2.

[16] "Christian monks writing in Syriac, Greek, and Arabic were the first to call attention to the doctrinal and moral challenges of Islam to Christians. Monks were also the first Christians to adopt Arabic as an ecclesiastical language, to write theology in Arabic, and to translate the Christian Bible and other classical Christian texts into Arabic. . . . Monasteries were often considered to be privileged places by Muslims and Christians alike, where help could be sought and interreligious conversations could take place." Sidney Griffith, "Monasticism and Monks," paras. 6–7.

[17] See L. Lechevalier, "*Le monachisme et l'Islam,*" *Cistercian Studies* 29, no. 4 (1967): 206ff.

[18] Asma Afsaruddin, formerly associate professor of Arabic and Islamic studies at the University of Notre Dame, Indiana; professor in the Department of Near Eastern Languages and Cultures, at Indiana University, in Bloomington. Author of *Excellence and Precedence: Medieval Islamic Discourse on Legitimate Leadership* (2002) and *The First Muslims: History and Memory* (2008).

agreed to disagree on key doctrinal issues, the Christian delegation concluded a pact with the Prophet, according to which they were granted full protection for their churches and their possessions in return for the payment of taxes. They were also allowed to pray in the mosque at Medina over the protests of some."[19] This example of early Christian-Muslim dialogue affirms what is stated in the Qurʾan—that Muslims should respect Christians provided the latter do not cause upset by trying to make converts. Christians should be respectful of Muslim law and customs and give an example that "[believers], argue only in the best way with the People of the Book, except with those of them who act unjustly. Say, 'we believe in what was revealed to us and in what was revealed to you; our God and your God are one [and the same]; we are devoted to Him'" (Qurʾan 29:46). Agreement about the Oneness of God opened up many opportunities for dialogue concerning faith, prayer, and devotion. Values such as integrity and justice, along with the knowledge that "good and evil cannot be equal" (Qurʾan 41:34-35), provided a basis for mutual respect, friendship, and the largeness of heart, which accepts difference.

On this basis there are many points of agreement even allowing partners in dialogue to "arrive at a statement that is common to us all: we worship God alone, we ascribe no partner to Him, and none of us takes others beside God as lords" (Qurʾan 3:64) for, as Afsaruddin comments, it is easier to find "common ground among fellow monotheists."[20] She offers a further item to the agenda for dialogue: to dissolve "epistemological and cognitive boundaries that separate us from one another—and thus ultimately from God,"[21] boundaries that have grown up over the years arising from the increasingly sophisticated lan-

---

[19] Asma Afsaruddin, "Discerning a Qurʾanic Mandate for Mutually Transformational Dialogue," in *Criteria of Discernment in Interreligious Dialogue*, ed. Catherine Cornille (Eugene, OR: Cascade Books, 2009), 101–21, here at 101–2.

[20] Ibid., 120.

[21] Ibid., 121. In the same book (pp. 122ff), the article by Mustafa Abu Sway, "Dialogue and Discernment in the Qurʾan," provides further encouragement for Muslims to dialogue with other religions.

guage of doctrinal statements. She puts her finger on a problem that can hinder dialogue: frequently a statement, obvious to one party, is interpreted differently by the other. Both Christians and Muslims have many distorted versions of each other's teachings and practices; a community dedicated to a dialogue of spirituality will have to work through such misrepresentations.

Contemporary Catholic-Muslim Dialogue

The enthusiasm of Pope John Paul II for dialogue with Muslims made it possible for others to make it a priority. His visits to many Muslim countries set new standards for dialogue with Islam, most notably when he prayed with young Muslims in Casablanca.

His successor, Pope Emeritus Benedict XVI,[22] was less enthusiastic about this dialogue. Two examples illustrate this. In his homily at the end of the Year of the Priest, he said, "The world religions, as far as we can see, have always known that in the end there is only one God. But this God is distant. Evidently he had abandoned the world to other powers and forces, to other divinities."[23] The failure to name specific world religions led listeners to conclude he was referring to them all, including Islam. Muslims would find his comments both inaccurate and offensive. Their belief in the One God is not distant: "We created man—We know what his soul whispers to him: We are closer to him than his jugular vein" (Qurʾan 50:16). Pope Benedict's

---

[22] Pope Emeritus Benedict XVI, Joseph Ratzinger (b. 1927), ordained priest 1951, professor of theology at Bonn University 1959–66, professor of theology at Tübingen University 1966–69, professor of theology at Regensberg 1969–77, archbishop of Munich and cardinal 1977–81, prefect of the Congregation for the Doctrine and Faith 1981–2005, elected 265th pope in 2005.

[23] Homily of His Holiness Pope Benedict XVI, para 2. Given at the Mass concluding the Year of the Priests, Solemnity of the Sacred Heart of Jesus, Friday, June 11, 2010. English translation used in the live Vatican Radio Commentary on the Mass. Also available at http://www .vatican.va/holy_father/benedict_xvi/homilies/2010/documents/hf_ben -xvi_hom_20100611_concl-anno-sac_en.html.

words were not an encouragement for a dialogue of spirituality with Islam.

A second example, from the postsynodal apostolic exhortation *Verbum Domini* (On the Word of God), includes a paragraph headed "Dialogue between Christians and Muslims." There is neither mention of the Qur'an, their "Word of God," nor any encouragement for Christians to dialogue with their sacred texts.[24] These negative comments suggest that the progress in Catholic-Muslim dialogue achieved during the pontificate of Pope John Paul II was not maintained by his successor, indeed by limiting himself to the words of *Nostra Aetate* he was trying to re-focus the dialogue, something quickly spotted by the many Muslim scholars engaged in dialogue with Catholics in many parts of the world. Wiser heads would have omitted both references; neither was essential.

There is another side. Pope Emeritus Benedict wrote, "During my visit to Turkey, I was able to show that I respect Islam, that I acknowledge it as a great religious reality with which we must dialogue,"[25] and continued that the dialogue must be about the two things we have in common: "faith in God and obedience to God."[26] He concluded, "the important thing here is to remain in close contact with all the currents within Islam that are open to, and capable of, dialogue, so as to give a change of mentality a chance to happen even where Islamism still couples a claim to truth with violence."[27] Though he offers welcome encouragement, it is also one sided. A Muslim, hearing these references to violence, would ask about what Muslims consider to be "Christian" violence, sponsored by states with an established Christian culture, in ways not so unlike the relationship of extremist Islam to mainline Muslim communities. Such naivete or misrepresentation dissolves trust and shows the need for dialogue at the spiritual level.

[24] Pope Benedict XVI, postsynodal apostolic exhortation, *Verbum Domini* (Rome: Libreria Editrice Vaticana, 2010), 226, para. 118.

[25] Pope Benedict XVI, *Light of the World* (London: CTS, 2010), 98.

[26] Ibid., 99.

[27] Ibid., 101.

The word from the Vatican still favors dialogue. Pope Francis has already shown his own commitment: washing the feet of a Muslim woman in the Maundy Thursday liturgy in 2013 has shown his intent to serve all people in the way Jesus did. One Middle East news site wrote, "The inclusion of two Muslims in a foot-washing ceremony by Pope Francis is one of several gestures of openness towards the Muslim world that could change perceptions of the Vatican."[28] He will surely rekindle the whole-hearted enthusiasm of Pope John Paul II for this dialogue.

The "One God": Same for Muslim and Christian?

Nicholas of Cusa

Miroslav Volf in his book, *Allah, a Christian Response* presents Nicholas of Cusa[29] as an early exponent of dialogue with Islam. He much preferred it to war, quoting John of Segovia, "war could never solve the issues between Christendom and Islam."[30] Nicholas asserted that all people, whether they know it or not, worshiped the One God. He proposed that notions of One God lie prior to any notion of Trinity, "as the infinite and

[28] See "Pope Francis Ritual Raises Hope for Better Ties with Islam," *Gulf-News* (March 30, 2013), http://gulfnews.com/news/world/other-world/pope-francis-ritual-raises-hope-for-better-ties-with-islam-1.1164771.

[29] Nicholas of Cusa (1401–64), fifteenth-century polymath—theologian, philosopher, mathematician, astronomer, canon lawyer, spiritual writer, and commentator on mysticism, also bishop and cardinal. Studied at Heidelberg, Padua, Cologne (1418–25). Taught in Cologne, then secretary to archbishop of Trier. Attended Council of Basel (1431–39). Supported Pope Eugenius IV in his efforts to reunite with the Eastern Church. In 1448 made papal theologian to Nicholas V, made bishop of Brix 1450, and made papal legate to German lands. Tried to reform his diocese, opposed by local prince. Significant because he wrote a commentary on the Qurʾan in which he showed Islam to share in the Truth and suggested there is but one eternal religion, manifested in different ways.

[30] Miroslav Volf, *Allah: A Christian Response* (New York: HarperCollins, 2011), Kindle edition, location 806.

incomprehensible one, God is 'not said to be one or three or good or wise or Father or Son or Holy Spirit'; God 'infinitely excels and precedes all such names.' "[31] He adds that numbers do not apply to God because they belong to the realm of creatures. So "the Trinity in God is no composite or plural or numerical, but is most simple oneness."[32] This is an important opinion, one not widely articulated by Christians, but nevertheless an opinion that encourages dialogue with Islam.

Miroslav Volf and Allah: A Christian Response

Miroslav Volf argues, as *Nostra Aetate* did before, that the God of Islam and the God of Christianity are the same One God, Creator, All-Powerful and Merciful. Many Christians oppose this view, hence the loud criticism of Volf's magisterial work. But it is a view well articulated by Pope John Paul II in his address to the Muslim youth at Casablanca when he said, "We believe in the same God, the one God, and the living God, who created the world and brings his creatures to their perfection."[33]

John Piper, a Baptist pastor from Minneapolis, has argued against this conclusion. He quotes the apostle Philip's request from the Fourth Gospel, "Lord, show us the Father" (John 14:8) and Jesus' reply, "Whoever has seen me has seen the Father" (John 14:9). Jesus elaborates his answer by first asking the question, "Do you not believe that I am in the Father and the Father is in me?" (John 14:10). It challenged Philip's faith. For Piper this is the key question defining what is distinctive about the

[31] Ibid., location 891, quoting Nicholas of Cusa, "*Cribratio Alkorani*" (A Sifting of the Qur'an), and 88.

[32] Miroslav Volf, *Allah: A Christian Response*, location 909. Quoting Nicholas of Cusa, "de Pace fidei," 23. The footnote adds that Thomas Aquinas in *Summa Theologiae* insists "the supreme unity and simplicity of God exclude every kind of plurality of absolute things" (ST I, q. 30, a. 3).

[33] Pope John Paul II, "To the Young Muslims of Morocco," in *Interreligious Dialogue: The Official Teaching of the Catholic Church from the Second Vatican Council to John Paul II*, ed. Francesco Gioia (Boston, MA: Pauline Books & Media, 2006), 336–44, here at 337.

Christian God, a God distinct from the "God" of any other religion, however similar the words used. To illustrate the point, he quotes a story of two people arguing about a fellow college classmate of thirty years back. Eventually they ask themselves whether they were talking about the same person. They decided to check the yearbook. There the evidence showed they were not talking about the same person. Applying this to Jesus Christ as portrayed in the New Testament, "the Yearbook equivalent," he put the question to a Muslim, "Is that your God?" The answer is bound to be "No."[34] He concludes the Muslim understanding of God is so different from the Christian understanding; they cannot be referring to the same God.

He goes on to suggest that by using the more general confession of faith in a single God, All-Powerful, All-Merciful, and Creator of the world, there is a danger of confusion or, worse, watering down the role of Jesus Christ as God made man. The God of Islam and the God of Christianity cannot be the same. If Christians continue to dialogue on this basis, they end up diminishing their faith in the incarnation, the distinctive element of Christian faith.

Volf replies with his own challenge. If Christians and Muslims are both monotheists, and, if the One God is not the same, then each is obliged to defend their own and accuse the other of idolatry, making dialogue impossible. The Christian and Muslim confession of faith in One God allows for the dialogue in which similarity and difference can be clearly defined from which a dialogue of spirituality can develop.

Piper proposes to get around this difficulty by focusing the dialogue on Jesus, presented differently in their respective Inspired Scriptures. To this Volf replied by pointing out that discussions about Jesus would lead ultimately to questions about God. Without a shared understanding of God, discussions would quickly focus on whose was the "true God"; there can be no

[34] David Mathis, "A Common Word between Us?," *Desiring God* (January 23, 2008), http://www.desiringgod.org/Blog/1032_a_common_word _between_us/. See also Miroslav Volf, *Allah: A Christian Response*, Kindle edition, location 607–14.

compromise on this fundamental truth. Volf concludes, a shared understanding of key elements of the nature of God is the only sure foundation for a dialogue.

Volf takes the discussion forward by focusing on the two basic commandments of Islam and Christianity: love of God and love of neighbor. He writes,

> It is possible to be benevolent and beneficent toward those who worship a different God and with whom we therefore disagree on ultimate principles, but it's very difficult. In that situation love strains mightily. If, on the other hand, Muslims and Christians worship the same God, albeit partly differently understood, the love of each for God will help them live together and make neighborly love easier.[35]

If both allow the One transcendent God to be represented differently by each, a dialogue of spirituality can be fruitful.

In developing the meaning of the One God, acknowledged by Muslims and Christians, Volf affirms that both accept that the One God is "God, the sovereign creator, not a malleable creature to be designed according to human need or fancy."[36]

In his examination of Benedict XVI's Regensburg speech, Volf suggests the emeritus pope's view is that the God of Islam and the God of Christianity are not the same One God. Christians see God as Reason, committed to thinking and freedom, while the Muslims think of God as inscrutable and arbitrary, inclined to submission of the will and prone to violence. Volf concluded that, expressed this way, he left too many questions unanswered.

Among the many comments the Regensburg speech provoked was a letter from 138 Muslim leaders called "A Common Word between Us," inviting Christian leaders to enter a dialogue around this common Word.

On Benedict XVI's visit to Jordan there was an exchange of addresses at the baptism site, when what was opaque was cleared

[35] Ibid., location 621.
[36] Ibid., location 626.

up in the speeches of HRH Prince Ghazi bin Muhammad bin Talal (the initiator of the letter) and the emeritus pope.

The emeritus pope affirmed that Christians and Muslims are believers in One God, that each accepted the role of reason as a gift from God, reaching its highest point when bathed in the light of God's truth and then affirmed with the unbreakable bond between the love of God and love of the neighbor.

For Volf, these were words of reconciliation that brought greater clarity to what the emeritus pope meant in his Regensburg speech; he clearly affirmed "a shared belief in one God and a common commitment to love God and neighbor."[37]

Volf's essential point is that this showed enough agreement about the nature of the One God to affirm that Islam and Christianity believe in the same God, while allowing for significant differences in the way the One God relates. Piper's concern is noted as a major point of difference, but it is not large enough to deny the truth of the confession of belief in One God. By exaggerating the difference dialogue is put at risk and by overemphasizing the similarity there is a danger of misrepresentation. One way forward is a dialogue of spirituality in which similarity and difference are accepted, each being open to insights from the "other."

What Do Christians Think of Muhammad?

Daniel Madigan raises the question of how Christians view Muhammad. If there is agreement in the respective confessions of faith in One God, then those who are inspired by God, with a message for humans, have a right to be heard with respect; their insights are valuable.

Madigan states that Muhammad's teaching "is invaluable, since it contains a salutary critique of Christian faith and behavior."[38] By engaging with Muhammad's teaching, Christians

[37] Ibid., location 654.
[38] Daniel Madigan, "Jesus and Muhammad," in *Bearing the Word*, ed. Michael Ipgrave, 96.

have an opportunity to reflect on the way their own teaching is articulated and, perhaps, consider rephrasing some of it to put more emphasis on their belief in God as One. The trinitarian doctrine, in particular, would not suffer if it was more clearly stated that the "three persons" do not mean three gods, an obvious misunderstanding by non-Christians, especially Muslims. Christians could make clear that the "religious language of fatherhood, motherhood and sonship was figurative rather than simply literal."[39] In that way it would help to remove this cause of misrepresentation and could lead to a reformulation to completely remove this danger, while not, of course, altering the teaching.

The strong affirmation of the role of the "Word" in the lives of both Muslims and Christians is a better starting point for a community dedicated to dialogue of spirituality with Islam, because the riches gained from the power of the "Word of God," spoken in Arabic to Muhammad and becoming Jesus for Christians, will lead to greater mutual understanding of what is shared and what is different.

This encouragement from Madigan is not reflected in the Vatican document *Dominus Iesus*.[40] Writing in general terms, it states the salvation of "individual non-Christians"[41] is achieved "in ways known to [God] himself."[42] The document goes on to warn of the dangers of "religious relativism."[43] Both Christians and Muslims hold their revelation to be unique and specific, both are committed to "mission," and both realize the importance of dialogue. Both also reject any possibility of syncretism or relativism. Neither seeks to undermine the integrity of the "other."

[39] Ibid.

[40] Congregation for the Doctrine of the Faith, Declaration *Dominus Iesus* on the Unicity and Salvific Universality of Jesus Christ and the Church (Vatican City, 2000).

[41] Ibid., 32, para. 21.

[42] Ibid.

[43] Ibid., 33, para. 22. It does not link it to para. 16 of *Gaudium et Spes* (Church in the Modern World of Vatican II) on the dignity of the moral conscience, "for man has in his heart a law written by God. To obey it is the very dignity of man; according to it he will be judged."

A community in dialogue will surely face the problem of authority, respectively, of Jesus and Muhammad. The principle: respect what is shared and be tolerant of what is different.

Can Christians Pray with Muslims?

John Paul II

On several occasions John Paul II encouraged the dialogue of spirituality: "On my part, I wish therefore to do everything possible to help develop the spiritual bonds between Christians and Muslims."[44] He saw Muslims and Christians as brothers and sisters, sharing faith in the One God: "We are grateful for this faith, since without God the life of man would be like the heavens without the sun. Because of this faith that we have in God, Christianity and Islam have many things in common, the privilege of prayer, the duty of justice accompanied by compassion and almsgiving, and above all, a sacred respect for the dignity of man."[45] For him prayer was an essential part of human life. Given this commitment, there is space both to be together at prayer and to pray together.

Faith in One God takes its starting point from the truth that the divine presence is everywhere throughout the created world, for "his loving presence accompanies us throughout each day. In prayer, we place ourselves in the presence of God to offer him our worship and thanksgiving, to ask forgiveness for our faults and to seek his help and blessing."[46] To illustrate this, John Paul II's most innovative words came in his own prayer with the young people of Morocco:

[44] John Paul II, "To the Muslim Leaders of Kenya" (Nairobi: May 7, 1980), no. 350, in *Interreligious Dialogue*, ed. Francesco Gioia, 265.

[45] John Paul II, "To the Communities of the State of Kaduna (Nigeria), and in Particular to the Muslim Population" (February 14, 1982), no. 390, in *Interreligious Dialogue*, ed. Francesco Gioia, 289.

[46] John Paul II, "To Representatives of the Muslims in Belgium" (May 19, 1985), no. 444, in *Interreligious Dialogue*, ed. Francesco Gioia, 323–24.

O God, You are our Creator.
You are limitlessly good and merciful.
To You is due the praise of every creature.
O God, You have given to us an interior law by which we should
    live.
To do Your will is to perform our task.
To follow Your ways is to find peace of soul.
To You we offer our obedience.
Guide us in all the steps that we undertake on earth.
Free us from evil inclinations which turn our heart from Your
    will.
Do not permit that in invoking Your Name we should ever
    justify human disorders.
O God, you are the One Alone whom we make our adoration.
Do not permit that we should estrange ourselves from You.
O God, judge of all mankind, help us to belong to Your elect
    on the last day.
O God, author of justice and peace, grant us true joy and au-
    thentic love, as also a lasting fraternity among all peoples.
Fill us with your gifts, forever. Amen![47]

Pope John Paul II set a standard with this prayer. When ques-
tioned, he defended it because prayer "disposes people to accept
God's will for them. It also affects the relationship of those who
pray together, for coming together before God in prayer people
can no longer ignore or hate others."[48] He went on to say that
in prayer each learns to see the other as pilgrim, a searcher for
the same goal, and acknowledges that each has a responsibility
to care for the neighbor. Prayer plays an essential role in dialogue, where it reveals its power to transform attitudes to share
belief in One Revealing God and be in dialogue with the partner.
Refusing to pray in dialogue is like driving a car without fuel.

    [47] John Paul II, "To Young Muslims" (August 19, 1985), no. 475, in *Inter-
religious Dialogue*, ed. Francesco Gioia, 344.
    [48] John Paul II, "Address to Representatives of the World Council of
Churches" (Rome: April 11, 1986), no. 517, in *Interreligious Dialogue*, ed.
Francesco Gioia, 370.

In the meeting of the leaders of the world religions at Assisi he said, "We cannot 'pray together,' namely, to make a common prayer, but we can be present while others pray. In this way we manifest our respect for the prayer of others and for the attitude of others before the divinity; at the same time, we offer them the humble and sincere witness of our faith in Christ, Lord of the Universe."[49]

This explanation took account of the diversity of religions represented at that meeting; the diversity of theologies of God made prayer together impossible.

John Paul II on many occasions explained his view of prayer: "prayer is the breath of the soul. Every adorer of the living and true God believes in the limitless value of prayer and feels, welling up from his inmost being, the need to pray."[50] The world needs fervent and persistent prayer if it is to become "a place of true and permanent peace."[51] "Prayer entails conversion of heart on our part. It means deepening our sense of ultimate Reality."[52] While these remarks were made to clarify a particular occasion, they also offer encouragement to a community in a dialogue of spirituality with Islam. Prayer has many echoes, one with the other; when Muslims and Benedictines meet "one another at a level where inequalities, misunderstandings, bitterness and hostility are overcome, namely before God, the Lord and Father of all,"[53] the Word, revealed to each, builds mutual respect.

In Sarajevo, John Paul II addressed Muslim communities with the hope that all "can join in the prayer which all people of good will raise to Almighty God, to implore, with unity of purpose,

---

[49] John Paul II, "To the Faithful in General Audience" (October 22, 1986), no. 531, in *Interreligious Dialogue*, ed. Francesco Gioia, 380.

[50] Ibid., 381.

[51] John Paul II, "To Representatives of Various Religions on the World Day of Prayer for Peace" (October 27, 1986), no. 536, in *Interreligious Dialogue*, ed. Francesco Gioia, 381.

[52] Ibid., no. 537.

[53] John Paul II, "Message for the World Day of Peace" (Rome: December 8, 1991), no. 732, in *Interreligious Dialogue*, ed. Francesco Gioia, 508.

an active peace"[54]—the only way forward for two communities at war in this ethnically divided state.

The sharing of faith and its expression in prayer brings both Christians and Muslims together; each honors "their places of prayer, as oases where they meet the All Merciful God on the journey to eternal life, and where they meet their brothers and sisters in the bond of religion."[55] Weddings, funerals, and other celebrations provide occasions when Christians and Muslims can be alongside each other in prayer, respecting the other's prayer and bearing witness to their union in the One Creating and Merciful God, but also enabling members to recognize the reality of difference. Given the pope's affirmation of this form of dialogue, there can be little objection to a community dedicated to a dialogue of spirituality.

This positive and encouraging attitude of John Paul II was greatly appreciated by Muslims. He was seen as a man of prayer, open to pray with others who shared belief in a transcendent God. Committed Christians in dialogue with Islam know the importance of prayer. It builds tolerance of the "other," affirms the faith of the "other," and offers the love, which is gift from the One God.

Pope Emeritus Benedict XVI

Benedict XVI has said little specifically about Islam and prayer; the nearest is an essay he wrote on the possibility of Christians praying with non-Christians at the time of John Paul II's invitation to religious leaders to pray for peace at Assisi. In it he offers three criteria by which a Christian can judge whether prayer is genuine. First, there should be agreement about the nature of God—Creator, One, Transcendent—having a personal

---

[54] John Paul II, "To the Islamic Community of Sarajevo" (April 13, 1997), no. 907, in *Interreligious Dialogue*, ed. Francesco Gioia, 646.

[55] John Paul II, "Address to the Muslim Leaders at the Umayyad Great Mosque of Damascus" (May 6, 2001), no. 1111, in *Interreligious Dialogue*, ed. Francesco Gioia, 841.

interest in each person. Muslims would have no difficulty with this. Second, there should be agreement about the content of the prayer, for which, he suggests, the Our Father could be the model. Again, Muslims would see this as the Christian equivalent to their prayer in Surah 1, *Al- Fātihah*. And, third, the one praying must recognize that Jesus Christ, the unique Savior of all, is active in that prayer. He adds, "If the non-Christian should be able to see the participation of a Christian as the relativizing of faith in Jesus Christ, the Savior of all, or be bound to see it thus, then such participation cannot take place."[56] Such prayer would not be in line with the Christian revelation. He claimed it would look back to the time before Christ, not forward to the moment of resurrection in Christ.

This statement is concerned not with the truth about the presence of Christ in the prayer of the Christian but with whether that presence has to be explicit in order to ensure validity.

But it *is* possible for Christians to pray with someone whose spirituality is based on the revelation of the One, Creating, and Merciful God, provided the latter accepts the role of Christ in that prayer and the former allows God to determine the validity of the prayer of the Muslim praying alongside. In this way Christians accept the essential importance for Christ in their prayer without having to make it explicit. A Christian's prayer has to be through Christ because that is a consequence of baptism, but it does not need Christ's name to be explicitly mentioned. None of the psalms make specific mention of Jesus as the Christ, but when the Christians use them in prayer, they do so with reference to him.

Nor would Muslims, aware of Christian teaching about Christ, see it as watering down that teaching. They would be supported by the prayer, not worried about its framework; both accept the One God.

[56] Joseph Cardinal Ratzinger, *Truth and Tolerance: Christian Belief and World Religions* (San Francisco: Ignatius Press, 2004), 109.

Christian W. Troll, SJ[57]

Troll has challenged Benedict XVI's view. He suggests that Islam's belief in a single, transcendent, creating God allows prayer with all who share this faith. Christians and Muslims acknowledge the example of Abraham and can stand before God, as revealed to Abraham, in prayer. Muslims and Christians at prayer, Troll writes, "give God the absolute priority and so recognize that it is God himself who unites us and grants us this encounter. Just that will help us, Christians and Muslims, to live our profound differences in true respect for each other, in loyalty to the voice of our conscience."[58] Being aware that both Christian and Muslim stand before God, in prayer as in life, is an important step for building greater understanding and respect. It means "an inner coming together and at the same time an opening to God. In addition, everybody can, in his own prayer, so to speak, carry the others 'before God.'"[59] Prayer, both Muslim and Christian, helps dialogue to proceed with honesty, openness, patience, and charity—gifts God shares with all participants.

Troll concludes, "Common prayer of Christians and Muslims in its various forms and on various occasions can create something lasting. It will promote the quality of the Christians and Muslims living together as neighbors."[60] It also provides the framework, so essential for a Benedictine community dedicated

[57] Christian W. Troll, SJ (b. 1937), Jesuit, studied in Tübingen, Bonn, and Beirut (philosophy, theology, and Arabic); 1970–75 studied at the School of Oriental and African Studies, University of London (BA and PhD); 1976–80 professor of Islamic studies at the Institute of Religious Studies, Vidyajyoti, New Delhi; 1988–93 senior lecturer for the study of Islam-Christian relations at the University of Birmingham (UK); 1993–99 professor at the Pontifical Institute for the Study of Arabic and Islam, Rome; 1999–2001 head of the Forum of Catholic Academy, Berlin; 2001–7 honorary professor at the School of Philosophy and Theology, Sankt Georgen, Frankfurt.

[58] Christian W. Troll, SJ, "Common Prayer of Christians and Muslims?" in *Stimmen der Zeit*, no. 6 (June 2008), para. 367, taken from www.con-spiration.de/texte/english/2008/troll-e.html; translation by Ernst Förster, SJ.

[59] Ibid., para. 374.

[60] Ibid., para. 376.

to dialogue with Islam, in which prayer together would be essential. Both sides accept this will involve a sort of *kenosis*,[61] becoming powerless before God. This prayer, made in faith, expressed differently by Christian and Muslim but directed to the one God, provides, through word, song, and silence, the essential framework for this Christian-Monastic dialogue of spirituality.

The fears of Benedict XVI would not be realized in a community dedicated to dialogue with Islam. Both parties understand and accept the integrity of their respective faith and their prayer.

Is Dialogue with the Qurʾan Possible? Mustansir Mir

Mustansir Mir offers an important challenge to those wanting to engage in dialogue with Islam. He writes, "Even a cursory reading of the Qurʾan will leave one with the unmistakable impression that it is marked by a very high degree of self-assurance."[62] That, at one level, is what one would expect. God does not reveal in order to confuse, and once a particular truth has been communicated, there can be little room for discussion of its meaning or attempts to reinterpret its revelation. Self-doubt is not an option for God. Divine truth is what it is, and the question for believers is whether

---

[61] The Greek word *kenosis* means literally "self-emptying," which in this context means removing anything that might distort or manipulate what is articulated by the "other." For Christians it is used by Paul to describe the extent to which God let go of divinity in becoming man as Jesus Christ who "emptied himself, taking the form of a slave" (Phil 2:7). If God in Christ can "empty himself of divinity" to identify more closely with the people, so the partners in dialogue should be ready to empty themselves of their own beliefs and practices to listen accurately to what the other is saying.

[62] Mustansir Mir, "Scriptures in Dialogue: Are We Reckoning without the Host?" in *Bearing the Word*, 14. Mustansir Mir is University Professor of Islamic Studies at Youngstown State University. Originally from Pakistan, he has taught at colleges in Lahore, at the University of Michigan, and at the International Islamic University in Malaysia. His main interests are Qurʾanic studies and Iqbal studies. He earned his PhD from the University of Michigan.

they accept and believe it. In some cases a truth is revealed to settle disputes. The Qur'an "establishes two diametrically opposed camps, one of the believers and the other of disbelievers."[63] The clarity of this statement reflects its sacred and authoritative character, typical of canonical literature, essentially directed to divide believers from unbelievers. The authoritative nature of the Qur'an is, of course, matched by similar authoritative statements by Christians, as shown by this quotation from the Second Vatican Council: "The Christian dispensation, therefore, as the new and definitive covenant, will never pass away, and we now await no further new public revelation, before the glorious manifestation of our Lord Jesus Christ" (DV 4).

Mir has four concerns: His first is that such authoritative texts concerning divinely revealed teachings leave participants in dialogue little room to move. That is true, but there is a prior responsibility: to make sure the other understands accurately the meaning of the revelation being used in dialogue and its practical effect in daily life. This process should be carried out with integrity and, in Mir's judgment, the participants in dialogue should not "do violence to the context of scripture in order to wrench out of it supposedly politically correct responses."[64] A community dedicated to a dialogue of spirituality should have too much respect for "difference" to engage in the superficiality of the politically correct.

Mir's second concern is that Muslims have failed to develop a "Qur'an based theology of inter-faith dialogue."[65] If true, this opens an agenda for a community dedicated to dialogue, to be undertaken with sympathetic help from the "other."

His third concern is that the prophet's revelation is clear. As Mir puts it, "A prophet does not invite people to tea parties at which to hold academic discussions with them on issues of common interest. Decisiveness is one of the hallmarks of a prophet's

[63] Ibid.
[64] Ibid., 18.
[65] Ibid.

speech."[66] Accepting that these revelations are nonnegotiable, there is still space to discuss how a particular qur'anic teaching can be understood by the "other." This is an important discussion for a Muslim-Christian community of dialogue: each has to challenge and explain elements of theology for the "other."

In his fourth concern, Mir argues that contemporary theologians, Muslim and Christian alike, should find a language that can be the basis of an "authentic theology of inter-faith dialogue."[67]

Mir's comments provide an important balance: a community dedicated to dialogue will be challenging for both parties. A constructive way of working will minimize the chance of conflict and encourage the patience needed for a true understanding of difference. The concerns he identified are important and will surely be part of the ongoing dialogue of spirituality.

Will They Do It?

Christian-Muslim relationships have a troubled history. It continues today in some parts of the world. Many on both sides have taken up hardened positions against a dialogue that includes spirituality. From a Christian perspective, such a dialogue opens an opportunity for a new initiative at the local level. In many places it would be welcomed by both, especially where Muslims and Christians live peacefully together; it challenges each to go deeper into their respective faiths. It can be done.

[66] Ibid.
[67] Ibid., 19.

Part 3

Defining the Dialogue of Spirituality: Can They Do It?

Chapter

8

Memory: The Heart of a Dialogue of Spirituality

Introduction

Memory is the key to this dialogue of spirituality. We have seen that Muslims and Christians share belief in a God Who communicates through the Revealed Word. While pondering that Word, each gains new insights into its depths of meaning. In this community of dialogue these insights will be shared, at once clarifying a point of difference, appreciating a new idea, or enhancing an existing understanding.

It is suggested that at the end of each session of sharing a written record is compiled by each to be edited later into a single account, representing an agreed record of that particular moment. Taken together, these individual records will come together to form a new shared memory, a tapestry of spiritual insights.

The Importance of Memory

An essay by Richard Bulliet[1] posted on the Agence Global web site[2] offers a challenge to those involved in Christian-Muslim dialogue. He gives a wide-ranging survey of the "forgetfulness" or "misinformation" that circulates among many Western-educated people concerning their understanding of Islam and its role over the last twelve hundred years of European history. He concludes, "Throughout contemporary Europe the debate over Islam and Muslims proceeds at a fevered pace. But without a comprehensive understanding of the past, all sides in the debate build on weak foundations."[3] The failure to ensure that the Western memory of Islam is accurate—historically, politically, and theologically—has resulted in an ongoing memory of prejudice. When the memory of a community, however large, is distorted, the attitude of the whole becomes unbalanced, a counterweight to positive dialogue. The records of this proposed dialogue of spirituality will be a corrective.

Walter Ong[4]

In a community of dialogue, this new "memory" arises from oral communication. Walter Ong has made an important study of this and offers this useful insight: "Oral communication unites

---

[1] Richard W. Bulliet, BA history, MA Middle East studies, PhD history and Middle East studies, Harvard. Columbia University, professor of history, 1978–; Director of Middle East Institute, 1984–90, 1992–2000.

[2] Richard Bulliet, "Islam and the West: A Case of Selective Memory," *Agence Global* (July 10, 2007), http://www.agenceglobal.com/index.php ?show=article&Tid=1312.

[3] Ibid., para. 12.

[4] Walter Ong (1912–2003), 1933 BA Rockhurst College, 1935 entered Society of Jesus, 1946 ordained Catholic priest. In 1941 MA English, St. Louis University; 1955 PhD Harvard; 1954–84 professor at St. Louis University.

people in groups."[5] Our world is still in the habit of reading published material in written or electronic form. For this dialogue of spirituality, however, the power of the spoken word is essential because the most effective way of communicating is still face-to-face, in small groups, so that each can listen and question, speak, and clarify. It is not just the words, however inspirational, but also the tone of voice and the body language of both the speaker and listener that influence the way the content is received. In these communications, the hidden power is the faith of the speaker, to which all are attentive as believers listening carefully to the inspiration behind the words. This is what distinguishes a dialogue of spirituality; the words point to the One Revealing God, present behind the voices.

As already noted, listening to the other does not imply agreement with all that is said. The counter-echo highlights "difference," requiring further reflection and clarification to discover ever more precisely where the difference lies. It is the echo and counter-echo that bring life to the dialogue. Oral communication, then, enhances honesty among participants and builds community, while increasing respect grows from appreciation of echoes and counter-echoes. In addition, the face-to-face meeting makes it easier to respond to questions and correct misunderstanding, and participants learn the language of empathy, patience, and tolerance.

Ong also stresses the value of learning texts by heart—a skill much prized by Muslims, many of whom learn at least parts of the Qurʾan by heart. This enables the text to become easily accessible in daily life. Sadly, it is a skill that has lost favor in Western education, and many Benedictines have lost the early monastic discipline of reciting the Psalter (the 150 psalms in the Bible) each week. Through in the Egyptian Coptic monastic tradition, the monks say the same seventy psalms every day.

What is learned by heart can be recalled and repeated at any time in any place. The Voice behind the remembered words

---

[5] Walter J. Ong, *Orality and Literacy* (1982; repr. London: Routledge, 2000), 68.

enables richer intimacy with God. In Ong's words, "God is thought of always as 'speaking' to human beings, not as writing to them."[6] Participants in a dialogue of spirituality will become familiar with some words and phrases from their respective Inspired Scriptures. In this way all can keep the memory of these moments in mind, recognize the powerful presence of God, and grow in mutual respect for one another.

Role of God

In approaching the task of creating the shared spiritual memory, each participant is aware, as Gerald May puts it, of the "inborn desire for God. . . . This desire is our deepest longing and our most precious treasure. It gives us meaning."[7] These desires give energy to the reflections on the Word. But participants must be ready, as May puts it, to take "risks of faith, trying to trust the incomprehensibly loving presence of God whether we feel it or not."[8]

On that journey each faces weakness. Emotions unchecked will transform energy, block the process of dialogue, lead to heightened self-preoccupation, and build a barrier. The cure, in May's words, is "the greening of desert into garden through the living water of grace. There is no geographic journey here; it all takes place within our hearts."[9] Commitment through prayer helps each to control emotion and make that journey. The power for this journey comes from God, radiating through the inspired texts of the Qur'an and the Bible. Mulholland writes that in silent

[6] Ibid., 74.

[7] Gerald G. May, *Addiction and Grace* (New York: HarperCollins, 1988), Kindle edition, location 70–77. Gerald G. May, MD (1940–2005), practiced medicine and psychiatry for twenty-five years before becoming a senior fellow in contemplative theology and psychology at the Shalem Institute for Spiritual Formation in Bethesda, Maryland. He was the author of many books and articles blending spirituality and psychology, including *Addiction and Grace, Care of Mind/Care of Spirit, Will and Spirit,* and *The Dark Night of the Soul.*

[8] Ibid., location, 1665–69.

[9] Ibid., location 2098–2102.

listing "we stand before scripture, and it opens up before us; it addresses us. It draws us into that order of being, that is shaped by the Word."[10] The Word enlivens and, as Mulholland writes, "we find ourselves drawn into that life where our 'word' begins to resonate with the Word. We begin to discover that all of the old structures of meaning, value, purpose, identity, fulfillment, and wholeness become turned around, taking wholly new shape."[11] This dialogue in most cases requires a difficult walk across a desert, with few landmarks and a challenging climate and harsh terrain. But even in these conditions, the Revealed Word continues to inspire, encourage, and affirm, while creating something new between us. For the work of God will not be finished until every Muslim and every Christian can look each other in the eye and recognize God, alive and active in that mind and heart.

Creating the Process

In this dialogue participants will move out from their own way of pondering and praying the Inspired Word to a new place where they will be free to hear the words of the other. By dismantling the inner *filter*, built from years of meditative prayer, the voice of the other will be more clearly heard. At the same time it will be in a mood ready both to identify the positive echo and to absorb the counter-echo. At the beginning, each should be free enough to walk outside the walls of their chapel or mosque and be ready to dialogue effectively in an unfamiliar place. The words will be different, but the Voice will be recognizable; the message will be challenging, whether positive or negative—a sign that this dialogue of spirituality is working well.

The skills come with time and experience; listening carefully to pick up undertones, expressing one's insight with clarity, without technical language, to make it easier for the other to understand. To work like this in dialogue will require patience and the

[10] M. Robert Mulholland Jr., *Shaped by the Word*, rev. ed. (1985; repr. Nashville: Upper Room Books, 2000), 70.

[11] Ibid., 71.

commitment to keep going, especially when loud counter-echoes are testing the agreed upon code of behavior.

As participants become more skilled, Gerald May writes, "we become less self-preoccupied, more free to be attentive to the needs of others,"[12] opening up wider channels of communication and revealing new levels of meaning in the Inspired Scriptures. This is the point, in Mulholland's words, each allows "the text to probe deeper levels of your being . . . to become that intrusion of the Word of God into your life, to address you."[13] From such intimacy, the Word will magnify faith, and as the community matures, insights will become become richer, echoes affirmed with greater clarity, and the clash of counter-echoes less threatening.

Meetings will not always be smooth. As insights become more sophisticated, greater clarity will, rightly, be required, and the participants, in Ong's words, will learn that progress can only come "within a context of struggle,"[14] perhaps most acute in the struggle to agree on the record of earlier sessions.

The Way of Dialogue

As the dialogue progresses, trust in each other grows and friendship strengthens. In this atmosphere participants become ever more skilled in the creation of the new shared memory. At the same time, the spiritual understanding deepens, allowing each to become more comfortable with the inclusion of both the familiar and the unfamiliar.

Reflections based on the Inspired Scriptures and recognized spiritual writers will grow richer: participants drawing on their own experience of prayer-filled pondering, their journey of faith, and their silent reflection will find their new insights bring an added quality to the community of dialogue, each respected more enthusiastically for their contribution.

---

[12] Gerald G. May, *Addiction and Grace*, location 1668–76.

[13] M. Robert Mulholland Jr., *Shaped by the Word*, 56.

[14] Walter J. Ong, *Orality and Literacy*, 43–44.

Discussion focused on an area of difference is the moment when the shared memory is at its most creative. It may take days or weeks to arrive at a final version. Time is not important; the accuracy of the finished product is the objective. This is a moment not of academic wrangling but of putting onto paper the varied threads of opinion, creating a tapestry of unity in difference. Each understands difference, each affirms and respects it. The themes discussed and the insights recorded in community discussion form this new tapestry of old spiritualities, now expanded by virtue of the sharing in dialogue. The record is there for others to take forward, in other places, at other times.

As the dialogue continues, the community becomes stronger, appreciation of the other goes deeper. Each becomes aware that *home* takes on a new meaning; the voice of God is heard from a different, unfamiliar direction. What has been two traditions of spirituality now comes together in the firm conviction that the revealing God speaks to each through difference.

Walter Ong offers a useful insight. Referring to oral culture, he describes its way of working as having "nothing corresponding to how-to-do-it manuals. . . . Trades are learned by apprenticeship . . . which means from observation and practice with only minimal verbalized explanation."[15] This would be the starting point for the community in this dialogue. The processes outlined above will develop with experience. Likewise the creation of the shared memory is not compiled from memoranda provided by participants but through oral exchange in dialogue. There are no instruction manuals for dialogue, only voices, truly heard and accurately recorded.

There will be moments of difficulty and tension, when voices are raised. May offers a concrete analogy: "The saga of the desert tells of a journey out of slavery, through the desert, toward the garden that is home. But it is much more than a journey; it is the discovery of the depths of weakness, the power of grace, and the price of both."[16] The community dedicated to dialogue is on

---

[15] Ibid., 43.
[16] Gerald G. May, *Addiction and Grace*, Kindle location 2098–2013.

a journey to find God in the spirituality of the other. No one is seeking to make agreements through compromise. It is enough to listen for the echo with an ear attuned to a different voice, coming from a different place, in phrases that echo enough to create a positive memory for the other. This is a moment not of conversion of one to another but of freedom gained by hearing the voice of God inspired by the words of the other. It will be a deliverance from an isolation, made possible by engaging with, in Benedict's phrase, "the ear of your heart" to the revelation of God in an unfamiliar tongue, in an unfamiliar way (RB Prol. 1, RB 1980).

The Record

As already noted, the themes discussed and the insights recorded in community discussion will form a new tapestry of old spiritualities, now expanded by virtue of the dialogue.

Once a record has reached its first step, it finds a temporary home in the minds and hearts of the participants. The content is pondered by each privately, for an agreed period of time, allowing each to affirm or edit the text. Later these modifications are collected and inserted, before a second meeting of participants to affirm or to require further editing, using the same process. This process will be repeated until approval is given by all and the text becomes formally part of the shared spiritual memory. This is not just text; it is a living dialogue of faith. It is both believers speaking about their own spirituality and the voice of God speaking through each, forming an organic whole.

The final version, agreed and canonized, becomes a reference point. A new session can then start and the process repeated. The first document becomes archived, able to be taken on by others to inspire future dialogue. Other texts can be associated with it, but it cannot be altered. With time the record gets longer, "threads of faith-filled" insights link more strongly, and counter-echoes get louder. With the addition of more agreed-upon texts the record of this dialogue of spirituality grows ever bigger.

Final Comment

These guidelines show how a community in a dialogue of spirituality might work, but they are not fixed rules. Each community works out its own to suit its members. Each participant takes responsibility for the shared spiritual memory that emerges, and most important of all, the community alone confirms the record.

"Remember God": Living in the Presence of God, Muslims and Christians

Introduction

Our next step is to go into greater detail about how Christians and Muslims engage with the presence of God in their Inspired Scriptures. The high level of similarity already identified will enable greater fluency in dialogue, while at the same time demanding greater sophistication in definition.

"Remembering God" in the Inspired Scriptures

The Inspired Scriptures of Each

The most effective way of being aware of the presence of God, for both Muslims and Christians, is by remembering God's presence in the Word, for the divine eye does not blink even for a second, such is Divine Love. The response of believers is to discipline themselves to remember that God is present at every moment in their lives. They overcome distractions by repeating words from

God and constantly growing in familiarity with their respective Scriptures; the best way to ensure God is not forgotten.

After spending time in dialogue with the Word of God, Muslims and Christians should be able to say, "Your Word of God is also the Word of God for me"—not meaning the Word of each is identical but that there are enough echoes from the Word of the other to hear something of the voice of God.

Remembering God: Examples from the Inspired Scriptures

A survey of the Inspired Scriptures shows that remembering God has several meanings, eight of which are given in the points that follow.

First, Muslims and Christians are remembered by God: "I remember my covenant with Jacob; I will remember also my covenant with Isaac and also my covenant with Abraham, and I will remember the land" (Lev 26:42) echoed by the other: "remember Me; I will remember you. Be thankful to Me" (Qurʾan 2:152). One focuses on memory and the other on a covenant, but both imply direct involvement with the God who creates. God gives a high priority to a tangible covenant as the way to securing greater intimacy with the Chosen People. The Muslim phrase reinforces and extends this—no longer limited to one people but now offered to all. In both accounts this sense of being special is weakened by human disobedience.

Second, Muslims and Christians must acknowledge their sin, repent, and renew their commitment to obey as God instructs: "You shall remember and do all my commandments, and you shall be holy to your God" (Num 15:40). The reward: growth in intimacy with God, stronger faith, and frequent affirmation from the Word. So a community of dialogue would share this common commitment to holiness and give priority to a disciplined life, which will include sharing prayer, pondering Inspired Scriptures, and growing in mutual love and friendship.

Third, Muslims and Christians share a memory of God, acknowledged as Creator, Lover, and Forgiver. This God is the center of daily life now and promises future fulfillment in eternity.

To "remember God" is the most important element in the spirituality of this community; it will enable it to grow and develop. Through the dialogue the members gain a larger understanding of and confidence in the God-Who-Never-Forgets. "I formed you, you are my servant; O Israel, you will not be forgotten by me" (Isa 44:21), and all remember, "God's blessing on you and the pledge with which you were bound when you said, 'We hear and we obey'" (Qurʾan 5:7). In the never-forgetting-mind of God, there is space for all. The richness of the Word inspires participants, opens them to its meaning, from whatever page it is read or from whichever mouth it is uttered.

Fourth, through the revealing Word of God a triple agenda emerges: first, the memory of inspiration will make the community stronger in faith ("He brought your hearts together and you became brothers"; Qurʾan 3:103); second, to warn against forgetfulness ("I will remember in their favor the covenant with their ancestors whom I brought out of the land of Egypt in the sight of the nations, to be their God"; Lev 26:45); and third, both share the obligation to acknowledge blessings received and never forget the One who gave them. So from the Word each learns the will of God, and through the Word each responds with gratitude.

Fifth, remembering God makes God accessible at all times. To achieve this requires training: remember God always, "remember the former things of old; for I am God, and there is no other" (Isa 46:9). God's tireless work recorded in these Inspired Scriptures should be remembered "in all humility and awe, without raising your voice, in the mornings and in the evenings" (Qurʾan 7:205). With this advice participants encourage each other to keep their focus on God throughout the day. When difficulties come, remembering God helps to put the problems into context.

Sixth, God reveals qualities appropriate for faith-filled people. This is reassuring because God not only commands the faithful to obey the divine rules, "Remember the Sabbath day, and keep it holy" (Exod 20:8), but is also "close to [true] believers" (Qurʾan 3:68). The stronger the sense of the presence of God, the greater the sign of virtuous living and the more powerful the witness to the love emanating from God. People will say, "Yet in far countries they shall remember me, and they shall rear their children and return" (Zech 10:9). And, "It is in the remembrance of God that hearts find peace—those who believe and do righteous deeds" (Qur'an 13:28-29).

Seventh, the awareness of sin and failure causes believers, Christian and Muslim, to feel guilty, but this enables their faith in the God who forgives at the slightest sign of repentance, as God in the Qur'an states, "It is He who shows you [people] His signs and sends water down from the sky to sustain you, though only those who turn to God will take heed" (Qur'an 40:13-14). Forgetting one's guilt clouds Truth and God punishes the unrepentant. The story of Noah, recorded in both Inspired Scriptures, shows divine anger in action, but from it emerges a new covenant "that is between me and you and every living creature of all flesh; and the waters shall never again become a flood to destroy all flesh" (Gen 9:15).

Eighth, in another intervention, God rescues the people enslaved in Egypt. This was so momentous that it immortalized God's power; it was also memorable because of the lengths God took to secure the safety of the faithful and effective as it led to another covenant. So, all are exhorted to "remember that you were a slave in Egypt, and diligently observe these statutes" (Deut 16:12). In the future, "celebrate the name of your Lord, and devote yourself wholeheartedly to Him. He is the Lord of the east and the west; there is no god but Him, so take Him as your Protector" (Qur'an 73:8-9).

The parallels in these stories define a space for a dialogue of spirituality. In that dialogue there will be focus on the gift which led to faith, the weakness that brought further difficulties, and the intimacy that God was prepared to share with believers. God has the power but also allows the freely chosen cooperation of the individual, an essential element of the divine plan. In a community of dialogue, the acknowledged freedom to choose will open up new avenues of enrichment.

Chapter **10**

Techniques for "Remembering God": Muslim and Christian

Definition of *Lectio Divina* and *Dhikr*

The Arabic word *dhikr* has many meanings, which can be summarized as ways of listening, reading, pondering, and expressing the Word. These skills are developed in different ways: by means of posture, in song, with movement, and in states of ecstasy, for "remembrance constitutes the very essence of religious devotion, both in principle and in practice."[1] Its aim is to increase awareness of God by the continual recitation of the Word, in that way removing distractions, a frequent cause of worry. To remember God is to be looked after by God. Another meaning of *dhikr* is "recollection, or . . . of recollectedness . . . of invocation and of worship, especially under its aspect of the

---

[1] Reza Shah-Kazemi, "The Principles and the Practice of the Remembrance of God: An Islamic Perspective," in Anthony O'Mahony, *Catholics and Shi'a in Dialogue: Studies in Theology and Spirituality* (London: Melisende, 2004), 214–24, here at 214.

invocation of the Name of God."[2] Regular practice stimulates ever greater awareness of the presence of God.

Lectio divina might be called the Christian equivalent of *dhikr*. It is also the conscious hearing, pondering, praying, and applying of the Word, following Jesus' example, who went into the synagogue in Capernaum and read a passage from Isaiah 61 and interpreted it for his listeners,[3] who were "awestruck before God's Word."[4] The Christian learns, in Magrassi's words, "to resonate with the words that come from God and to let them work in us, to allow the Holy Spirit to judge our hearts as we read and to let it penetrate to the core of some life situation where the Word itself will resound."[5] Magrassi continues, "When I go beyond the letter of Scripture to its spirit, I personally encounter the living Christ. . . .

---

[2] Constance E. Padwick, *Muslim Devotions* (London: SPCK, 1961), 14. Constance E. Padwick (1886–1968), leading British woman missionary in Student Christian Movement; studied Arabic, Arab folklore, and Islam at School of Oriental and African Studies. Joined the Church Mission Society in 1912, went to Cairo where she studied at the American University and worked with the Nile Mission Press until 1921. Returned to London, wrote thesis on Arab folklore, returned to Egypt 1923, and remained for thirty years, including time in Palestine. In 1947 moved to Sudan. Expert in writing textbooks.

[3] "When he [Jesus] came to Nazareth, where he had been brought up, he went to the synagogue on the sabbath day, as was his custom. He stood up to read, and the scroll of the prophet Isaiah was given to him. He unrolled the scroll and found the place where it was written: 'The Spirit of the Lord is upon me, because he has anointed me to bring good news to the poor. He was sent me to proclaim release to the captives and recovery of sight to the blind, to let the oppressed go free, to proclaim the year of the Lord's favor.' And he rolled up the scroll, gave it back to the attendant and sat down. The eyes of all in the synagogue were fixed on him. Then he began to say to them 'Today this scripture has been fulfilled in your hearing'" (Luke 4:16-21).

[4] Enzo Bianchi, *Praying the Word: An Introduction to* Lectio Divina, Cistercian Studies 182 (Kalamazoo, MI: Cistercian Publications, 1998), 30. Enzo Bianchi (b. 1943) read economics at University of Turin; founded an ecumenical community at Bose, Italy 1965; still prior, mixed community, men and women, Christians from all denominations, with its own publishing house, Qiqajon. Has published at least nineteen books translated into English.

[5] Ibid., 31.

Understanding the Bible is like having a conversation with him."[6] But "when our spiritual life loses its dynamic character we need to look around for a source of renewal that will reactivate our sensibilities by exposing us to something fresh."[7] Faithful *lectio divina* both opens our vulnerability and reassures us because "we come to the Scriptures aware that our souls are perishing through starvation and we allow ourselves to express our desire to be fed."[8]

Aims of *Dhikr* and *Lectio Divina*

The simplicity of *dhikr*[9] is its most attractive characteristic; "in its primary form—it is permitted in any place and at any time; its practice is restricted neither to the exact hours of ritual prayer nor to a ritually clean place."[10] Muslims see it as the way to holiness,

---

[6] Mariano Magrassi, *Praying the Bible: An Introduction to* Lectio Divina (Collegeville, MN: Liturgical Press, 1998), 21–22. Mariano Magrassi, b. Tortona, Italy, monk, abbot of Santa Maria della Scala in Noci 1972, archbishop of Bari 1977. PhD in theology, LSS in Scripture.

[7] Michael Casey, *Sacred Reading* (Barnhard, MO: Liguori, 1996), 30. Michael Casey: a Cistercian monk of Tarrawarra Abbey in Australia. Well-known retreat master and lecturer on monastic spirituality; author of many books, including *Toward God: The Ancient Wisdom of Western Prayer*, *A Guide to Living in the Truth: Saint Benedict's Teaching on Humility*, and *Fully Human, Fully Divine: An Interactive Christology*.

[8] Ibid.

[9] Relevant texts from the Qurʾan: "Recite what has been revealed to you of the Scripture; keep up the prayer: prayer restrains outrageous and unacceptable behaviour. Remembering God is greater: God knows everything you are doing" (29:45). "God . . . guides to Himself those who turn towards Him, those who have faith and whose hearts find peace in the remembrance of God—truly it is in the remembrance of God that hearts find peace" (13:28). "Believers, remember God often and glorify Him morning and evening; it is he who blesses you" (33:41). "Remember God often so that you may prosper" (62:10). "God makes things easy for those who are mindful of Him" (65:4). "It is the one who brings the truth and the one who accepts it as true who are mindful of God; they will have everything they wish for with their Lord. Such is the reward of those who do good" (39:33-34).

[10] Annemarie Schimmel, *Mystical Dimensions of Islam*, rev. ed. (1975; Chapel Hill, NC: University of North Carolina Press, 2011), 167. Annemarie

and its final goal is to "become prayer"; the soul, so identified with prayer, God present "at the centre of one's heart."[11]

There are many ways of praying *dhikr*. Some join groups[12] so they can benefit from sharing experiences, encouraging others, and hearing their problems and joys. A Hadith Qudsī justifies this: "When my worshipper's thought turns to Me, there am I with him. And when he makes mention of Me within himself, I make mention of him within Myself: and when he makes

---

Schimmel (1922–2003), born Erfurt, Germany; 1939 studied at University of Berlin; doctorate in Islamic languages and civilization at 19; 1946 professor of Arabic and Islamic studies at the University of Marburg, where she gained a second doctorate in history of religions; 1954 appointed professor of History of Religion at University of Ankara; five years teaching in Turkish. From 1967 to 1992 at Harvard. She was honored for her work on Sufism in Pakistan and Germany. Published over fifty books on Islamic mysticism, literature, and culture, and translated Persian, Urdu, Arabic, Sindhi, and Turkish poetry.

[11] William C. Chittick, ed., *The Essential Seyyed Hossein Nasr* (Bloomington, IN: World Wisdom, 2007), 80.

[12] Constance E. Padwick, *Muslim Devotions*, 15, offers this description: "The fascination of this semi-hypnotic experience, as well as religious ardour, draws to the '*dhikr*' circles some whose lives are poor and starved of rich sensation. Such village '*dhikr*' circles as those of the Mirghaniyya Order, so common among Berber servants or in the Sudan, of the Shīdhilī Order, so common in the Egyptian Delta, of the little Khalīlī Order, once so common in Southern Palestine, or the '*dhikr*' circles on the Baiyūmi Order in some Cairo slums consist of lesser bourgeoisie, peasants or workmen living in the world, led by one adept who knows the '*dhikr*' of an order. The only connection of this group with the order may be attendance at these meetings, when, hypnotized by rhythm of sound and action, they may escape the immediate pressure of hard lives. . . . The writer knows men of education and position who sought in this way food for spiritual hunger. The man who enters the '*dhikr*' seriously and with instruction has, in the suspense of all sensation, save that of the rhythmic beat of the uttered Name, a goal of the spirit. The suspension of all other consciousness is to be in favour of the flooding and interpenetration of his whole being by the influence, the Divine Reality, behind one the Divine Names. So his being is to be transfused and unified through the Living Reality."

mention of Me in company, I make mention of him in a better company,"[13] clearly the language of intimacy.

Benedict's description of *lectio divina*[14] describes it as the agent of conversion, requiring three hours each day, with particular guidance about the choice of book, encouraging the reader to read well enough for the listeners to memorize it. Benedict imposes no obligation "to read the Bible from beginning to end."[15] The readings focus on the way to salvation, running "counter to our perceptions and expectations. . . . God's saving of us takes place by dragging us beyond our own comfort zone into new territory and new adventures."[16] The culture of Benedict's time was an oral society and the listener was often surprised by the Word read aloud; its power could penetrate the heart.

Today, beginners in *lectio divina* liken it to entering a darkened cave: "We need to give our eyes time to adjust to the dimmer light. . . . '*Lectio divina*' is a sober, long term undertaking and, as such, better reflected in sustained attention to whole books than in seeking a quick fix from selected texts."[17] It is a discipline to be learned; "we cannot listen attentively to the Word of God if we do not quiet what is going on inside us."[18] So it is a determined desire to penetrate further into the mystery of God, allowing oneself to be "suspended in the love of God."[19] Then, one thing leads to another, "reading invites application. Constant application produces familiarity. Familiarity produces faith and makes it grow."[20] The text penetrates the mind, heart, and memory, until the reader is soaked in its language and imagery: the Lord's voice then echoes strongly.

---

[13] Ibid., 18, whose source is *Usūlu 'l-Kāfī* of *al-Kulīnī*. She adds that it is constantly quoted in Sunni as well as Shi'a devotions.

[14] RB 48.

[15] Michael Casey, *Sacred Reading*, 5.

[16] Ibid., 6.

[17] Ibid., 8, 9.

[18] Enzo Bianchi, *Praying the Word*, 43.

[19] Ibid., 45, quoting Gregory the Great.

[20] Ibid., 51, quoting Jerome, *Epistola ad Eustochium*, 22.17 (PL 22:404).

The Origin of *Dhikr*

Many Muslims consider the origin of *dhikr* to go back to the first moment of creation, before anything existed. Reza Shah-Kazemi writes, "This implies that man's being 'remembered' is equivalent to his being created: thus for God to 'create' man is tantamount to a divine 'remembrance' of man."[21] The result: the life of each individual is seen as the playing out of this divine memory. The covenant, recorded in that divine memory, is prehistorical. It becomes alive in the memory of each person, who, during life, relives that original covenant—a process best described by the Greek word *anamnesis*, reliving in the present, an event of the past, without repeating it.[22] This offers reassurance and perspective, for, in the daily search for God, each begins with the assumption of already being a memory in the mind of God. By *dhikr*, remembrance is fulfilled. Ibn al-'Arabi writes, "Whenever one of the letters from the Book appears to you, the letter will become a source of inspiration and understanding to the extent of your proximity and your presence in Him."[23] This explains why the Qur'an is sometimes called a reminder.

[21] Reza Shah-Kazemi, "The Principles and the Practice of the Remembrance of God, an Islamic Perspective," in Anthony O'Mahony, *Catholics and Shi'a in Dialogue: Studies in Theology and Spirituality*, 223.

[22] *Anamnesis* is the word Catholic theologians use to describe how each Eucharist can be a reenactment of the sacrifice of Jesus Christ on the cross, without multiplying the number of times Jesus was crucified. It is the one historical event, which by a process of remembering is reenacted, not reproduced or multiplied.

[23] Ibn Al-'Arabi, *The Meccan Revelations*, vol. 2, trans. and ed. Micehl Chokkiewicz, Cyrille Chodkiewicz, and Denis Gril (1988; repr. New York: Pir Press, 2004), 136. Ibn Al-'Arabi (1165–1240), b. Murcia, Spain. Early Muslim formation in Spain, at sixteen went into seclusion, encouraged by a vision of the three great prophets—Moses, Jesus, and Muhammad. In 1190 in Cordoba, he had a vision of all the prophets from Adam to Muhammad. Started writing, probably many more than the existing one hundred in manuscript form. In 1194, after death of parents, went to Fes, Morocco, where his friendship with 'Abdallah Badr al-Habshi started. In 1202 to Tunis, Cairo, during a famine, then Mecca, where he married, had a son, and

The opening words of John's gospel, might be the Christian equivalent, "In the beginning was the Word, and the Word was with God, and the Word was God" (John 1:1),[24] showing both the Word as present in creation and as the foundation of God's revelation to believers and at the same time reminding them of the continual divine presence. The Christian is, then, both "the passive receiver of revelation, and an active follower, who strives to render life responsible to its dictates."[25] This is possible because the constant living remembrance "is like the soul's embrace by which it clings to God without any trace of forgetfulness."[26] This embrace of love magnifies human love, enlarges the memory, and leads to firmer commitment and greater appreciation of God's gift of intimacy.

The Obligation

Reza Shah-Kazemi offers a similar explanation. He proposes that the duty to remember God arises from the nature of the relationship, for God is " 'greater' than the prayer, in the very measure that the goal transcends the means, the essence surpasses the form, and inner realization takes priority over outward practice."[27] The divine-human relationship is

---

wrote. Travels to Syria, Egypt, Palestine, Anatolia, Jerusalem, and Baghdad, before dying in Damascus.

[24] Words that echo, "The LORD created me at the beginning of his work, the first of his acts of long ago. Ages ago I was set up, at the first, before the beginning of the earth. . . . When he established the heavens, I was there. . . . When he marked out the foundations of the earth, then I was beside him, like a master worker; and I was daily his delight, rejoicing before him always, rejoicing in his inhabited world and delighting the human race" (Prov 8:22-23, 27a, 29b-31).

[25] Michael Casey, *The Undivided Heart* (Petersham, MA: St. Bede's Publications, 1994), 62.

[26] Ibid., 72, quoting St. Aelred, *Sermo in Nativitate Domini*, ed. C. H. Talbot, *Sermones Inediti*, Series Scriptorum S. Ordinis Cisterciensis 1 (Rome: Editiones Cistercienses, 1952), 38.

[27] Reza Shah-Kazemi, "The Principles and the Practice of the Remembrance of God: An Islamic Perspective," in Anthony O'Mahony, *Catholics*

beyond measurement. Only sin conceals the presence of God. The antidote is to be constant in the practice of *dhikr* because constant awareness of God's presence dissolves the cloud of sin and reveals its cure: repentance and forgiveness.

Lectio divina, in a similar way, creates the memory of God's actions on behalf of Christians. By munching or repeating a chosen Word, their minds are focused on God. Each should read with care, "done slowly and always vocalized,"[28] in this way it helps Christians to pray as much "as shall be necessary to sanctify [their] . . . vocation"[29]—that is, to avoid anything that distracts attention from the ever-watchful eye of God.

Liturgical prayer, combined with the reading of books by spiritual authors and silent contemplative prayer, provides other frameworks conducive to remembering God. But *lectio divina* is unique. It unites the voice of God speaking through the Word and the listening ear obliged to live at all times in the presence of God.

Techniques: *Dhikr* and *Lectio Divina*

"'*Dhikr*' is the first step in the way of love; for when somebody loves someone, he likes to repeat his name and constantly remember him."[30] When applied to God, this reveals a deeper motive: to secure "man's obedience and submission to God

---

and Shi'a in Dialogue: Studies in Theology and Spirituality, 214.

[28] Columba Stewart, *Prayer and Community: The Benedictine Tradition* (London: Darton, Longman & Todd, 1988), 36.

[29] Augustine Baker, *Holy Wisdom* (1964; repr. Wheathampstead: Anthony Clarke Books, 1972), 316. Fr. Augustine Baker, OSB (1575–1641), b. Abergavenny, 1590 law at Oxford, 1590 recorder of Abergavenny, 1603 became Catholic, 1605 monk of St. Justina, Padua, 1607 took vows in London with English monks of the Italian Congregation, 1613 ordained priest at Rheims, 1613–24 missioner in England, 1624–33 assistant chaplain at Cambrai with English Benedictine nuns (now Stanbrook, Yorkshire), 1633–38 at St. Gregory's Douai, 1638 returned to English mission. Died in London, 1641, buried in Holborn.

[30] Annemarie Schimmel, *Mystical Dimensions of Islam*, 168.

and his service,"[31] perfected when the "heart and tongue are in harmony"[32]—a harmony broken when self-interest clouds the memory, when "you forget your own soul in your remembrance."[33] Repetition of words or simple sentences is the best way to maintain this focus on God.

Different styles of *dhikr* have been developed. Some involve the heart, others the tongue, and others both. The highest form is described in this enigmatic statement: "when the heart is wandering in recollection and lets the tongue be silent and the worth of such a recollection is known only to God,"[34] suggesting the subject makes no attempt to disengage from distractions while the will continues to be focused on its intention to live in the divine presence; the rest is left to God.

Group *dhikr* can induce a state of intense concentration on God; it requires careful planning and uses "rhythmical speech and breathing and rhythmical movement, so as, by a kind of self-hypnotism, to banish any external sight or sound or thought,"[35] ensuring God alone is remembered. At this moment, God gives "some of that knowing of Him, of those divine secrets and supernatural understandings, which He granted to His servant al-Khadir."[36] Once the faithful are enveloped by God, they lose all self-awareness and are in a state sometimes referred to as " 'saturation' of self in Allah";[37] participants

---

[31] Ayatollah Mushin Araki, "The Remembrance of God," in Anthony O'Mahony, *Catholics and Shi'a in Dialogue: Studies in Theology and Spirituality*, 185–213, here at 186.

[32] Reza Shah-Kazemi, "The Principles and the Practice of the Remembrance of God: An Islamic Perspective," in Anthony O'Mahony, *Catholics and Shi'a in Dialogue: Studies in Theology and Spirituality*, 214–24, here at 221.

[33] Ibid.

[34] Annemarie Schimmel, *Mystical Dimensions of Islam*, 171, quoting Farīduddīn 'Attār, *Tadhkirat al-auliyā*, ed. Reynold Nicholson, vol. 2 (London and Leiden: Luzac & Co. and E. J. Brill, 1907), 44.

[35] Constance E. Padwick, *Muslim Devotions*, 15.

[36] Ibn Al-'Arabi, *The Meccan Revelations*, vol. 1, p. 14.

[37] Malise Ruthven, *Islam in the World*, 3rd ed. (1984; repr. London: Granta Books, 2006), 256. Malise Ruthven (b. 1942 Dublin), MA in English, PhD

transcend their immediate surroundings and have an intense experience of God.

In contrast the essential technique of *lectio divina* is to move from reading the Word to meditating its meaning and, from that, discerning its relevance for the subject, who is then challenged to live that insight. Fidelity to daily *lectio divina* strengthens commitment, changes priorities, and builds stability. This journey in the Word can be undertaken alone or with others in shared *lectio*, when participants may share their insights and offer each other support.

Benedict proposed that the Word should be prayed by slow recitation, eventually learned by heart—particularly relevant for Christians in dialogue with Islam. The " '*lectio*' time provided the opportunity to commit the Bible to heart allowing '*lectio*' the continual repetition of text throughout the day, especially at the Work of God."[38] Columba Stewart quotes this advice from a thirteenth-century monk who urged "his readers to remember each evening's common reading so that throughout the night, whether desiring sleep or prayer, they would have something to ruminate, lest the devil find them at loose ends,"[39] an anxiety shared by Muslim teachers. Memorized texts provide a Word from God, alive in the mind at every moment so God can be praised "with psalms, hymns and spiritual songs; either on our lips, when that is possible and edifying, or at least in our hearts. Else, how could we reconcile these two ideas of St. Paul: pray unceasingly and labor without respite,"[40] sometimes called the gift of "interior recollection."[41] After years of *lectio divina*, the subject becomes more silent, creating expectation, emptying the heart, listening for an echo, alert to the signs of the Holy Spirit, usually gentle, subtle, and quiet. For appreciation to grow there

---

social and political sciences, University of Cambridge; writer, journalist, and teacher focusing on fundamentalism and Islamic affairs.

[38] Columba Stewart, *Prayer and Community*, 37.

[39] Ibid., 37–38.

[40] Marcel Driot, *Fathers of the Desert: Life and Spirituality* (Slough: St. Paul Publications, 1992), 64. Marcel Driot was a French monk and hermit.

[41] Ibid., 70.

has to be ever greater sensitivity illustrated by this analogy from a monk of Mt. Athos. To get close to a dove means becoming quieter and stiller, and "the more we give it our careful attention, the closer to us it will come."[42] So when the Word comes, it should be welcomed as if it "were spoken today for the first time."[43]

Lectio divina provides an opportunity to have a view of the Bible as a whole, to gain "an understanding of the Bible by means of the Bible itself."[44] This is achieved by reading the whole Bible regularly as Muslims read the whole of the Qurʾan. After a few years, familiarity with the whole of Scripture enables better understanding of the particular; the Word in one text is now echoed more clearly in another.

With these skills, the Word penetrates to the deepest level of the soul, conversing "silently with God, with no other desire than to remain close . . . we know God's thoughts in our deepest being. We feel that we have discovered God's heart in the Scriptural text and we give ourselves to him."[45]

Dhikr and *Lectio Divina* in Prayer and Life

Dhikr integrates by being "woven into the texture of everyday life,"[46] and it is self-perpetuating because "the one who remembers God the most, and is best known to serve Him is the most respectable person near God."[47]

Lectio divina increases the desire for God and provides the best defense against forgetfulness. As Abba Lucius said, "While

[42] Enzo Bianchi, *Praying the Word*, 43.

[43] Ibid., 53.

[44] Ibid., 54.

[45] Ibid., 63.

[46] Reza Shah-Kazemi, "The Principles and the Practice of the Remembrance of God: An Islamic Perspective," in Anthony O'Mahony, *Catholics and Shi'a in Dialogue: Studies in Theology and Spirituality*, 219.

[47] Hassan Ibn Fazl Ibn Hassan Tabarsi, *Mishkat Ul-Anwar Fi Ghurar Il-Akhbar, The Lamp Niche for the Best Traditions* (2001; repr. Qum: Ansariyan Publications, 2007), 146, no. 261.

performing my manual tasks, I pray unceasingly. I sit down with God, moistening my rushes for plaiting my cords and saying, 'have mercy on me, God in your great kindness, and in keeping with the greatness of your compassion take away my sin.' "[48] This shows that "when the Spirit establishes his abode in a human being this person can no longer stop praying for the Spirit prays unceasingly in him or her."[49]

[48] Marcel Driot, *Fathers of the Desert: Life and Spirituality*, 63, quoting J-Cl Guy, "Les Apophtegmes des Pères du desert" (Bellefontaine: Spiritualité orientale, 1966), 162.

[49] Ibid., 66, quoting Pl. Deseille, "Guide Spiritual," 282.

Chapter 11

The Holiness of the Word: Muslim and Christian

Aspects of Holiness

For Muslims, The Qurʾan is "God's very own words. To hear its verses chanted, to see its words written large on mosque walls, to touch the pages of its inscribed text creates a sense of sacred presence in Muslim minds and hearts"[1] to over a billion Muslims worldwide. Not just a book but the living voice of God. Its miraculous qualities are described by Ali Bin Uthaman Al-Hujwiri[2] as "the most beneficial audition to the mind and the most delightful to the ear is that of the Word of God. . . . It is

---

[1] Jane Dammen McAuliffe, "Preliminary Material: 'A Description of the Qurʾan,'" item 2, in *Encyclopaedia of the Qurʾān*, ed. Jane Dammen McAuliffe (Leiden and Boston: Brill, 2005), CD-ROM.

[2] Ali Bin Uthaman Al-Hujwiri (d. 1073), b. Ghazna, Afghanistan, came to Lahore 1039 where he died. Popular spiritual leader known as "The Giver." Few details are known, but his tomb is popular among Sufis of all classes.

a miraculous quality of the Qur'an that one never grows weary of reading and hearing it."[3]

Christians use more sober language: "God speaks only one single Word, his one Utterance in whom he expresses himself completely,"[4] elaborated as the single divine Word that "extends throughout Scripture, that it is one and the same utterance that resounds in the mouths of all the sacred writers, since he who was in the beginning God with God has no need of separate syllables, for he is not subject to time."[5] This Word is communication from God, spoken out of the depth of the Oneness of the Divine Being, into time, in voice, in language, for Muslims and for Christians, "the sacred Scriptures contain the word of God and, since they are inspired, really are the word of God" (*Dei Verbum* 24), and to emphasize the point, it quotes St. Jerome, who said, "ignorance of the Scriptures is ignorance of Christ" (St. Jerome, Commentary on Isaiah, Prol.: PL 24, 17). By reading these Scriptures the faithful can say, "we speak to Him when we pray; we hear Him when we read the divine sayings,"[6] for the texts "have been written down under the inspiration of the Holy Spirit" (11).[7]

---

[3] Ali Bin Uthaman Al-Hujwiri, *The Kashf Al-Mahjub*, trans. Reynold A. Nicholson (New Delhi: Adam Publishers and Distributors, 2009), 394.

[4] *Catechism of the Catholic Church* (London: Geoffrey Chapman, 1994), 29, para. 102.

[5] Ibid., quoting Augustine of Hippo, *Enarrationes in Psalmos*, 103, 4, 1 (PL 37, 1378).

[6] The inspiration of Scripture is summarized therein: "Holy Mother Church, relying on the belief of the apostles, holds that the books of both the Old and New Testament in their entirety, with all their parts, are sacred and canonical because, having been written under the inspiration of the Holy Spirit . . . they have God as their author, and have been handed on as such to the Church herself" (Dogmatic Constitution on Divine Revelation 11).

[7] DV 11. It continues: "In composing the sacred books, God chose men and while employed by Him they made use of their powers and abilities, so that with Him acting in them and through them, they, as true authors, consigned to writing everything and only those things which He wanted."

For Muslims, the Word in the Qurʾan has similar power. By recitation, it leads, in the words of Annemarie Schimmel, "the spirit into a meditative state or even of producing a mystical rapture."[8] This is illustrated by an anecdote about Shibli, who, hearing the command to remember God, said, " 'remembrance (of God) involves forgetfulness (of self), and all the world have stopped short at the remembrance of Him'; then he shrieked and fell senseless. When he came to himself, he said: 'I wonder at the sinner who can hear God's Word and remain unmoved' "[9]—a vivid reminder of the transforming power of the Word of God. Many Muslims seek "total immersion in *dhikr* (remembrance) of Allah, and his constant awareness of the Possessor of Majesty."[10] Stories are told of retired people sitting with their Qurʾan, praying, fasting, and learning more about God, who say, "This is real work! All that other activity is nothing!"[11] for, as the Prophet said, "An hour of meditation is worth sixty years of worship."[12]

[8] Annemarie Schimmel, *Mystical Dimensions of Islam*, 26.

[9] Ali Bin Uthaman Al-Hujwiri, *The Kashf al-Mahjub*, 395. Shibli is also known as Abû Bakr Dulaf, b. Jahdar al-Shiblî, "a great and celebrated Shaykh," the opening words of a section about him, no. 57, p. 155.

[10] Muhammad Al-Ghazālī, *Remembrance and Prayer* (1986; repr. Markfield, UK: Islamic Foundation, 2000), 25.

[11] Sharafuddin Maneri, *The Hundred Letters* (New York: Paulist Press, 1980), letter 51, p. 206. Sharafuddin Maneri (c. 1263–1381), known as 'The Spiritual Teacher of the Realm', venerated as one of the most famous Islamic saints. He attended first a local mosque-school and then under Abu Tawwama al-Hanbali for his education in all branches of Islamic learning. According to tradition he married the daughter of Hanbali, had a son by her. After his father's death he adopted a life of celibacy, entrusted the boy to the care of his mother, and went to Delhi in search of a spiritual guide probably during the late 1280's. There he found a little known master, Najibuddin Firdausi. Next he moved to Bihar Sharif where he taught and wrote the Letters to the Governor of Chausa in Western Bihar who was unable to attend his lectures. He died there on Jan 2nd 1381. The third volume *A Mine of Meaning*, Louisville, Kentucky, Fons Vitae 2012, appeared too late for my research.

[12] Ibid., letter 60, p. 243.

Given time for pondering and reflecting, the Word penetrates to the heart of believers.[13]

In silent reflection the hidden meanings are revealed, of these the spiritual meanings open a window into the mystery of faith, as Henri de Lubac[14] has written, the "spiritual understanding is, in its principle, identical to the process of conversion,"[15] which shows the Word, alive and active, enabling the reader to turn to Christ, "a conversion which can never be said to have been fully achieved."[16]

Likewise, Muslims recognize their engagement with the Inspired Scriptures as a lifelong task. The reader learns to appreciate that every word has an eternal existence, as Ibn Al-'Arabi writes, it is "perpetually new; since there is an incessant renewal of creation, there is an incessant renewal of the Divine Word."[17] The Word is never the same twice and in that way offers new challenges, ordering me "that all my talking should be in remembrance of God, my silence should be accompanied by thinking

---

[13] An example: "One of the most famous conversion stories in early Sufism is that of Fudayl ibn 'Iyād. He was a highway man, albeit a magnanimous one, between the cities of Abiward and Sarakhs. One day, on the way to his beloved, he happened to hear a verse from the Koran and immediately gave up banditry, thereafter devoting himself to the study of the Prophetic tradition in Kufa. He died in Mecca in 803." Quoted in Annemarie Schimmel, *Mystical Dimensions of Islam*, 35.

[14] Henri de Lubac (1896–1991), b. Cambrai, entered Jesuits 1913, moved to UK for formation; military service in WWI, wounded, returned to study in UK until 1926. Then to Lyon, ordained priest 1927. Taught fundamental theology at the Catholic University of Lyon 1929–61, served in the resistance in WWII and was "suspended" by Vatican authorities 1950–58. First book *Catholicism* (1938). Founder of *Sources Chrétiennes*, greatest work on respective roles of Scripture and Tradition. Peritus at Vatican II and member of the Theological Commission. Appointed cardinal 1990, with the dispensation of not being ordained a bishop.

[15] Henri de Lubac, *Scripture in the Tradition* (New York: Crossroad Publishing, 2000), 21. Original published in French in 1967, *L'Ecriture dans la Tradition*.

[16] Ibid., 21.

[17] Ibn Al-'Arabi, *The Meccan Revelations*, vol. 2, p. 30.

and my looking should be accompanied by learning,"[18] living in the presence of God, recognizing "the Qurʾan is the language of all knowledge,"[19] for he who does "not know the Koran is as if he were never born,"[20] words paralleling Christian teaching.

Benedictine communities are organized so that all can spend, as Michael Casey puts it, "several hours every day reading or listening to books being read,"[21] originally in common, for "there was always respect for the text; in the case of the Bible and the words of the great Christian teachers this grew into a deep sense of reverence."[22] Reading established the framework for living, "it did not foment isolation."[23] The members grew into the Word, which becomes "an instrument of salvation,"[24] challenging attitudes and inviting new thoughts.

[18] Hassan Ibn Fazl Ibn Hassan Tabarsi, *Mishkat Ul-Anwar Fi Ghurar Il-Akhbar, The Lamp Niche for the Best Traditions*, 152, no. 278.

[19] Ibn Al-'Arabi, *The Meccan Revelations*, vol. 2, p. 139.

[20] Annemarie Schimmel, *Mystical Dimensions of Islam*, 331, quoting Yūnus Emre, *Divan*, ed. Abdülbâki Gölpinarli (Istanbul, 1943), 508. Another expresses it: "for the Muslim [the Qurʾan] is the revelation of God and the book in which His message to man is contained. It is the Word of God revealed to the Prophet through the archangel Gabriel. The Prophet was therefore the instrument chosen by God for the revelation of His Word, of His Book of which the spirit and the letter, the content and the form, are Divine. Not only the content and meaning come from God but also the container and form which are thus an integral aspect of the revelation." Seyyed Hossein Nasr, *Ideals and Realities of Islam* (1966; repr. London: George Allen & Unwin, 1971), 42. Seyyed Hossein Nasr (1933–), Tehran, came to USA at age 13, to MIT to study physics, became a disciple of Frithjof Schuon, earned PhD at Harvard on the history of science in 1958. Returned to Iran, professor at Tehran University, where he was dean of the Faculty of Letters, 1968–72, then to Arya Mehr University where he became president in 1972. Then returned to USA, eventually becoming, in 1984, professor of Islamic studies at George Washington University. Has written many books.

[21] Michael Casey, *Sacred Reading*, 3.

[22] Ibid., 3–4.

[23] Ibid., 4.

[24] Ibid., 7.

The process of transformation is slow; patience is essential, well illustrated as these words of Abba Poemen, the desert father, show: "The nature of water is soft, that of stone is hard; but if a bottle is hung above the stone, allowing the water to fall drop by drop, it wears away the stone. So it is with the word of God; it is soft and our heart is hard, but the (one) who hears the word of God often, opens his heart to the fear of God."[25] A determined commitment to be transformed in heart by the Word is needed for the power to be effective.

A different analogy has been used for Muslims. The Prophet revealed, "This is the Truth" (Qur'an 41:53), the Truth that activates the spiritual memory. The one who seeks God needs to be attracted before conversion, as the fish needs to be trapped before it can be landed. So God, seeking conversion of believers, places, in Seyyed Hossein Nasr's words, "a net before them into which they run and in which they are caught."[26] Once caught, they see the light guiding them to union with God.

The Christian is challenged to read the Word regularly to develop an ever more intimate relationship with God. Those who get close will grasp the "magnitude of God's gift [and] will be in awe of every aspect of the divine bounty"[27] but, at the same time, intimate enough for the divine speaker to be, in Mariano Magrassi's words, "present before me as a divine 'Thou.' At that moment God speaks those words for me. God wishes to create a dialogue of love, to take hold of my life and insert it into God's life."[28] Once the believer is truly listening, the transformation begins; Enzo Bianchi explains that "the Word of God is . . . a seed that contains life in itself and within which life itself develops until it becomes the great tree of the Kingdom";[29] the result is a slowly transforming dialogue.

[25] Benedicta Ward, *The Sayings of the Desert Fathers: The Alphabetical Collection* (Oxford: AR Mowbray, 1977), 192–93, no. 183.

[26] Seyyed Hossein Nasr, *Ideals and Realities of Islam*, 54.

[27] Michael Casey, *Sacred Reading*, 29.

[28] Mariano Magrassi, *Praying the Bible*, 83.

[29] Enzo Bianchi, *Praying the Word*, 24.

Both Muslim and Christian teachings echo the other, with each describing an ever-deeper love affair with the Word—affirming, challenging, tantalizing, reminding, forgiving, and giving life. For both faiths, the revealed Word is a gift, incomplete now but containing the promise of fulfillment.

Chapter 12

Engaging with the Word of God:
Muslim and Christian

For the Muslim, regular dialogue with the Word "softens the heart and removes its veils, the heart becomes worthy of being the receptacle of the Divine Peace or *al-sakīnah*."[1] As the dialogue continues, the Word acts like polish, in Reza Shah-Kazemi's words, "by which they hear after being deaf, and see after being blind and yield after being resistant."[2] With growing clarity, the desire for "the mystery of loving communion"[3] becomes clearer; the roles changed and "the seat of consciousness has shifted from the invoker to the Invoked."[4] God has taken the initiative; "man's invocation is but a shadow, a reflection or a consequence of this

---

[1] William C. Chittick, ed., *The Essential Seyyed Hossein Nasr*, 87.

[2] Reza Shah-Kazemi, "The Principles and the Practice of the Remembrance of God, an Islamic Perspective," in Anthony O'Mahony, *Catholics and Shi'a in Dialogue: Studies in Theology and Spirituality*, 2004.

[3] Ibid., 221.

[4] Ibid., 222.

divine invocation."[5] The moment of fulfillment is achieved when the believer is one, transformed into the everlasting God.[6]

Many Christians describe reading the Word as a journey without an identifiable end, or in Magrassi's words, "a mystery whose dimensions are the same as those of the mystery of Christ. It is infinite in extent; no reading can ever reach the bottom."[7] He then goes on to quote Origen, who was "overcome with fear upon entering the vast, deep, and mysterious sea of God's Word with his fragile boat"[8] and uses this analogy: "Just as one who goes to sea in a small boat feels extremely anxious about entrusting a small vessel to such huge waves, so we too suffer when we dare to penetrate such a great sea of mysteries." To engage with the Word of God is dangerous: its demands can be life changing.

Similarly, in the Muslim journey, by remembering, pondering, and growing, each gets closer to the Word, enabling the believer to pass from moments of repetition to continual prayer, driven by the memory of that Word. The goal now is "to become prayer. The very substance of the soul must become prayer. It must become totally identified with prayer,"[9] made possible because God is at the center of the heart guiding toward, as Allameh Jafari[10] writes, "constant remembrance of and calling out for God."[11] The inner heart now becomes "the supreme Name of God, by virtue of the mystery of the creation of man as a being at whose centre resides the All-Merciful."[12] Such intimacy with

---

[5] Ibid.

[6] See Annemarie Schimmel, *Mystical Dimensions of Islam*, 172.

[7] Mariano Magrassi, *Praying the Bible*, 38.

[8] Ibid., referring to Origen, *Homilies on Genesis*, Homily 9.1, *PG* 12, 210.

[9] William C. Chittick, ed., *The Essential Seyyed Hossein Nasr*, 80.

[10] Allameh M. T. Jafari (1923–98) studied at Talebieh Seminary, moved first to Tehran and Qum then to Najaf for studies in jurisprudence, earning the highest degrees. Returned to teach in Qum and Tehran. He has an institute named after him.

[11] Allameh M. T. Jafari, *The Mystery of Life* (Tehran: Allameh Jafari Institute, 2005), 273. (tenth point in a section titled "Having God in Mind").

[12] William C. Chittick, ed., *The Essential Seyyed Hossein Nasr*, 93.

God changes every aspect of life for "there is no prayer, no rite, no ritual that is separable from remembrance."[13]

Muslims are assured "there is nothing needful for the people in religious or worldly affairs which We have not placed in the Holy Qurʾan,"[14] but to gain access to this information, Muslims have to be ready to be truly open to the Word to gain "intimate knowledge of the secrets of the Qurʾan."[15]

The first step is to learn the discipline of regular reciting and listening to the words of the Qurʾan.

The second is to find a spiritual adviser who will speak, as Ibn Al-'Arabi writes, words that come "from the presence of the Qurʾan and Its treasures,"[16] who will facilitate the Word, not replacing it, enabling it to guide to conversion, not being part of it, because all know "the Glorious, Exalted God is found within you."[17]

The third is to attain purity of heart, to ensure "prayer, recitation of the Quran and remembering God or meditating upon Him"[18] are effective in deepening understanding of God, achieved by the fourth step, which is spending time "remembering God and reading the Qurʾan, especially during the last part of the night,"[19] a particularly important hour for inspiration. When followed enthusiastically, the desire for God becomes stronger, in Whom all hearts can "find peace in the remembrance of God—truly it is in the remembrance of God that hearts find peace" (Qurʾan 13:28), not just individuals but also "the community . . . find peace

---

[13] Reza Shah-Kazemi, "The Principles and the Practice of the Remembrance of God: An Islamic Perspective," in Anthony O'Mahony, *Catholics and Shi'a in Dialogue: Studies in Theology and Spirituality*, 214.

[14] Sharafuddin Maneri, *In Quest of God: Maneri's Second Collection of 150 Letters* (Gujarat, KT: Mathew SJ Gujarat Sahitya Prakash, 2004), 235, letter 119.

[15] Ibid.

[16] Ibn Al-'Arabi, *The Meccan Revelations*, vol. 1, p. 80.

[17] Sharafuddin Maneri, *In Quest of God*, 190, letter 90, quoting Qurʾan 51:21.

[18] Sharafuddin Maneri, *The Hundred Letters*, 123, letter 32.

[19] Sharafuddin Maneri, *In Quest of God*, 76, letter 29.

and satisfaction by remembering God."[20] The ultimate aim of the faith-filled person is to love in "conformity to the inner order of the universe, governed and dominated by God and His will."[21]

The teaching of Islam does not exclude any aspect of human living from the presence of God. The Qur²an advises believers not only to remove "the 'rust' of worldliness, of egotism and of sin"[22] but also to remember God in the most intimate moments of life, such as "in the matter of sexual contact, each partner is expected to link his or her desire to the name of Allah,"[23] and, when in pain, remembering God "soothes the aching body and causes time to pass unnoticed,"[24] further, in a crisis, remembering God in prayer "restrains outrageous and unacceptable behavior" (Qur²an 29:45), while, when distracted, remembering God helps from falling "for worldly and materialistic affairs,"[25] and, finally, invoking the name of God effects a change: enmity is "replaced by love. . . . selfishness by . . . self-sacrifice, violence by benevolence, wrath and retaliation by forgiveness and mercy."[26] These examples show how believers learn to pray, live every moment in the divine presence, and grow in intimacy with the revealing God.

Ibn'Abbad of Ronda[27] advises the spiritual teacher that he should "give thought to his ultimate reward and be as gentle in his teaching as possible, never treating a student harshly or

[20] Angelika Brodersen, "Remembrance," in *Encyclopaedia of the Qur²ān*, ed. Jane Dammen McAuliffe (Leiden and Boston: Brill, 2005), CD-ROM. In first section "Remembrance of God," para. 7.

[21] Ayatollah Mushin Araki, "The Remembrance of God," in Anthony O'Mahony, *Catholics and Shi'a in Dialogue*, 185–213, here at 185.

[22] Reza Shah-Kazemi, "The Principles and the Practice of the Remembrance of God: An Islamic Perspective," in Anthony O'Mahony, *Catholics and Shi'a in Dialogue: Studies in Theology and Spirituality*, 216.

[23] Muhammad Al-Ghazālī, *Remembrance and Prayer*, 51.

[24] Ibid., 80.

[25] Allameh M. T. Jafari, *The Mystery of Life*, 272.

[26] Ayatollah Mushin Araki, "The Remembrance of God," in Anthony O'Mahony, *Catholics and Shi'a in Dialogue: Studies in Theology and Spirituality*, 188.

[27] Ibn Abbad of Ronda (1333–90), b. in Ronda, attracted to the famous madrassahs of Morocco, went there and stayed for most of his life, buried near Fes. Known for his letters on the Sufi Path.

unjustly. He must at all times focus his attention on his Lord."[28] The responsibility of the Muslim teacher is not merely to offer accurate teaching but also to show how the teaching is put into practice, leading to his Friend and then "sit[ting] down at the feast of the gracious manifestation of the Beloved."[29] The reward for a life of faithful teaching is to be eternally in the presence of the One. With time the teacher not only knows the journey but will show his student too.

One chapter of Benedict's Rule has relevance to all Christians with regard to the Word of God. Chapter 4, "Tools of Good Works," offers guidance for daily living. First, "love the Lord God with your whole heart, your whole soul and all your strength, and love your neighbor as yourself" (RB 4.1-2, RB 1980); second, *"never do to another what you do not want done to yourself"* (RB 4.9, RB 1980; quoting Tob 4:16, Matt 7:12, Luke 6:31), the foundation commandment for living in community. Third, "your way of acting should be different from the world's way; the love of Christ must come before all else" (RB 4.20-21, RB 1980); and the fourth teaches, "never give a hollow greeting of peace or turn away when someone needs your love . . . but speak the truth with heart and tongue" (RB 4.25-26, 28, RB 1980). Facing challenge each should "be certain that the evil you commit is always your own and yours to acknowledge" (RB 4.43, RB 1980). This advice, based on the Word, reveals the divine will in ways that can be followed in daily living in family or community.

The main work for the Christian is, as Benedict states, to "take delight in listening to sacred reading" (RB 4.9, NPB), because it inspires prayer and increases awareness of sins, preparing all to confess them with heartfelt sorrow "to God in prayer" (RB 4.57, RB 1980), never losing "hope in God's mercy" (RB 4.74, RB 1980). By keeping faithfully to this daily routine, Christians grow ever closer to God. On Judgment Day these tools will be

[28] Ibn 'Abbad of Ronda, *Letters on the Sūfī Path*, trans. and intro. John Renard (New York: Paulist Press, 1986), 182, letter 15.

[29] Sharafuddin Maneri, *The Hundred Letters*, 265, letter 65.

returned to God and they will receive "the reward the Lord has promised" (RB 4.76, RB 1980).

Mature Christians know they will face boredom in their spiritual life, sometimes leading to laziness, lethargy, and a lack of enthusiasm, defined by Benedict as an "unwillingness to make an effort to do something that our mind approves."[30] It is sometimes called *acedia*, that "lack of commitment to spiritual values which leaves a person unable to settle down to anything serious, for any length of time."[31] In modern terms it is the "fantasy world," which reduces the "capacity to discern what is of permanent value and what is merely ephemeral."[32] This may make it difficult to ponder the Word, or, in Cassian's words, renders a person incapable of entering "into the very heart and core of heavenly utterances, to contemplate with the heart's purest gaze the deep and hidden mysteries."[33] Such people should be encouraged by these words: when "God 'knows' a being, he cares about it, loves it, chooses it, showers it with gifts and binds it as if it shared the same destiny."[34]

From the above we can see that both Muslims and Christians need training to engage with the Word of God—encouragement both to make it a daily commitment and find inspiration and hope in it.

---

[30] Michael Casey, *Sacred Reading*, 19.

[31] Ibid.

[32] Ibid.

[33] Mariano Magrassi, *Praying the Bible*, 58, quoting John Cassian, *Collationes XIV*, and c. 11 (Paris: Sources Chrétiennes, 1942), 54, 195. English trans. Colm Luibheid—CWS.

[34] Mariano Magrassi, *Praying the Bible*, 71.

Chapter 13

Engaging with the Word as Revelation and Guidance: Muslim and Christian

As we have seen, Muslims and Christians see the Word both as revelation from God and as guidance for the journey to ever greater intimacy with God.

Muslims hear the Word of God and believe, as Seyyed Nasr wrote, it "alone can actualize the intellect in man and allow it to function properly."[1] The Word acts as counterbalance to secular thinking. To keep persevering remains a challenge. As Tabarsi explains, "The spirit's perseverance is attained through sincerity in repentance. The heart's perseverance is attained through properly begging for pardon. The intellect's perseverance is attained through properly learning from one's mistakes. . . . The wisdom's perseverance is attained through proper pride, and the head's perseverance is attained through awareness of the

---

[1] Seyyed Hossein Nasr, *Knowledge and the Sacred* (Albany: State University of New York Press, 1989), 148. Seyyed Hossein Nasr (1933–), Teheran, came to USA at 13, to MIT to study Physics, became a disciple of Frithjof Schuon, moved to Ph.D at Harvard on the History of Science, and graduated 1958. Returned to Iran, Professor at Teheran University, where he was Dean of the Faculty of Letters, 1968–1972, then to Arya Mehr University, where he became President in 1972. Then returned to USA, eventually becoming, in 1984, Professor of Islamic Studies at The George Washington University. Has written many books.

secrets of the world."[2] Taken together, they all lead to a clearer understanding of the God Who Reveals.

The early Christian hermits abandoned everything and went into the desert to seek advice of one who had already spent long years in that search. One asked Antony for ways to please God. He gave these instructions: "Wherever you go, keep God in mind; whatever you do, follow the example of holy Scripture; wherever you are, stay there and do not move away in a hurry."[3] Stay still, remember God, and ponder God's Word, creating the right mood to hear God's revelation. In the past, as Ivan Illich[4] writing about monks states, even an "unlettered servant or un-couth dullard . . . attends the seven daily assemblies in the choir and, in front of the book, sings the Psalms. They become part of his being, and like the most learned brother, he can mouth them while he watches his goats."[5] Regular repetition of the Inspired Word invites all to become one with that revelation. Benedict's Rule makes "provision for that solitude; it enables 'creative monotony,' the skill necessary for heightened awareness,"[6] aided by the virtually unchanging routine.

When the Muslim sits in a mosque and the Christian sits in a church, both are learning to live the stillness, *munching* the oft-repeated divine Word. In this silent memory, God is close, inspiring new insights, offering a fragment of divine wisdom. Michael Casey describes this as a moment of spiritual growth,

---

[2] Hassan Ibn Fazl Ibn Hassan Tabarsi, *The Lamp Niche for the Best Traditions*, 146, no. 265.

[3] Benedicta Ward, ed., *The Desert Fathers: Sayings of the Early Christian Monks* (London: Penguin Books, 2003), 3.

[4] Ivan Illich (1926–2002), b. in Vienna, Croatian father and Jewish mother, studied in Florence, Pontifical Gregorian University in Rome, and Salzburg. In 1956 appointed vice rector of the Catholic University of Puerto Rico. Later founded the Intercultural Documentation Centre at Cuernavaca, Mexico, where he offered critical evaluation of Third World Development Schemes; author of many books.

[5] Ivan Illich, *In the Vineyard of the Text* (1993; repr. Chicago: University of Chicago Press, 1996), 60.

[6] Michael Casey, *The Undivided Heart*, 70.

which "demands a change of heart by which a person is simultaneously the passive receiver of revelation and an active follower."[7] Such revelations are remembered. With time the presence of God enlarges the heart.

Muslims follow their obligations, which include the repetitive reading of the Word, obedience to the disciplines of charitable giving, observing Ramadan (the month of fasting), and making plans to go on pilgrimage to Mecca. Each helps the memory of God to grow stronger.

The Sufis put more emphasis on the Inspired Scripture, training their members to see its deeper meanings. They are taught to recognize the Word's multiple meanings, as Gerhard Böwering expresses it,[8] "the outer, literal meaning and the inner, hidden meaning of the Qurʾānic text,"[9] or for the more advanced, the four meanings, the outer, inner, norm, and anagose similar to the four meanings used by Christians, literal, allegorical, moral and anagogical.[10] The more time spent with the Inspired Scriptures in study and prayer, the easier it is to discover these hidden meanings.

Marcel Driot writes that prayer is not "something, but someone. Prayer is God and the one who is praying. If the prayer passes completely into his prayer—and only then it is truly

[7] Ibid., 62.

[8] Gerhard Böwering, 1964–67 Urdu language study, Lahore, Pakistan; Diploma, Islamic studies, Panjab University; Arabic language study, Cairo. From 1967 to 1971 ThL Montreal; 1971–75, PhD Islamic studies, McGill University. From 1975 to 1984 assistant/associate professor University of Pennsylvania, Philadelphia; 1984– professor of Islamic studies, Yale University. In 1980, wrote *The Mystical Vision of Existence in Classical Islam: The Qurʾānic Hermeneutics of the Sūfi Sahl al-Tustari* (d. 283/896).

[9] Gerhard Böwering, "The Scriptural Senses," in *With Reverence for the Word*, ed. Jane Dammen McAuliffe, Barry D. Walfish, Joseph W. Goering, 346–65, here at 346 (Oxford: OUP, 2003).

[10] See Gerhard Böwering, "The Scriptural Senses," in *With Reverence for the Word*, ed. Jane Dammen McAuliffe, Barry D. Walfish, Joseph W. Goering, 346–65, here at 350, quoting Sahl al-Tustarī. Anagogical can be defined as a mystical interpretation of scriptural passages alluding to heaven.

prayer."[11] What may start as an obligation should become a love affair, aiming "to intensify this act of faith."[12] Far from giving up when difficulties arise, Christians should strengthen their commitment by creating, in Columba Stewart's words, "the whole atmosphere of . . . mindfulness of God."[13]

The Sufi mystics and spiritual imams possess the "the greatest possible insight into the depth of the Qurʾan. They understand the full meaning of the qurʾanic verses the way God himself understands them."[14] But once in formation, Nasr describes how "an unbridgeable hiatus between intelligence sanctified by revelation and the intelligence which, cut off from this source and also from its own root, is reduced to its reflection upon the human mind."[15] This can cause division, named by Christians as the distinction between the rational systematic theology and the spirituality focused on prayer, well expressed by Augustine Baker: "All the things we do we ought to do them in order to our last end, which is God,"[16] but "there is no question of the '*memoria Dei*' being a substitute, alternative or rival to common sense and practicality."[17] This is a warning against unrealistic idealism.

Reading the Inspired Scriptures "slowly and distinctly" (Qurʾan 73:4), ensuring the voices bring out the best in the text, and revealing, as Constance Padwick puts it, "their gospels are in their hearts,"[18] the Word has become the "stuff of their daily lives taking for them the place of a sacrament. For to them these are not mere letters or mere words. They are the twigs of the burning bush,

---

[11] Marcel Driot, *Fathers of the Desert: Life and Spirituality*, 74–75.

[12] Ibid., 79.

[13] Columba Stewart, *Prayer and Community*, 39.

[14] Gerhard Böwering, "The Scriptural Senses," 352.

[15] Seyyed Hossein Nasr, *Knowledge and the Sacred*, 149.

[16] Augustine Baker, *Holy Wisdom* (1964; repr. Wheathampstead: Anthony Clarke Books, 1972), 316.

[17] Michael Casey, *The Undivided Heart*, 72.

[18] Constance E. Padwick, *Muslim Devotions*, 114, a description of the community of Muhammad in *Munājātu Mūsā*.

aflame with God."[19] Using that image, Christians and Muslims can come to an ever-deeper sense of the presence of God.

Participants in a dialogue focused on the Sacred Word can hear the voice of God on their journey in moments of contemplative stillness. From Word to silence, from dialogue to contemplation, all become ever more familiar with their inner voices, challenging each to be patient. In this stillness each can access their common respective goals. Their skills of munching, speaking, pondering, and praying the Word will lead to a deeper understanding, which both enriches the present and offers hope for the future.

Ivan Illich finds that in such a community, "an effective and in-fallible search for wisdom is founded in the fact that all things are impregnated with sense, and this sense only waits to be brought to life by the reader."[20] In a dialogue this sense is a greater under-standing of the One God articulated by each participant.

Can They Do It?

Both Christians and Muslims receive the gift of the Divine Word revealed, historically at particular moments and preserved as their respective sources of revelation. There are echoes one with the other; there are techniques each can use to gain deeper understanding of and inspiration from both these revelations of the Divine Word. In an encouraging atmosphere, this dialogue will strengthen friendship, provide ever deeper insights of one to the other, and promote greater mutual trust. It can surely be done.

[19] Ibid., 119.
[20] Ivan Illich, *In the Vineyard of the Text*, 123.

Part 4

The Higher Forms of Spiritual Experience Compared: How Far Can They Get?

14

Comparing the Mystical Life: Muslim and Christian

Introduction

Muslim and Christian spiritualities converge in mystical experience—the deepest union with God. Though very few people are involved, their respective experiences warrant comparison in the context of a dialogue of spirituality. Ian Richard Netton has written that there is "powerful equivalence and emphasis on the image of 'the Way' or 'the Road' which must be undertaken in one form or another in the soul's journey towards perfection."[1] Elements of that "equivalence" will be outlined here.

Comparing Theory and Practice

Story

In Islam the best descriptions of mystical experience are found in the writings of Sufis, whose goal is total union with God.

[1] Ian Richard Netton, *Islam, Christianity and the Mystic Journey: A Comparative Exploration* (Edinburgh: Edinburgh University Press, 2011), 88.

Having renounced this world and its attractions, being purged of Self and its desires, inflamed with a passion of love to God, journeyed ever onward, looking towards his final purpose, through the life of illumination, with its ecstasies and raptures, and the higher life of contemplation, until at last he achieved the heavenly gnosis and attained to the Vision of God, in which the lover might become one with the Beloved and abide in Him forever.[2]

For Christians the mystical life is confined to those committed to a life of prayer. Contemplative prayer is part of any formation in prayer, but mystical experience is gift and, historically, rarely experienced. It has been well described by Aelred of Rievaulx[3] as the "soul's embrace, by which it clings to God without any trace of forgetfulness";[4] only in the memory does the "soul embrace God without any sense of weariness."[5] Occasionally, Christians called to the eremitical life are graced with mystical experiences, but it is a gift, not an outcome of a human ambition.

[2] Margaret Smith, *Rābi'a the Mystic and Her Fellow-Saints* (1928; repr. Felinfach: Llanerch Publishers, 1994), 1. Margaret Smith, 1884–1970, b. in Southport, MA in Cambridge and PhD, DLit London. A fine scholar of Islam and one of the first women to work in the field of Islamic mysticism. She taught in various Arab countries and lived in Damascus, Beirut, and Cairo. Her writings include *Studies in Early Mysticism in the Near and Middle East* (1931), *Readings from the Mystics of Islam* (1950), and *The Sufi Path of Love* (1954).

[3] Aelred of Rievaulx (1109–67), b. Hexham, in service of King David of Scotland. In 1133 entered the monastery at Rievaulx, the first Cistercian house in England, founded in 1132. In 1142 appointed abbot of new foundation at Revesby, Lincolnshire, and 1147 returned to Rievaulx as abbot. Known for his "On Spiritual Friendship" and "Mirror of Charity." In his time the number at Rievaulx rose to over six hundred, and he also had responsibilities to other Cistercian communities.

[4] Michael Casey, *The Undivided Heart* (Petersham MA: St. Bede's Publications, 1994), 72, quoting Aelred of Rievaulx. First, from ed. C. H. Talbot, *Sermo in Natitivate*, *Sermones Inediti*, Series Scriptorum S. Ordinis Cisterciensis 1 (Rome: Editiones Cistercienses, 1952), 38, 108.

[5] Ibid., quoting Aelred of Rievaulx, from *Sermo in die Pentecosten*, *Sermones Inediti*, Series Scriptorum S. Ordinis Cisterciensis 1, 108.

Women Mystics: Muslim and Christian

In Islam, women saints were acknowledged from the earliest times, a status conferred on "women as much as on men."[6] For, "in the spiritual life there could be 'neither male nor female.' "[7] Prayer offered to God with such dedicated spiritual desire may lead "to the most radical 'forgetting.' . . . You will not remember God . . . 'until you forget your own soul,' "[8] where "the remembrance itself continues, but is no longer conditioned by individual consciousness."[9] God now utters the invocation, "the invocation by man being but an outward appearance."[10]

The long history of Christian women mystics affirms the importance of this insight.[11] One contemporary makes this comment:

> The mystical marriage is not a state of psychic bliss, not a comprehensive fulfillment. It is utterly remote from such paltryness; it has nothing to do with self-states. It is to be with Jesus a total "for-Godness" which must mean being totally for others; it is an ecstasy of devotedness with no concern for self; it is to be Fire on earth purifying, enkindling others at a depth far below what we can discern. We have insisted throughout that the direct action of God in the human being is wholly secret. It can be known only by its effects and even these are not easily assessed by "flesh and blood."[12]

[6] Margaret Smith, *Rābi'a the Mystic and Her Fellow-Saints*, 1.

[7] Ibid.

[8] Reza Shah-Kazemi, "The Principles and the Practice of the Remembrance of God: An Islamic Perspective," in Anthony O'Mahony, *Catholics and Shi'a in Dialogue: Studies in Theology and Spirituality*, 214–24, here at 222.

[9] Ibid.

[10] Ibid.

[11] As examples, see the works of Gertrude of Helfta (1256–1301/2) and Hildegard of Bingen (1098–1179).

[12] Ruth Burrows, *Interior Castle Explored* (London: Sheed and Ward, 1981), 118.

The Process

The Sufi arrives at this state after a period of initiation. Techniques of *dhikr* were, as Reynold Nicholson[13] writes, "inspired by the spiritual director, and constantly controlled by him."[14] Facing many difficulties on the way, the trainee learns patience and realism, shown in this anecdote: "A man asked Abū 'Uthmān al-Hīrī: 'I recollect with the tongue but my heart does not become friends with the recollection.' He answered: 'Be grateful that one of your limbs obeys and one of your parts is led aright: maybe later your heart too will come into accord.' "[15] The path to mystical union faces the same human distractions as ordinary believers.

Permanent recollection is a skill acquired when the subject is "lost in the object, in which recollection, recollecting subject, and recollected object become again one. . . . What has been created disappears, and the only true subject, the everlasting God, is as He had been and will be."[16] For the Sufi, "true '*dhikr*' is that you forget your '*dhikr*,' says Shiblī. Since even the word or thought 'O God!' implies the consciousness of subject and object, the last mystery of recollection is complete silence."[17] Others agree, saying that "worshipping has ten parts, of which nine are silence. . . . Sincere recollection is beyond letter and thought; rosary and beads are, for the advanced Sufis, 'like the

---

[13] Reynold A. Nicholson (1868–1945), b. Keighley, Yorkshire, educated at Aberdeen and then settled in Cambridge, as lecturer in Persian (1902–26), then Sir Thomas Adam's Professor of Arabic (1926–33). Able to study major Sufi texts in Arabic, Persian, and Ottoman Turkish. Major work on Rumi's Masnavi, published in eight volumes between 1925 and 1940.

[14] Annemarie Schimmel, *Mystical Dimensions of Islam*, rev. ed. (1975; Chapel Hill: University of North Carolina Press, 2011), 169.

[15] Ibid., 171. See Farīduddīn 'Attār, *Tadhkirat al-auliyā*, ed. Reynold A. Nicholson, vol. 2 (1907; repr., Leiden: Brill, 1959), 59.

[16] Annemarie Schimmel, *Mystical Dimensions of Islam*, 172.

[17] Ibid., quoting Abū Nasr al-Sarrāj, *Kitāb al-Luma' fī't-tasawwuf*, ed. Reynold A. Nicholson, Gibb Memorial Series, no. 22 (Leiden and London: Brill, 1914).

lion painted in the bathroom' i.e., dead, without meaning and value."[18] This state of emptiness creates the disposition for total immersion in God.

From a Christian perspective, Augustine Baker shows that God works on the internal senses, producing "raptures or ecstasies, likewise internal visions and apparitions, which go together sometimes and sometimes are separated."[19] With these inner experiences the subject loses the use of the external senses, becomes totally focused on God, who calls "souls to a nearer and more perfect active union by love whereof one perfect act framed by the will is of more worth and more grateful to God, than all the visions and revelations of all things that pass in heaven and earth can be"[20]—a view echoed by the Sufis.

In this state, all existing knowledge passes as "mere darkness and a knowledge of the outward letter only whereas now she penetrates into the internal spirit of the writings."[21] Then the soul "perfectly feels her own nothing and God's totality and thereby is strangely advanced in humility and the divine love."[22] Such gifts celebrate the fullness of love: being able to *give* love and *receive* love. The result: "all our perfection consists in a state of love and an entire conformity with the divine will."[23] Self-giving love is gift for others, not personal possession but an indication of the dimension of God's love.

[18] Annemarie Schimmel, *Mystical Dimensions of Islam*, 172. The first quotation comes from Walter Braune, *Die Futūh al gaib, des 'Abdul Qādir* (Berlin and Lepzig: 1993), 98. The second is from Rūzbihān Baqlī, *Sharh-I shathiyāt, Les paradoxes des soufis*, ed. Henry Corbin (Tehran: Département d'iranologie de l'Institut franco-iranien, 1966), para. 509.

[19] Augustine Baker, *Holy Wisdom* (1964; repr. Wheathampstead: Anthony Clarke Books, 1972), 467.

[20] Ibid., 475.

[21] Ibid., 480.

[22] Ibid.

[23] Ibid., 487.

Schools of Mystical Union

Sufi schools teach the road to mystical union with distinctive elements; some describe different phases relating to different parts within the body.[24] Others allow themselves to be carried away by " 'rhythmical *dhikr*,' with its increasing tempo and its reduction of words until a kind of permanent sighing is reached."[25]

The Christian hermit develops the habit of remembering God's gifts like the hidden sap that keeps trees alive. In this case providing enough energy for "actions performed in mindfulness somehow have the power to produce a disproportionate effect on the recipient."[26] In this state of knowing, not fully understanding, the mystic arrives at the human limit and reaches out to a perfection available only within the gift of God.

The Unitive State

The final state for the Sufi is called unitive. It is a process of simplifying prayer so that "the soul is gradually isolated from all that is foreign to itself, from all that is not God. . . . He who dies to self lives in God, and '*fanā*,' the consummation of this death, marks the attainment of '*baqā*' or union with the divine life,"[27] realizing "his essential oneness with God."[28] Prayer is described as the "praise of God, proceeds from God and his knowledge is God's knowledge."[29] This is not the human becoming God, but where he or she "goes forth from his [or her] own will and enters into the will of God."[30]

[24] See Annemarie Schimmel, *Mystical Dimensions of Islam*, 174.

[25] Ibid., 176.

[26] Michael Casey, *The Undivided Heart*, 73.

[27] Reynold A. Nicholson, *The Mystics of Islam* (1914; repr. London: Penguin, 1989), 149.

[28] Ibid., 155.

[29] Ibid., 156.

[30] Ibid., 157, quoting from Abū Nasr al-Sarraj, *Kitāb al-Luma*.

Hujwīrī writes of Love as "the annihilation of the lover in His attributes and the confirmation of the Beloved in His essence."[31] In this state, the mystic becomes totally obedient, thus, "if you would say 'Die!' I would die in full obedience, and would say 'welcome to him who calls me to death,' "[32] for in death what is removed is "the disturbing 'I' that stands between lover and beloved."[33] In the end in the words of Hujwīrī, "the lover's clay is wholly converted into love and all his acts and looks become so many properties of love. This state is named 'Union.' "[34]

For Christians the lover of God will move beyond this world, becoming, in the words of Augustine Baker, "totally dead to the world and it to them and all the intellectual exercises and operations which formerly they pursued with propriety are altogether dead in them. They do neither by intention nor love, seek themselves nor any proper honor nor profit in time or eternity; they have utterly lost themselves."[35] In this state, imperfection is obliterated and God is "all in all,"[36] a union that dominates all else. What is unworthy is obliterated, what is worthy is transformed. Such people lose themselves to find themselves in God. Only when deprived of all securities—spiritual and material—can God "enjoy a secure and perfect possession of it."[37] Then, "when the memory is filled with God . . . joy, grace and love flood the soul, understanding and love are activated and temptation and infidelity are kept at bay,"[38] made possible by the gift, arising

---

[31] 'Alī ibn 'Uthmān al-Hujwīrī, *Kashf al-Mahjūb* (The Oldest Persian Treatise on Sufism), trans. Reynold A. Nicholson, Gibb Memorial Series 17 (1911; repr. London: 1959).

[32] Annemarie Schimmel, *Mystical Dimensions of Islam*, 135, quoting Maulāna 'Abdurrahmān Jāmī, *Nafahāt al-uns*, ed. M. Tauhīdīpūr (Tehran: 1336sh./1957).

[33] Annemarie Schimmel, *Mystical Dimensions of Islam*, 135.

[34] See Reynold A. Nicholson, *The Mystics of Islam*, 160, the quotation from Hujwīrī, *Kashf al-Mahjūb*.

[35] Augustine Baker, *Holy Wisdom*, 489.

[36] Ibid., 491.

[37] Ibid., 492.

[38] Michael Casey, *The Undivided Heart*, 72–73, quoting from William of St. Thierry, in *Cant* 127 (Paris: Sources Chrétiennes, 1942).

from a union in grace. The subject is filled with the Word of God, increasing the desire for fuller union with God.

The Spiritual Heart

At the moment of entry to the spiritual path, Muslim initiates are taught "they must reserve their heart for God alone, for He alone is the master of the house of the heart." [39] An Arab poem tells the story of one knocking on the door of a Sufi's heart to hear the reply that there is no one at home except the Master of the House, the one who is Creator and Sustainer of that heart. In the inner heart of every human being there is inscribed God's name, the all-merciful One.

Christians using the words of a medieval English mystic can be "so spiritually refined by grace and so intimate with God in prayer that they seem to possess and experience the perfection of this work almost as they like, even in the midst of their ordinary daily routine, whether sitting, standing, walking or kneeling." [40] But if they were asked, they would only admit to being sinners: to their brothers and sisters, they are shining examples of the transformation achieved through faithful following of Christ, the same effect is shown, in the words of Michael Casey, as "an inner radiance," [41] transforming the humblest service.

[39] William C. Chittick, ed., *The Essential Seyyed Hossein Nasr* (Bloomington, IN: World Wisdom, 2007), 93.

[40] William Johnston, ed., *The Cloud of Unknowing* (London: Harper Collins, Fount Paperbacks, 1997), 101. Originally written by an unknown mystic of the fourteenth century, it has become a much-loved guide to the ways of contemplation.

[41] Michael Casey, *The Undivided Heart*, 74.

Chapter 15

Comparing Two Mystics: Rābi'a al-'Adawiya Al-Qaysiyya and Paul Giustiniani, OSB

The similarity in mystical experience is illustrated by two mystics, the Muslim Rābi'a al-'Adawiya Al-Qaysiyya and the Benedictine Paul Giustiniani, made possible because both spoke about their experience and their words have been recorded.

Their Lives Compared

Rābi'a, born about 717 CE in Basra, became part of an ascetic movement established as a counter to growing worldliness. Its members focused on the Day of Judgment and encouraged fasting and prayer during the night as a means of strengthening their memory of God. Rābi'a emphasized that God should be loved not just as a way to avoid hell but as an appropriate way to respond to the gift of faith. Her way to God arose from the circumstances of her life. Both parents died when she was young. Rābi'a was sold in the slave market, worked for her "owner" by

131

day and prayed and fasted at night. One night her master saw her praying with a light suspended above. Disturbed by this, he freed her the next day. She went to the desert, set up a house of retreat, and made her pilgrimage to Mecca. On the way her ass died. Others in the caravan offered to take her belongings, she refused, telling them to continue. She prayed, trusting that help would come from God; the animal came back to life. Later in life, she refused all suitors, saying, "God can give me all you offer and even double it. It does not please me to be distracted from Him for a single moment. So farewell."[1] She added, "My peace, O my brothers, is in solitude, / And my Beloved is with me always, / For His love I can find no substitute, / And His love is the test for me among mortal beings."[2]

Paul Giustiniani (1476–1528) came from a wealthy noble family of Venice and was trained as a lawyer at the University of Padua. Then, aged thirty-four, he became a member of the Camaldolese Benedictines, a community who lived an eremitical life. He reformed the community by taking it back to its original eremitical life as established by the founder St. Romuald. He himself became a hermit and died at age fifty-two.

Their Mystical Lives Compared: Rābi'a and Paul

Rābi'a dedicated her life to prayer; it attracted others. When a man asked her to pray for him, she said, "Who am I? Obey your Lord and pray to Him, for He will answer the suppliant when he prays."[3] Under Sufi masters she was treated no differently from others. Filled with prayer and remembrance of God,

---

[1] Margaret Smith, *Rābi'a the Mystic and Her Fellow-Saints*, 11, quoting Munāwī, *Al-Kawākib al-Durrīya*, fol. 510. Sibt Ibn al-Jawzī, *Mir'āt al-Zamān*, fol. 265b.

[2] Margaret Smith, *Rābi'a the Mystic and Her Fellow-Saints*, 12, quoting Al-Hurrayfish, *Al-Rawd al-Fā'iq*, 214.

[3] Margaret Smith, *Rābi'a the Mystic and Her Fellow-Saints*, 17, quoting Sibt Ibn al-Jawzi, *Mir'āt al-Zamān*, fol. 265b.

she showed exemplary detachment. When asked whether she needed anything, she replied, "For twelve years I have desired fresh dates and you know that in Basra dates are plentiful and I have not yet tasted them. I am a servant and what has a servant to do with desire?"[4] She lived on the providence of God.

She was concerned that the destructiveness of her will against the will of God was too evident. To counteract it, she waited on the divine will rather than express her own desires. She summarized her position, "that should be willed which He wills."[5] This courageous trust in God was based on dedication to the will of God and summarized in her prayer, "O my God, my concern and my desire in this world is that I should remember Thee above all the things of this world, and in the next, that out of all who are in that world, I should meet with Thee alone. This is what I would say, 'Thy will be done.'"[6]

When invited by her servant to praise God in the beauty of spring she replied, "Come, you inside that you may behold their Maker. Contemplation of the Maker has turned me aside from contemplating what He has made."[7] Her faith enabled her to accept everything as from God, whether good or bad, pleasurable or painful. Her aim was to escape the world and its distractions; "My hope is for union with Thyself: for that is the Goal of my desire."[8] In this way she expressed her deep love affair with God, called "the Companion of my heart."[9] At the same time, she was ready to offer hospitality to whoever came,

[4] Margaret Smith, *Rābi'a the Mystic and Her Fellow-Saints*, 24, quoting Farīd al-Dīn 'Attār (d. 1230 CE), Tadhkirat *al-Awliyāa*, 70–71.

[5] Margaret Smith, *Rābi'a the Mystic and Her Fellow-Saints*, 25, quoting Farīd al-Dīn 'Attār (d. 1230 CE), Tadhkirat *al-Awliyāa*, 70–71.

[6] Margaret Smith, *Rābi'a the Mystic and Her Fellow-Saints*, 30, quoting Farīd al-Dīn 'Attār (d. 1230 CE), Tadhkirat *al-Awliyāa*, 73.

[7] Margaret Smith, *Rābi'a the Mystic and Her Fellow-Saints*, 62, quoting Farīd al-Dīn 'Attār (d. 1230 CE), Tadhkirat *al-Awliyāa*, 68.

[8] Margaret Smith, *Rābi'a the Mystic and Her Fellow-Saints*, 87, quoting Al-Hurayfish, *Al-Rawd al-Fā'iq*, 214.

[9] Margaret Smith, *Rābi'a the Mystic and Her Fellow-Saints*, 98, quoting Al-Ghazālī, *Ihyā 'Ulūm al-Dīn*, iv, 358.

recognizing every visitor as a pale image of the "Beloved of my heart [who] is the guest of my soul."[10] That love gave rise to some challenging comments, like "My love to God leaves no room for hating Satan,"[11] and her definition of love as coming "from Eternity and passes into Eternity and none has been found in seventy thousand worlds who drinks one drop of it until at last he is absorbed in God."[12] This was the one aim of her life, to be totally absorbed into God. The simplicity of her life, the direct way she spoke, and the long hours in prayer, testify to the totality of her commitment.

Paul saw the Inspired Scriptures as the starting point, saying, "It is sufficient to read and re-read the holy Gospels, which openly propose to everyone the doctrine and example of Jesus Christ."[13] The initiation and the culmination of the eremitical life was to carry the discipline of learning Jesus' words by heart, the foundation of a memory that would minimize the opportunity for entertaining temptations. From Jesus' words, "he who loves me keeps my words,"[14] Paul was inspired to propose that we should "fill our memory with them. Those who do not read the Gospel find it difficult to love Christ."[15] A memory enriched with stories and sayings is well prepared to contemplate Jesus. He required the hermits to read the whole Bible "each year and

---

[10] Margaret Smith, *Rābi'a the Mystic and Her Fellow-Saints*, 98, quoting Al-Ghazālī, *Ihyā 'Ulūm al-Dīn*, iv, 358.

[11] Margaret Smith, *Rābi'a the Mystic and Her Fellow-Saints*, 99.

[12] Ibid., 100.

[13] Jean Leclercq, *Alone with God*, trans. Elizabeth McCabe (1961; repr. Bloomingdale: Ercam Editions, 2008), 73. From French, *Seul avec Dieu: La Vie Eremetique*, quoting here *Un humaniste ermite* contains the inventory of Giustiniani's writings by Jean Leclercq, the quarto series, QII: 52. Jean Leclercq (1911–1993), Benedictine monk of Clervaux, Luxembourg, wrote *The Love of Learning and the Desire for God* and many other books in addition to translations and critical editions of the entire Bernardine corpus.

[14] Jean Leclercq, *Alone with God*, 77, quoting *Un humaniste ermite*, referring to the folio series F+:96, John 24:23.

[15] Ibid.

the whole Psalter should be recited in common each week."[16] In every spare moment he would come back to the psalms, learned by heart "so that I can say them without having to hold the Psalter in my hands . . . a love of the psalms is the mark of a true monk."[17] In this way he set an example of how the hermit should pray without ceasing, as important in the eremitical life "as breathing is to exterior life."[18]

Progress in the eremitical life is slow and unmarked. He likened it to a ship that leaves no trace as it makes its way through the ocean, "the soul, borne along by the Holy Spirit across the ocean of divine contemplation, cannot, even by turning around, see either the route it has followed or the point it has reached."[19] The eremitical life is one of faith; each hermit is unique.

To focus solely on God, the hermit needs to be detached "from all that is not God."[20] To renounce all and to depend totally on Christ means prompt obedience, as the Rule states (5.7), and enables the mind to be at peace with whatever comes, "for there is no point in exterior silence without interior peace."[21] In its search for complete selflessness, the soul prepares for "an experience of its nothingness. Keenly aware of its impotence, it plunges into God and receives all from His love."[22] In that nothingness the hermit is united with God in ways unattainable in earlier life.

Their Union in God Compared: Rābi'a and Paul

Rābi'a said in her final moment, "I have ceased to exist and have passed out of self. I am become one with Him and

---

[16] Jean Leclercq, *Alone with God*, 80, quoting *Regula vitae eremiticae* (Rule of the Eremitical Life), 1520, f.70V–71V.

[17] Jean Leclercq, *Alone with God*, 82–83.

[18] Ibid., 84, quoting the Rule of the Eremitical Life, 1520.

[19] Jean Leclercq, *Alone with God*, 86.

[20] Ibid., 93.

[21] Ibid., 107.

[22] Ibid., 111.

am altogether His."[23] By gazing upon the Vision and, in that moment, to be caught in the Divine, her deepest desire had been fulfilled, she had reached the goal of her guest, attained "not by annihilation, but by absorption and transmutation, so that the soul is transmuted into the Divine Image,"[24] now alive in God, enfolded in the Union of Love forever. It is a moment of silence; beyond words. This is the moment when personal otherness becomes subsumed into the Universal One; the wildest dream fulfilled.

Paul Giustiniani defined humility as the place where love is so pure that "no place remains for self-love."[25] This revelation came toward the end of his life. While at the Eucharist, he had an experience that showed him how to die to self in order to live for God alone. Later, this teaching was developed in a description of the third type of annihilation: "The soul is reduced to nothingness and knows it. Burning with love of God, it no longer lives in itself but in God alone, or rather God lives in it and it knows itself only in God."[26] This new identity is a sign of the maturing presence of Christ within his heart, showing that the intense love of God "transforms it [the soul] in God that it no longer loves itself in itself nor itself in God nor God in itself but only God in God."[27] This marks the total identification of the individual with God, dramatically described, as the soul "no longer knows anything but God, no longer loves anything but God, no longer is anything but God. . . . To love God alone in God means to be attached to nothing other than God Himself,

---

[23] Margaret Smith, *Rābi'a the Mystic and Her Fellow-Saints*, 110, quoting Farīd al-Dīn 'Attār (d. 1230 CE), Tadhkirat *al-Awliyāa*, 66.

[24] Margaret Smith, *Rābi'a the Mystic and Her Fellow-Saints*, 109. At this point a footnote offers a comparison with John of the Cross.

[25] Jean Leclercq, *Alone with God*, 116, quoting *Un humaniste ermite*, quarto series QIVbis: 134V.

[26] Jean Leclercq, *Alone with God*, 116–17, quoting from Paolo Giustiniani and Anselm Stolz, *Secretum meum mihi o dell'amor di Dio* (Frascati: Sacro Eremo Tuscolano, 1941), 19.

[27] Ibid.

to seek nothing but God's glory."[28] The one, so deeply in love with God, so absorbed into that love, recognizes that personal annihilation in God is a higher state of being than remaining individual. Rābi'a would agree with that conclusion, and she would share his final prayer: "Grant that I may be united to You in a way that the mind cannot grasp nor the pen express, that I may be so transformed into You that I may love You and enjoy You. I do not ask that Your joy may enter into me, but rather that I, like the faithful servant, may enter into it, and that reduced to nothing and annihilated to myself, I may taste Your love in a manner beyond all telling or understanding"[29]—a prayer summarizing the purpose of Rābi'a and Paul's mystical journey and the goal of every believer, Muslim or Christian.

Comment

These stories show that Christian and Sufi mystics can reach the same end, absorbed in the Love Who Is God, using similar language, disciplines, and lifestyle. They were driven by the same enthusiasm; only their starting points are different. Rābi'a and Paul Giustiniani lived centuries ago; their insights still resonate with those who seek this deep union. Their writings reveal parallel pathways to Union with God. At this point, Christian and Muslim spiritualities *touch*. From that *touch* comes the justification for a dialogue of spirituality, coming together as believers in the One God, seeking to be ever more closely united to the One God revealed in Word and fulfilled in Union.

---

[28] Jean Leclercq, *Alone with God*, 121.

[29] Ibid., 123, quoting from Paolo Giustiniani and Anselm Stolz, *Secretum*, 52–53.

Chapter 16

Thomas Merton and Sufism: His Dialogue with Abdul Aziz

Introduction

Trappists lead quiet, silent, even unnoticed lives, but there are always exceptions, and Thomas Merton[1] was one. His writings were much read both before his early death in 1968 and even more so since. Through them he attracted many to the Trappist life, especially by his focus on the development of spirituality, especially contemplative prayer. He developed a special interest in the monastic communities of Oriental religions and later with Sufism through a dialogue with the Pakistani Sufi Abdul Aziz,[2]

---

[1] Thomas Merton (1915–1968). Born in France, converted to Catholicism while at Columbia University and entered the Trappist community of Gethsemani (USA) in 1941. 1948 wrote his autobiography, *The Seven Storey Mountain*, a best-seller. 1949 Ordained Priest, 1951–1955 Master of Scholastics, 1955–1965 Master of Novices. From 1951 to 1968 he produced almost a book a year. He played an important part in monastic dialogue with Eastern Monks and Zen. In his last years became interested in Sufism.

[2] Abdul Aziz, "In December 1951, a young Pakistani Muslim assistant collector of customs in the Karachi Custom House, asked his boss, the collector of customs, one AE Wright, who happened to be a Catholic, to recommend to him a good book on Christian mysticism. Wright suggested a book by Thomas Merton, called *The Ascent to Truth*, which had just been published that same year." Later he started a correspondence with Louis Massignon (1883–1962). In 1959, Massignon visited Karachi, met Aziz, and gave him

with whom he started a correspondence in November 1960, continuing until his death in 1968; his last letter was dated April 24, 1968, a premature end to a dialogue that promised so much more.

This correspondence was important because each was able to challenge the other and affirm the common ground between them. It has been described as "one of the most interesting epistolary exchanges between a Muslim and a Christian in the twentieth century"[3]—such was the depth of their mutual understanding.

This led to a new initiative: Merton proposed and was given permission to offer conferences to the novices on Sufism, in this way showing the importance of this mystical tradition in the formation of Trappists, a bold step at that time.

Contemplative Prayer: Merton and Sufism

Seyyed Hossein Nasr writes that Merton taught the novices that "every authentic spirituality has its distinct perfume which is an extension of the perfume of paradise and reflects the celestial archetype,"[4] opening up the contemplative path. Novices were urged to appreciate the important insights from the Muslim contemplative tradition, a genuine path to God, different from the Trappist but with relevant lessons from its discipline and techniques.[5] Merton reached this conclusion having absorbed the spiritual writings of Sufi mystics, concluding that

---

Merton's address. The first letter from Aziz to Merton was dated November 1, 1960. The correspondence continued until Merton's death in 1968. Sidney H. Griffith, "'As One Spiritual Man to Another': The Merton-Abdul Aziz Correspondence," in *Merton & Sufism: The Untold Story*, ed. Rob Baker and Gray Henry (Louisville, KY: Fons Vitae, 1999), 101–29, here at 101.

[3] Sidney H. Griffith, "As One Spiritual Man to Another" in *Merton & Sufism*, 101–2.

[4] Seyyed Hossein Nasr, "What Attracted Merton to Sufism," preface to *Merton & Sufism*, 9–13, here at 9.

[5] Ibid., 11.

they represent "an enterprise of the human spirit as complex and deep as Christianity."[6]

Merton adopted Massignon's[7] phrase the *point vierge*, the culminating point of human despair, the ultimate desert experience, illustrated in Sufi literature by the story of Hagar's despair when, with her son Ishmael, she found herself at the moment of death in a waterless desert, abandoned by family, Abraham, and, apparently, by God too. As God intervened in Hagar's story, so too God intervenes in the mystic's story; the darkness of death and nothingness is transformed into the bright light of divine affirmation. Al-Hallaj describes this as a place where "our hearts, in their secrecy, are a virgin alone, where no dreamer's dream penetrates . . . the heart where the presence of the Lord alone penetrates, there to be conceived,"[8] from that moment comes transformation, the place where Merton realized the Christian and Sufi traditions "touch," using the same language to describe this moment. Sidney Griffith quotes Merton's self-description as evidence of his own experience, "I have no proper place in this world but for that reason I am in some sense to be the friend and

[6] William C. Chittick, "Sufism: Name and Reality," introduction to *Merton & Sufism*, 15–31, here at 21.

[7] Louis Massignon (1883–1962), "French Orientalist, dominated the field of Islamic studies for sixty years. A believer who rediscovered Christianity through Islam, a mystic involved in the political realities of his day, and an Islamophile who remained quintessentially French." From flysheet of Mary Louise Gude, *Louis Massignon: The Crucible of Compassion* (Notre Dame: University of Notre Dame Press, 1996).

[8] Sidney H. Griffith, "Merton, Massignon, and the Challenge of Islam," in *Merton & Sufism*, 51–78, here at 65 with a reference to Louis Massignon, "*Le 'coeur' (al-qalb) dans la prière et la meditation musulmanes*," in *Le Coeur: les études carmelitaines* (Paris: Desclee de Brouwer, 1950), 97. Massignon's article reprinted in *Opera Minora*, II:428–33. Sidney Griffith is a Professor in the Department of Semitic and Egyptian Languages and Literature at the Catholic University of America in Washington, DC. His speciality is Syriac and Arab Christian Literature, especially from the early Islamic period with a particular interest in Muslim-Christian relations.

brother of people everywhere, especially those who are exiles and pilgrims like myself."[9]

The Trappist tradition got Merton so far, but through Sufism, he found a way to handle his difficulties, especially with his monastic community. These words of Al-Hallaj he found particularly affirming: "He takes away every trace of earthly consolation so that the lover has only God to rely upon."[10]

Correspondence with Aziz on Dialogue

Taking the doctrine of God as an example, Merton affirmed the unique role of "the supreme transcendent Unity of God, and the fact that there is no other with Him or beside Him. He has 'no helper.' The word of creation and of the salvation of man is entirely His work alone."[11] He feared that Christianity tended to preach salvation through Christ, in such a way as to obscure the uniqueness of this divine initiative. This prioritization of the oneness of God over any trinitarian description removed a potential obstacle for Aziz. Merton was not denying the Christian teaching that God in Christ works salvation, nor was he downgrading the truth that Christ is alive in each person. He is careful to state that the presence of Christ is found not just within ourselves but also within the heart of those "most remote from our own. . . . If I insist on giving you my truth, and never stop to receive your truth in return, then there can be no truth between us . . . God speaks and God is to be heard, not only on Sinai, not only in my own heart, but in the *voice of the stranger*."[12] This was not just an

[9] Sidney H. Griffith, "As One Spiritual Man to Another," in *Merton & Sufism*, 105.

[10] Burton B. Thurston, "Merton's Reflections on Sufism," in *Merton & Sufism*, 33–39, here at 35.

[11] Sidney H. Griffith, "As One Spiritual Man to Another," in *Merton & Sufism*, 111.

[12] Ibid., 108.

expression of mutual friendship but Merton's conviction that Aziz speaks God's Word to him.

In their discussion about prayer Merton states that his prayers are centered "entirely on attention to the presence of God and to His will and His love. . . . One might say this gives my meditation the character described by the Prophet as 'Being before God as if you saw Him.' "[13] Affirming the truth of his intense prayer, Merton shows deep respect for "the purity of the divine Oneness, which is beyond any possible representation."[14] In this mystery, contemplatives too can recognize this description in the words of the other.

Sufism and Its Relevance to Formation According to the Rule of Benedict

Merton believed that formation in Sufism would help novices mature in monastic life. He said our desire is to seek "God and have ways of seeking to know God and this should have some success with us."[15] Merton introduced his novices to the Muslim practice of remembrance, *dhikr*, by which they could reach an ever deeper union with God so that ultimately "one is identified with God, and there is no further distinction between subject and object."[16] Merton linked the regular rhythmic breathing of the Sufi Master, in which there is "total renunciation of everything except God. . . . 'I want nothing, I love nothing, I seek nothing but God,' "[17] to the hesychastic prayer of Eastern monks,

[13] Ibid., 114.

[14] Ibid., 115.

[15] Burton B. Thurston, "Merton's Reflections on Sufism," in *Merton & Sufism*, 33.

[16] Erlinda G. Paguio, "Islamic Themes in Merton's Poetry," in *Merton & Sufism*, 88–100, here at 94.

[17] Burton B. Thurston, "Merton's Reflections on Sufism," in *Merton & Sufism*, 37.

affirming that the Jesus Prayer is not dissimilar to the Muslim devotion of rhythmic recitation of the ninety-nine names of God.

Merton explained to the novices that Muslims understand the Names of God as "clamouring to the invisible, unknown, absolute abyss of God for manifestation and God breathes on them and they are manifested in creatures."[18] In this way creatures themselves become manifestations of the Names of God but not of the essence of God, which is hidden. For a Christian this offers an insight into the belief that, at baptism, each is gifted with an inner presence of Christ, later to be enhanced through prayer and other sacraments. From this insight, each can discover, not only that there is One God for all but that "each person knows God by a special name,"[19] in this way maintaining the oneness of God but allowing each a unique relationship, expressed by living that name.

Christians seek the straight path to God by learning "to love the true good in everything without personal preference,"[20] for there is no partiality in the spiritual life—that is, "within me and it is God, and it's within everybody too. And there's one ground for everybody, and this ground is in the Divine Mercy,"[21] something acting from within; not made visible through events but alive within the believer all the time.

Merton's particular gift was to bring the respective insights of Sufis and followers of Benedict's Rule together, believing that each "has received from God the charge to seek what he has to seek."[22] The journey never ends; there is continual struggle and within this struggle the phrase "purity of heart," understood by Sufis as "non-preference, not preferring anything to What Is, taking What Is straight, without adding onto it any other

[18] Bernadette Dieker, "Merton's Sufi Lectures to Cistercian Novices 1966–68," in *Merton & Sufism*, 130–62, here at 138.

[19] Ibid., 139.

[20] Ibid., 143.

[21] Ibid., 144.

[22] Ibid., 147.

preference, without substituting something for it, without trying to make it better."[23]

Merton was struck by the close parallel between Sufi and monastic teaching about contemplative prayer and the insistence that its followers should cultivate the habit of living always in the presence of God. At the same time, in Merton's words, one feels "oneself completely penetrated by God's Knowledge of us, God as our Father, as our Creator, loving us, redeeming us."[24] Another way of expressing this is to say that Muslims and Christians come to know God by his name "not all his names, but by the name he speaks to us under the names of Allah,"[25] the One God.

The coherence of the Muslim and Christian understanding of the mystical life, as seen by Merton, resonates with that of Rābi'a and Paul, as shown above.

How Far Can They Get?

Both Islam and Christianity have produced women and men of deep spirituality, specially gifted with mystical experience of God. That these experiences should be defined in similar language and describe similar experiences suggests there is a depth to the prayer of a Muslim and Christian, which can benefit the other. The answer of each can help the other to reach that deepest union within his or her faith. This is the special gift of a dialogue of spirituality: it assumes the strength of the faith of the other and accepts the richness of its spirituality. It is not competitive.

[23] Ibid., 145–46.
[24] Ibid., 160.
[25] Bonnie Thurston, "Thomas Merton's Interest in Islam: The Example of *Dhikr*," in *Merton & Sufism*, 40–50, here at 43.

Part 5

God's Revelation and the Human Response: Examples from Inspired Scriptures

Is This the Encouragement to Do It Now?

Please Note: The next twelve chapters cover different approaches, Muslim and Christian, to the revelation of God in the Bible and the Qur'an. Specifically, these similarities and differences emerge in the lives of key people presented in both texts. Reflecting on them will provide some of the material for a dialogue of spirituality, in which insights can be shared. Later these insights could form the shared spiritual memory referred to above.

Affirming the Positive Echoes in the Understanding of God as Creator

Creation

Both the Hebrew Scriptures and the Qurʾan present a similar pictorial description of the origin of the world and the first human sin, but their interpretations differ: it shows the enduring relevance of the original story.

One fundamental difference with important consequences for the subsequent teaching of Christians and Muslims concerns Adam and his response to God's conviction of sin.

The similarities are clear from the start, "In the beginning when God created the heaven and the earth, the earth was a formless void and darkness covered the face of the deep" (Gen 1:1) and continue: God "created the heavens and the earth for a true purpose; He wraps the night around the day and the day around the night; He has subjected the sun and the moon to run their course for an appointed time" (Qurʾan 39:5).[1] This provides

---

[1] See also 13:3, 20:6, and 22:64-65.

a strong echo: the One God is at the origin of all that exists; God alone is all-powerful.

"A wind from God swept over the face of the waters" (Gen 1:2), then God spoke: the creation happened in seven days, for "He Is truly the Mighty, the Forgiving" (Qur'an 39:5-10). There are no rivals on this new earth for only God "gives breath to the people upon it and spirit to them that walk in it" (Isa 42:5), and only God "who created them in the first place will give them life again: He has full knowledge of every act of creation" (Qur'an 36:79); there is no loneliness in Creation, God has only "to say, 'Be'—and it is!" (Qur'an 36:82), for "all things came into being through him, and without him not one thing came into being. What has come into being in him was life, and life was the light of all people" (John 1:3-4). It was the deliberate intention of God to create variety, because *difference* is a reminder of God. Creation is a *sign* because "of His signs is the creation of the heavens and earth and the diversity of your languages and colors. There truly are signs in this for those who know" (Qur'an 30:22). These signs differ; for one, God is the light shining "in darkness, and the darkness did not overcome it" (John 1:5), for the other God is the "above all comparison in the heavens and earth" (Qur'an 30:25-30). But both texts acknowledge the supremacy of the One God beyond time and space.

Among the beings of creation, the first humans are the most important; they are created "in his image, in the image of God he created them; male and female he created them" (Gen 1:27) and, God "created him of a drop of fluid" (Qur'an 36:75-80). Again it is significant that both express an intimacy between human beings and God, the foundation of their respective faiths.

Daniel Carl Peterson emphasizes that the worship of God the Creator arises not because of a moment in the past but "from dependence upon him for existence at every instant."[2] For Muslims' "nature is constituted as it is 'that you might remem-

---

[2] Daniel Carl Peterson in *Encyclopaedia of the Qur'ān*, ed. Jane Dammen McAuliffe (Leiden and Boston: Brill, 2005), CD-ROM, s.v. "Creation," subsection "God as Sole Creator."

ber'"[3] that the whole created universe is a sign of the creating God, still actively maintaining it. He goes on to suggest that the stages of human development, from conception to birth, form a single process, which in every age the Qur'an "ascribes to the creative agency of God."[4] Pondering the sheer scale of the universe enlarges our appreciation of the Infinity of God.

In the *Catechism of the Catholic Church* there is an answer to God's motive in creation: "God created the world according to his wisdom. It is not the product of any necessity whatever or of blind fate or chance. We believe that it proceeds from God's free will; he wanted to make his creatures share in his being, wisdom and goodness."[5] This articulates a central theme of Christian faith: that *creation* is a dynamic concept, evolving toward a fulfillment, guided by the providential will of God.

From both Inspired Scriptures comes the same message: the world does not exist by chance or accident of evolution. It is the product of the divine will to create. In this, each act of creation is unique, and, within creation, each human being is endowed with the capacity for an intimate relationship with the creating God. Through a life of faith this is fulfilled in the paradise of the divine presence.

Human Responses to the Created World

Three positive echoes emerge from the similarities in these texts about the Creator:

1. The Qur'an states that it is God who "creates you weak, then gives you strength, then weakness after strength, together with your grey hair" (Qur'an 30:54), a comment on the cycle of human life, showing that humans are most active in their

---

[3] Ibid., subsection "A qur'anic Natural Theology."

[4] Ibid., subsection "Does the Qur'an Teach 'Creatio ex Nihilo'?"

[5] *Catechism of the Catholic Church* (London: Geoffrey Chapman, 1994), 69, no. 295.

middle years. A contrast comes from the Bible, where the psalmist tries to come to terms with the difference between the Creator and the created by asking, "What are human beings that you are mindful of them, mortals that you care for them? Yet you have made them a little lower than God, and crowned them with glory and honor. You have given them dominion over the works of your hands" (Ps 8:4-6). Both quotations echo the uniqueness of each human being, especially talented among all other earthly beings but still tiny within the scale of creation. From this perspective, creaturehood is a state of weakness, revealing both the fragility of human life and its disproportionate significance within the grandeur of Creation.

2. Both the Bible and the Qurʾan affirm the appropriate human response to the creating God is reverence. The Bible states you are "worthy, our Lord and God, to receive glory and honor and power, for you created all things" (Rev 4:11), while the Qurʾan encourages all to "worship your Lord, who created you and those before you, so that you may be mindful [of Him] who spread out the earth for you and built the sky" (Qurʾan 2:21-22). Both Muslim and Christian respect the created world, whose Creator deserves praise and thanks.

3. To the eyes of faith, God's presence in the created world is a sign of the divine purpose. Without this divine involvement, reason would suggest the Creator was distant, with no personal interest in it and unpredictable in the way it works. However, with the revelation that God is Love, people can be brought to "understand that the worlds were prepared by the word of God" (Heb 11:3) and learn to appreciate "He who made the sun a shining radiance, and the moon a light, determining phases for it so that you might know the number of the years and how to calculate time" (Qurʾan 10:5). These show that both Muslim and Christian accept, at least in outline, the same story of Creation.

Another theme from Islam offers a subtle link of the Creator to the Revealed Word. The same Arabic word *āyāt* means both "signs" in nature and "verses" in the Qurʾan. Showing that "nature, properly viewed, becomes a revealed book very much like the Qurʾan is itself composed of individual signs or miracles."[6] So the created world is not just an abstract discovery but a revelation of God speaking to those seeking a meaning in their lives. The human response is to praise "his glorious grace" (Eph 1:6), confirming the words of Irenaeus: "the glory of God is man fully alive. . . . If God's revelation through creation has already obtained life for all the beings that dwell on earth, how much more will the Word's manifestation of the Father obtain life for those who see God."[7]

Both Muslims and Christians see creation as the revelation of the Creating God, whose intention is to invite all to fulfillment in a world beyond creation, in heaven. Having outlined the similarities in the understanding of creation, the next chapter examines the story of Adam as understood by Christians and Muslims.

---

[6] Daniel Carl Peterson in *Encyclopaedia of the Qurʾān*, ed. Jane Dammen McAuliffe, s.v. "Creation," subsection "A qurʾanic Natural Theology."

[7] *Catechism of the Catholic Church*, 69, no. 294, quoting St. Irenaeus, *Adversus Haereses*, 4.20.7 PG. Irenaeus (ca. 130–ca. 200), bishop of Lyons. Little is known of his life but heard Polycarp as a boy, so perhaps from Smyrna. Studied in Rome, later priest in Lyons. To Rome in ca. 177, when persecution broke out in Lyons, in which the bishop was martyred; Irenaeus succeeded on his return in 178. His main writing is *Adversus Haereses*. Little is known of his later life, possibly martyred.

Chapter 18

Adam: The First Human and the One Responsible for the First Sin

The Common Elements

The Adam story, found in both Muslim and Christian Inspired Scriptures, has many common features. In both, Adam and Eve were created by God, placed in a garden, told the rules, heard a voice tempting them to disobedience, sinned by breaking the rules, then recognized their nakedness and their shame. At that point, both were summoned by God to explain their behavior and were expelled from the garden.

Behind these facts are differences of interpretation, which, as Abdel Haleem puts it, have "consequences and bearings on the status of men and women, on the concept of God and the moral standing of human beings in this world and in their destiny beyond it,"[1] put more succinctly by Anthony Johns,[2] "it is in the

---

[1] Muhammad Abdel Haleem, *Understanding the Qurʾan: Themes and Style* (1999; London: IB Tauris & Co., 2011), 126. Abdel Haleem, b. Egypt, learned the Qurʾan by heart from childhood, educated at al-Azhar, Cairo, and Cambridge Universities. He has taught Arabic at Cambridge and London Universities since 1966. Now King Fahd Professor of Islamic Studies at the School of Oriental and African Studies, University of London.

[2] Anthony Johns (1928–), b. London, Catholic with Polish roots, educated in Devon, National Service 1946–49 in Malaya, teaching Malays English.

way that the consequences of the fall are to be repaired"[3] and the way to salvation revealed.

The Christian Story

The first two chapters of Genesis are considered by Christians as presenting "a balanced picture of humanity. The creature made in the image of God, indeed invited into God's presence, is also the creature primarily responsible for the subsequent alienation and enmity within creation."[4] The act of disobedience to the divine command is "not to be blamed primarily on the woman in the garden, but is the responsibility of the whole human community."[5] In contrast to this the psalmist reflects on what God is prepared to do for those who trust: "I waited patiently for the LORD; he inclined to me and heard my cry. He drew me up from the desolate pit, out of the miry bog, and set my feet upon a rock, making my steps secure" (Ps 40:1-2).

For Adam this superiority is shown by "his naming them [the animals]. In the ancient world to give a name was a sign of authority; it also exhibits the intelligence of man."[6] After the sin and expulsion from the garden, a penalty is inflicted, "the curse of the man implies that the soil shall no longer be docile and fertile for him; he must wring his living from it by hard labor,

---

Then to SOAS for studies in Malay literature, BA, PhD 1954–58 to Indonesia for the Ford Foundation, teaching languages, married a Sumatran Muslim, 1958 founded the Department for Indonesian Language and Literature in Canberra University, elevated to professor in 1964, sabbatical 1964–65 in Cairo, learned Arabic.

[3] Anthony Johns, "Abraham—Our Father in Faith? A Reflection on Christian-Muslim Consociation," *St. Mark's Review* 206, no. 3 (November 2008): 15.

[4] Howard N. Wallace in *The Anchor Bible Dictionary*, ed. David Noel Freedman (New York: Doubleday, 1992), s.v. "Adam."

[5] Ibid.

[6] John L. McKenzie, *Dictionary of the Bible* (London: Geoffrey Chapman, 1965), s.v. "Adam."

and ultimately he must die. Neither toil nor death were found in the unspoiled simplicity of Eden."[7]

Paul's interpretation of the biblical message adds a new dimension; Adam brought sin into the world and with it, death; it was Christ who overcame death and brought new life for all. "While this analogy presents Adam and Christ as those who shape the destiny of the world, the contrast is not to be ignored. The reign of grace and righteousness which comes through the second Adam confronts the reign of sin and death introduced through the first Adam and overcomes it."[8] Paul expresses it in these words:

> Because of the one man's trespass, death exercised dominion through that one, much more surely will those who receive the abundance of grace and the free gift of righteousness exercise dominion in life through the one man, Jesus Christ. Therefore just as one man's trespass led to condemnation for all, so one man's act of righteousness leads to justification and life for all. (Rom 5:17-18)

Christian teaching is founded on Paul's statement, "for since death came through a human being, the resurrection of the dead has also come through a human being" (1 Cor 15:21). The first Adam gave way to "the last Adam [who] became a life-giving spirit" (1 Cor 15:45). In this way the Adam and Eve story is enriched for Christians when seen in the context of Christ's life, death, and resurrection.

Concerning the later life of Adam, Christian teaching is tentative, though some acknowledge his life with God. As Aphrahat of Syria[9] writes, "From the beginning God created Adam; molded him from the dust of the earth, and raised him up. For

---

[7] Ibid.

[8] Howard N. Wallace, in *The Anchor Bible Dictionary*, ed. David Noel Freedman, s.v. "Adam."

[9] Aphrahat of Syria (early fourth century), first of the Syriac church fathers, also known as the Persian Sage. An ascetic, held important offices. Lived through persecution of King Shapur II (310–79). His "Demonstrations" survived. First ten completed in 337, next twelve in 344, and final one

if, while Adam was not, He made him from nothing, how much easier now is it for Him to raise him up."[10]

The Muslim Story

Using the same story, Islam offers a different interpretation:

> Adam and Eve disobeyed God. They were expelled from the Garden. They repented. Their first home on earth was Mecca. There they built the first place of worship on earth, identified in the Qurʾan as the Kaʾba, where it all began. Adam was the father of all humankind. He was the first prophet, the first teacher. In him is established the basic template of divine revelation, of an economy of salvation that humankind must recognize that God is one.[11]

The Christian doctrine of original sin has no place in Islam. The sin of Adam is like all human sin: once repented, it can be forgiven, for "every individual is born in a state of grace with a natural disposition to the true religion: Islam."[12] A consequence of this is that Muslims sometimes speak of *reversion* rather than *conversion*. Corruption comes from family, society, or worldwide influences. To counteract this requires simply good teachers: "They do not need a redeemer, they do not need a Messiah, as understood in Judaism or Christianity."[13]

The Qurʾan presents Adam several times to remind readers of this primeval event and its effect on their lives. It makes this event more immediate "than if it were left at the beginning of

---

in 345. Much emphasis on asceticism, especially celibacy. Sheds valuable light on early Christianity in Persia.

[10] Aphrahat of Syria, *Demonstration VIII*, 6, in *Nicene and Post-Nicene Fathers of the Christian Church* 2, vol. 13, p. 376. All subsequent citations of *Nicene and Post-Nicene Fathers of the Christian Church* 2, trans. Philip Schaff and Henry Wace (New York: Christian Literature Company, 1890–1900), hereafter NPNF 2, are from this series.

[11] Anthony Johns, "Abraham—Our Father in Faith?," 16.

[12] Ibid.

[13] Ibid., 17.

Chapter 1 as in the Bible."[14] This memorable story shows the origin of disobedience, the consequences of this sin, and, most important of all, the effect of sincere repentance; "the Qurʾan employs it regularly in support of its teachings on beliefs and conduct, making the connections clear."[15]

The first lesson for Muslims is to accept the power of God, "one of His signs is that He created you from dust and—lo and behold!—you became human and scattered far and wide" (Qurʾan 30:20), and a second sign is that the Creating God intended the spouses to live in peace with each other. They failed, "There truly are signs in this for those who use their reason" (Qurʾan 30:24).

Repeating the story emphasizes to believers that all human beings were created from dust; in death they return to dust and from dust God can raise them to new life. God says, "From the earth we created you, into it We shall return you, and from it We shall raise you a second time" (Qurʾan 20:55). In the act of creation, Adam experienced the "spirit of God" breathed into him, enabling him to name all things, for it is those "who have knowledge who stand in true awe of God" (Qurʾan 35:28). Muslims emphasize that Adam was created without a Father, like Jesus, created by means of a single cell, showing the fundamental unity of humanity. Next, from a woman and a man came races and tribes, "in God's eyes the most honored of you are the ones most mindful of Him: God is all knowing, all aware" (Qurʾan 49:13). The role of Satan is clearly described; on several occasions warnings are given: "Did I not command you not to serve Satan, for he was your sworn enemy, but to serve Me?" (Qurʾan 36:60).

Later Reflections on Creation and Sin

A Christian Perspective

For Christians, the images of Genesis affirm an "event" at the very start of human history, but it is revelation that "gives us the

---

[14] Muhammad Abdel Haleem, *Understanding the Qurʾan*, 138.
[15] Ibid., 136.

certainty of faith that the whole of human history is marked by the original fault, freely committed by our first parents."[16] They deliberately chose self-interest and destroyed the promise, for "created in a state of holiness, man was destined to be fully 'divinized' by God in glory. Seduced by the devil, he wanted to 'be like God,' but 'without God.'"[17] The consequence of this disobedience is that "control of the soul's spiritual faculties over the body is shattered; the union of man and woman becomes subject to tensions. . . . Harmony with creation is broken"[18] and death marks the end of each human life. The condition of pained, wavering, and selfish human beings is derived from this action. They were powerless to change, as later stories in the Hebrew Scriptures show.

A Muslim Perspective

Muslims offer a different interpretation. The deliberate disobedience was the result of erroneous views of the world, seeing "the ego as real instead of God who alone is Real. Thus redemption from the Fall lies within the 'shahādah' in realizing the truth that there is no god, or autonomous reality, but Allāh."[19] Once a person confesses faith in God, then the effects of the Fall are

[16] *Catechism of the Catholic Church*, 87, para. 390. The quotation is from *Gaudium et Spes* of the Second Vatican Council, 1966, chap. 1, para. 13. The final sentence is inspired by a decision of the Council of Trent, quoted in Denzinger-Schönmetzer, *Enchiridion Symbolorum* (1965) 1513 and by Pope Pius XII in the same volume 3897, and by Pope Paul VI in *Acta Apostolicae Sedis* 58, 654.

[17] *Catechism of the Catholic Church*, 89, para. 398.

[18] Ibid., para. 400.

[19] Cyril Glassé, ed., *The New Encyclopedia of Islam* (1989; repr. New York: Altamira Press, 2002), s.v. "Adam." Cyril Glassé (b. 1944), graduate of Columbia University, practicing Muslim whose published works include *A Guide to Saudi Arabia* (Berlitz, 1981); *The Pilgrim's Guide to Mecca*, written for the Hajj Research Centre, King Abdul Aziz University, Jeddah; and *The New Encyclopedia of Islam* (1989, 2001). He has lectured on comparative religion around the world.

corrected, and the individual is restored to the original state, "that of Adam before the Fall."[20] By confessing the omnipotence of God, human thoughts are put into their proper perspective— that is, they are always relative to the thinking of God. This was the attitude of Adam before sin and clarifies the meaning of the vicegerent role. God "has given human beings power to dominate the earth, but on the condition that they remain obedient to God."[21] The human vocation is, first, to be "passive toward Heaven in submission to God's Will"[22] and, second, to be "active as God's agent and doing His Will in the world."[23] In this way Islam claims to avoid the worst consequences of the Christian teaching on original sin.

God Seeks Out the Sinner: An Encouragement to Repent

A Christian Perspective

Before his sin, Adam had no needs, as John Chrysostom[24] expresses it, "either of a garment or a shelter or any other provision of this sort; but rather [he] was like to the Angels; and many of the things to come he foreknew and was filled with great wisdom."[25] He "enjoyed much freedom, a certain tillage of the ground was enjoined upon him; not indeed a laborious

---

[20] Ibid.

[21] Seyyed Hossein Nasr, *The Heart of Islam* (San Francisco: HarperSan-Francisco, 2004), 13.

[22] Ibid.

[23] Ibid.

[24] John Chrysostom (ca. 347–407), b. in Antioch, became a hermit, then at 34, in 381, joined clergy of Antioch; gained reputation as a preacher. In 398 elected archbishop of Constantinople, reformer, especially attacking the misuse of wealth, antagonized the rich and aggravated Egyptian and Syrian bishops, deposed in 403, sent into exile, where he died in 407. Honored as one of the four Greek Doctors of the Church.

[25] John Chrysostom, *Homily XVII: On 1 Corinthians*[6:12], in *Nicene and Post-Nicene Fathers of the Christian Church* 1, vol. 12, p. 99, para. 4. All subsequent citations of *Nicene and Post-Nicene Fathers of the Christian Church* 1, ed.

or a troublesome one, but one which afforded him much good discipline."[26] But he still faced challenges, and, after sin, "paradise profited him nothing."[27] There was no excuse for him. Once they had eaten they hid. For at that time "there were neither letters, nor law, nor Moses. Whence then doth he recognize the sin, and hide himself? Yet not only does he so hide himself, but when called to account, he endeavors to lay the blame on another,"[28] showing how sin, once committed, multiplies easily.

Adam's statement provoked John Chrysostom to affirm the wisdom of God, "for when Adam said, 'I heard Thy voice, and I was afraid, for I was naked, and I hid myself,' God does not at once convict him of what he had done, nor say, 'Why hast thou eaten of the tree?' "[29] Instead he asks, who informed you of your nakedness? In other words, God neither remained silent nor immediately convicted him but tried to get him to admit and repent of his sin. To give him confidence, hoping it would lead him to repent and be forgiven, God "was Himself the first to call; cutting off much of Adam's distress by the familiar appellation, and dispelling his fear, and opening by this address the mouth that was shut."[30] Chrysostom was reminding his community that sin destroys the sinner, not God. But once the sinner hears the voice of God and understands the need for repentance, the gift of forgiveness is immediately available.

Chrysostom reflected, "Five thousand years and more have passed, and death hath not yet been done away, on account of

---

Philip Schaff (New York: Christian Literature Company, 1887–98), hereafter NPNF 1, are from this first series.

[26] John Chrysostom, *Homily XIX on the Sunday Called "Episozomenes": To Those Who Had Come to Antioch from the Country*, in NPNF 1, vol. 9, p. 465, para. 2.

[27] John Chrysostom, *Homily IV: An Exhortation to the People Respecting Fortitude and Patience*, in NPNF 1, vol. 9, p. 369, para. 10.

[28] John Chrysostom, *Homily XII: Thanksgiving to God for the Pardon Granted to the Offenders against the Emperor*, in NPNF 1, vol. 9, p. 422, para. 10.

[29] Ibid.

[30] John Chrysostom, *Homily VII: Recapitulation of Former Exhortations*, in NPNF 1, vol. 9, p. 393, para. 7.

one single sin."[31] From this perspective, Adam had heard no warnings from prophets, nor had he seen others punished for their sins, but he had disobeyed and was punished. Adam "died on the day that he ate of the tree."[32] The nature of that death concerns the relationship with God. It is not a physical death. It should be remembered that the Christian doctrine of original sin was formulated many years after the death and resurrection of Christ.

A Muslim Perspective

Adam had all the advantages of being sinless. Maneri writes, "Everything in paradise and in the abode of peace, that had the power to comfort and delight, fell in love with Adam, for the simple reason that, since he had not seen such wonderful things, all the hands of love took hold of his skirt. Adam, with great spiritual resolve, snatched his heart away from them all."[33] This presents Adam as one with moral strength. Earlier weakness did not erode all his moral strength; the ways of God are unpredictable, as these highs and lows of Adam's life indicate: "The messenger Adam was made the object of angelic prostrations. The kingdom of paradise was bestowed upon him. He was then expelled, naked, from paradise and, in the world, it was proclaimed: 'Adam disobeyed his Lord.' "[34] Punishment for failure is as instantaneous as is the glory of selfhood in a paradise garden. The key element is that people recognize their sin, repent, and continue trying to obey, knowing God is all merciful and forgiving. On the day of resurrection, "all the angels will exclaim in astonishment: 'Glory be to God! This is the man who

[31] John Chrysostom, *Homily IX: On 1 Corinthians iii:12–15*, in NPNF 1, vol. 12, p. 50, para. 2.

[32] John Chrysostom, *Homily XXVIII on John iii:17*, in NPNF 1, vol. 14, p. 97, sec. 1.

[33] Sharafuddin Maneri, *The Hundred Letters*, letter 63, 254.

[34] Sharafuddin Maneri, *In Quest of God: Maneri's Second Collection of 150 Letters* (Gujarat, India: Gujarat Sahitya Prakash, 2004), letter 60, 132.

was driven naked out of paradise.' From this you will realize that it is impossible to know what divine providence has in store for a person."[35]

Lack of foresight, however, does not excuse forgetfulness. "The messenger, Adam, had angels prostrate before him. The eight heavens were assigned to him. When his gaze penetrated the secret of poverty, however, he sold the eight heavens for a grain of wheat."[36] Remembering that blessings are gifts from God helps us turning them into possessions.

Simplicity of lifestyle attracts grace, for through it one is reminded of the transitory nature of this world. In Muslim teaching it is clear that Satan is a superior being to Adam, made of fire to Adam's clay, but Adam was favored. From this comes the teaching that "grace depends, neither on what one does, nor on who one is. In other words, activity and nature are not the cause of grace. Thus it is proved that grace is not given to anyone except the person to whom God gives it."[37]

Adam was unique because when the angels prostrated in front of him, "a trace of love came into existence within them. When they found the Way to God within Adam's soul, they hastened to offer him service without end."[38] Until creation happened and Adam appeared, the angels knew nothing of created beings or their meaning. Through Adam the key to the world of creation and the world of God was revealed. "Adam's nature was the receptacle of hidden mysteries, otherwise how could a handful of dust exhibit such worthiness that those who dwell in holy seclusion and are preachers from the pulpits of intimacy, should prostrate themselves before him?"[39]

This high view of Adam contrasts with that of Christians.

---

[35] Ibid.
[36] Ibid., letter 54, 119–20.
[37] Ibid., letter 61, 133.
[38] Ibid., letter 109, 222.
[39] Ibid., letter 109, 223.

Sin and the Descendants of Adam

A Christian Perspective

Adam had all he needed yet still sinned—that is the core mystery in the Adam story. Later sinners, more aware of their sin and less able to avoid it, can be grateful that a genuine act of repentance and sorrow can produce such a dramatic change; reuniting sinners with God. However, the devil saw Adam as a target and attempted to dispose of him by sinking his ship (by which is meant the soul). "But God made the gain greater than the loss, and brought our nature to the royal throne."[40] The true battle is between evil and God for which not even a paradise was secure protection: "Adam was in paradise yet he fell."[41] For those who follow Adam, there is no escape from the divine tribunal, for "'all things are naked and laid open to Him' who judges us, and we must submit to give an account not of deeds only but also of thoughts; for that judge is quick to discern the thoughts and intents of the heart."[42]

For Christians the death of Jesus opens up a new life. First he "'came to the place of a skull.' Some say that Adam died there, and there lieth; and that Jesus, in this place where death had reigned, there also set up the trophy. For He went forth bearing the Cross as a trophy over the tyranny of death: and as conquerors do, so He bare upon His shoulders the symbol of victory."[43] Christians conclude, that "the death of Adam was for our sakes, that we might be corrected; and the death of Christ, that we might be saved."[44] The role of Adam in Christianity is

---

[40] John Chrysostom, *Homily against Those Who Say That Demons Govern Human Affairs*, in NPNF 1, vol. 9, p. 179, para. 2.

[41] John Chrysostom, *Against Eutropius*, in NPNF 1, vol. 9, para. 254.

[42] John Chrysostom, *An Exhortation to Theodore after His Fall*, in NPNF 1, vol. 9, p. 113, letter 2, para. 2.

[43] John Chrysostom, *Homily LXXXV on John, XIX:16–18*, in NPNF 1, vol. 14, p. 317, sec. 1.

[44] John Chrysostom, *Homily on 1 Corinthians 3:18, 19*, in NPNF 1, vol. 12, p. 55, homily 10, para. 4.

to be the forerunner of the real Savior; his disobedience made a Savior necessary, and he remains the cause of the weakness that every human being inherits.

A Muslim Perspective

Islam does not allow any human act, however wicked, to distort the human will. The disobedience of Adam is not interpreted so catastrophically: "Man by being man is imperfect, only God being perfection as such. Being imperfect man has a tendency to forget and so is in constant need of being reminded, through revelation, of his real nature."[45] The weakness is more one of forgetfulness, in the sense that God's will is given lower priority than the believer's own wishes. The evil one, Iblis, in Rumi's words, "saw only Adam's form, made of dust. . . . He overlooked the decisive fact that God had breathed His breath into man and formed him according to His image."[46] This suggests Iblis' power was limited. Significantly, "never in the history of Islam has Satan been given absolute power over men: he can tell them lies and seduce them as he did with Adam, but they have the possibility to resist his insinuations."[47] Iblis is never seen as the embodiment of evil, as Satan is for Christians. Rather Iblis is a creature of God, part of the divine drama, which in this case, challenged Adam's human will. He could have resisted. Within every human being there is a hidden treasure waiting to be discovered; to discover it, accurate self-knowledge is essential, for "whoever knows himself also knows his Lord."[48] Adam was ignorant of his true self and was expelled from the garden.

---

[45] Seyyed Hossein Nasr, *Ideals and Realities of Islam* (2nd impression; London: George Allen & Unwin, 1971), 24.

[46] Annemarie Schimmel, *Mystical Dimensions of Islam* (Chapel Hill: University of North Carolina Press, 1975), 195. Reference to Jalāluddin Rūmī, *Mathnawī-ī ma'nawī*, ed. and trans. Reynold A Nicholson, 6 vols. (London, 1925).

[47] Annemarie Schimmel, *Mystical Dimensions of Islam*, 193.

[48] Sharafuddin Maneri, *In Quest of God*, letter 142, 276.

He had to find his inner beauty in the desert: "I expelled Adam from the garden and displayed My beauty in the wilderness."[49]

Satan is the ultimate cause of sin, as a hadith of Sahih al-Bukhari[50] shows: "There is none born among the off-spring of Adam, but Satan touches it. A child therefore, cries loudly at the time of birth because of the touch of Satan, except Mary and her child."[51] But "Satan runs in the body of Adam's son (i.e. man) as his blood circulates in it,"[52] leading to this realistic assessment of human weakness: "If the son of Adam (the human being) were given a valley full of gold, he would love to have a second one, for nothing can fill the belly of Adam's son except dust, and Allah forgives him who repents to Him."[53]

Significantly, when two people fight, they avoid the face for, as Sahih Muslim[54] records, "Allah created Adam in His own image."[55] Mercy and forgiveness are the key; the sinner has only to obey; "the son of Adam was commanded to prostrate, and he

---

[49] Ibid., letter 142, 276.

[50] Sahih al-Bukhari gave his name to one of the six canonical hadith collections of Sunni Islam. Persian scholar who traveled widely from the age of sixteen, collecting the trustworthy traditions. From the many thousands collected, 2,602 were included, meeting his criteria for authenticity, a sound chain of the narratives, back to firsthand recorders, who lived the teachings and fitted his own understanding of Islam. Work completed 846; last twenty-four years of his life were spent visiting cities and teaching the hadith he had collected.

[51] *Sahih al-Bukhari*, vol. 4, book 55, no. 641. Unless otherwise noted, all hadith were accessed from www.sahih-bukhari.com.

[52] Ibid., vol. 8, book 73, no. 238.

[53] Ibid., vol. 8, book 76, no. 446.

[54] Sahih Muslim (817–875), b. Naysabur, Iran, traveled widely throughout Iraq, Arabian Peninsula, Syria, and Egypt to make his collection. Some dispute about the number recorded, between 1400 and 2200, all authentic. Second in importance after *Sahih al-Bukhari*; 4,000 chosen from thousands collected, divided into forty-three books. Differs from *al-Bukhari*: all versions of a narrative placed together. And authenticity required two companions.

[55] *Sahih Muslim*, book 32, no. 6325. See Compendium of Muslim Texts, available at http://msawest.net/component/content/article/10-funda mentals-hadith-a-sunnah-muslim/308-sahih-muslim-book-32-the

prostrated and Paradise was entitled to him."[56] If it is natural for human beings to sin, it is also true that "the sinner who repents is like a person who hasn't sinned. Dear friend, it is not astonishing that man sins, for a hundred kinds of desires and appetites have been kneaded into his composition. From him repentance is astonishing."[57] So "beg to be excused for whatever fault you commit, for Adam, by that very repentance, attained his rank"![58] In repentance the sinner is forgiven and the relationship with Adam "is cemented, but whoever persists in sin till the end of his life and does not repent links himself to Satan inextricably."[59] Each person has the choice.

Context for Dialogue

The respective descriptions of the original paradise, the rules of the garden, the first sin, and subsequent expulsion form a strong echo. On the other hand, the different interpretations of the first sin, in the one Adam repents and is forgiven while in the other Adam's sin marks all humans throughout history, provide a strong counter-echo. Taken together this is a firm base for dialogue.

-book-of-virtue-good-manners-and-joining-of-the-ties-of-relationship-kitab
-al-birr-was-salat-i-wal-adab.

[56] Ibid., book 1, no. 144.

[57] Sharafuddin Maneri, *In Quest of God*, letter 137, 265.

[58] Sharafuddin Maneri, *The Hundred Letters*, letter 82, 339.

[59] Ibid., letter 88, 362.

Chapter **19**

Affirming the Positive Echoes in the Understanding of God in Whom We Trust

By means of the creation, God has provided a link to the human mind and heart. Without this link, the scale of difference between God and human beings would make communication impossible. In both traditions, believers are invited to a relationship of faith with the Creating God, made accessible through revelation and invited as a God who can be trusted.

Listening to these words inspires wonder, what "no eye has seen, nor ear has heard, and nor the human heart conceived, what God has prepared for those who love him" (1 Cor 2:9). These words encourage the listener for "when you have decided on a course of action, put your trust in God: God loves those who put their trust in Him" (Qurʾan 3:159), and thus become ready to follow the divine path, for "it is He who has guided us to this way we follow" (Qurʾan 14:12). But still people must be circumspect: "You who stand in need of God—God needs nothing and is worthy of all praise—if He wills, He can do away with you and bring in a new creation, that is not difficult for God"

(Qur'an 35:15-17). For Christian and Muslim human life remains fragile—a condition that is overcome by faith in a merciful God.

God becomes "angry" when people reject divine revelation. Better to seek "the LORD while he may be found, call upon him while he is near . . . for my thoughts are not your thoughts, nor are your ways my ways, says the LORD" (Isa 55:6, 8). Believers learn to deal with the unpredictability of God, sometimes the cause of great pain, tempting some to turn away from God whom they consider no longer trustworthy.

The divine promises offer a tantalizing future. Al-Ghazālī[1] writes, the "religious fruit . . . for a man is that God alone suffices for him . . . He wants only God—great and glorious. He should not want paradise nor should his heart be preoccupied with hell, trying to be on guard against it, but his intention should be absorbed by God alone, the most high."[2] This heartening vision points to a fulfillment beyond human reach: a divine gift. There may be a hint of difficulties, but God, as the Catholic Catechism explains, "does not abandon his creatures to themselves. He not only gives them being and existence, but also, and at every moment, upholds and sustains them in being, enables them to act and brings them to their final end."[3] Here the approaches of Muslim and Christian coincide: only full union with God will satisfy the deepest of human desires. The promise

---

[1] Al-Ghazālī, Abū Ḥāmid Muḥammad (1058–1111). Born and died in Tūs, Persia. Appointed professor of law in Baghdad, became well known but after four years faced crisis of faith. Gave his post to his brother and went to Damascus and lived in solitude, from there visited Jerusalem and Hebron, as well as Mecca and Medina. Reflected on philosophy, theology, and ended with mysticism, returning to Sufism. He said: "I arrived at Truth, not by systematic reasoning and accumulation of proofs, but by a flash of light which God sent into my soul." In all he wrote about seventy books. He concluded the Sufis were the heirs of the Prophet. He ushered in the second age of Islam (source: Cyril Glassé, *Encyclopedia of Islam*).

[2] Al-Ghazālī, *The Ninety-Nine Beautiful Names of God*, trans. David B. Burrell and Nazih Daher (1992; repr. Cambridge, UK: Islamic Texts Society, 2009), 112.

[3] *Catechism of the Catholic Church*, 71, no. 301.

is clear: reaching it is difficult. Believers are challenged to find a way of discovering that God's promises are trustworthy.

Benedict in his Rule advises: "Place your hope in God alone. If you notice something good in yourself, give credit to God, not to yourself" (RB 4.41-42, RB 1980), in this way countering a tendency to praise ourselves for our achievements. Both Muslims and Christians agree that all goodness comes from God as a gift. The human task is to make proper use of God's gift and not to take pride in an achievement more properly belonging to God. This is the way Muslims and Christians build into their memory the truth that God is trustworthy.

20

Joseph: An Example of the God Who Can Be Trusted

Joseph: Two Memories of a Spiritual Journey

Joseph is the only biblical figure whose story is present in a single surah of the Qurʾan, making comparison easier. In comparing the two accounts there arises the question of whether the two accounts have the same agenda. Both stories encourage readers to see that even in the most difficult of circumstances God never abandons human beings.

The Christian Story

The biblical story "transports Joseph, the brash but abused brother in Jacob's family, from his position in Canaan to his position in Egypt, where, in his new position of power, he may in turn choose to be brash and abusive."[1] Later, "at the mercy of the strange Egyptian who controls the food reserves, Joseph toys with them before he breaks the tension of the scene. . . . At the

---

[1] George W. Coats, in *The Anchor Bible Dictionary*, ed. David Noel Freedman, vol. 3, s.v. "Joseph, Son of Jacob."

highest point of tension, Joseph breaks the charade and identifies himself as Joseph to his brothers."[2] One could speculate how the brothers reacted to the news that their lost brother is now the Pharaoh's national food manager, but "the storyteller controls the scene by observing that the brothers were dismayed when they learned Joseph's identity. Joseph, even as brother, had the power of life and death over the guilty group. He could now openly seek his revenge."[3] Joseph's love and forgiveness of his brothers was more powerful than their guilt for he "kissed all of his brothers and wept on them."[4] The family was reconciled and reunited. In Egypt, the family was protected and lived in peace. Joseph understood his life, from teenage shepherd to all-powerful minister, as fulfilling a divine plan. The brothers' action was part of that plan. For this Joseph was particularly gifted; his virtue led to his imprisonment, his skills as a dream inter-preter outshone the local experts and was his way to freedom. Furthermore, his advice led to an imaginative job description and appointment to it, the second highest official in the country; all this accomplished under the guidance of God.

The Muslim Story

The qur'anic account of Joseph focuses on how the evil done to him was transformed and turned "to his advantage and through him to the advantage of Jacob and his wife, as well as all his children, who will need Joseph and benefit from his elevated position in Egypt."[5] In the Qur'an, the key moment is Joseph's dream, repeated to his father. Alongside the sun and the moon, he had dreamt of eleven stars, all of which bowed down before him. His father replied, "My son, tell your brothers nothing of this dream, or they may plot to harm you—Satan is man's sworn enemy. This is about how your Lord will choose you, teach you

---

[2] Ibid.
[3] Ibid.
[4] Ibid.
[5] Muhammad Abdel Haleem, *Understanding the Qur'an*, 143.

to interpret dreams and perfect His blessing on you and the House of Jacob" (Qurʾan 12:5-6). This made Jacob happy: Joseph had been chosen as a prophet, a recipient of God's blessing.

This surah was revealed at the time of Muhammad's response to "the challenge made him by the Meccans, that if he is indeed a prophet he will be able to tell them the story of Joseph and why Jacob's family moved from Syria to Egypt."[6] The resulting surah was constructed "out of a rapidly moving series of scenes, something like a morality play and the events of the story are communicated through the dialogue."[7] But the story has wider implications, "God's grace, a reward for Joseph, is, at the end of the verse, universalized, 'this is how we reward those who do good.' "[8]

Coming when surrounded by problems and difficulties, the revelation strengthened the Prophet's heart. In the same year he faced persecution of his Muslim community, the deaths of his wife and uncle, and the migration to Medina, "it remains in the Qurʾan a moral to men of understanding; especially as the protection and aid of God to Joseph has . . . been generalized."[9]

The effectiveness of the surah "derives from its inner coherence and thematic unity . . . a series of replays: incidents which occur a first time to result in evil then a second time to result in good, the effect of which is heightened by juxtapositions and inversions."[10] This is well illustrated by the meetings Joseph had with Zulaikha. First she tried to seduce him, failed, and her husband supported Joseph. Later, her revenge came with his public refusal to obey her leading to his imprisonment. But later "on his release from prison, she admits her guilt and he forgives her."[11]

---

[6] Anthony H. Johns, *Joseph in the Qurʾan: Dramatic Dialogue, Human Emotion, and Prophetic Wisdom* (Rome: Pontificio Istituto di Studi Arabi e Islamici, in Islamochristiana, 1981), no. 7, 31.

[7] Ibid.

[8] Muhammad Abdel Haleem, *Understanding the Qurʾan*, 148.

[9] Ibid., 159.

[10] Anthony H. Johns, *Joseph in the Qurʾan*, 34.

[11] Ibid.

The first visit to Egypt to buy food led to a curious request that the youngest brother should accompany them on a second visit. This reminded the brothers of their first request to their father to take Joseph; his affirmative reply led to their betrayal of his trust. When their food was again finished, they made a second request to take Benjamin; this time their father was forced to agree, but he did not trust them. It turned into a happy re-union with Joseph. The story of "a son lost and found" showed the strength of Jacob's faith in God. Without wavering, though overcome with sadness, Jacob trusted, saying, "It is best to be patient, may God bring all of them back to me—He alone is the All Knowing the All wise" (Qurʾan 12:83).

As in the biblical account above, the most striking element following the reconciliation with Joseph is the resolution of the family conflict. From that moment, the family was gifted with peace and harmony, a contrast with the Qurʾan's presentation of Noah and Abraham as will be seen later. "Neither Jacob nor Joseph make threats or need to exact vengeance. Jacob accepts his trials and forgives his penitent sons for the pain they caused him. His patience and endurance never waver. Joseph likewise forgives Zulaikha for her lies and his brothers for their envy, declaring: 'No reproach is held against you today.'[12] Muhammad applied this lesson on his return to Mecca when he addressed "the Quraysh at the Kaʿba: 'I say to you the words of my brother Joseph, no reproach is held against you today.'"[13] The parallels become clear: "Joseph's rejection as a parallel to Muhammad's rejection, his imprisonment, a parallel to the restriction of Muslim activities to the house of Arqam, and his establishment as a ruler in exile, a parallel to Muhammad's leadership in Medina."[14] In this revelation, around 619–620 CE, Muhammad heard these words, "Joseph came to you before with clear signs, but you never ceased to doubt the message he brought you. When he

[12] Ibid., 43.
[13] Ibid.
[14] Ibid., 44.

died, you said, 'God will not send another messenger'" (Qur³an 40:34), on which Muhammad Asad[15] offers this useful insight:

> It would seem that Joseph had been accepted in Egypt as a prophet only by the ruling class, the Hyksos, who were of Arab origin, spoke a language closely related to Hebrew . . . and were, therefore, emotionally and culturally predisposed towards the spirit of Joseph's mission, while the rest of the population was and remained hostile to the faith preached by him.[16]

The Example of Joseph in the Spiritual Journey of Christian-Muslim Dialogue

The stories are similar but there are differences in interpretations and their practical applications to the lives of their respective believers. The story in the Qur³an offers a powerful lesson about forgiveness and reconciliation: Joseph is an exemplar for Muslims to follow.

Joseph: The Man Who Trusted God

A Christian Perspective. Some Christians see Joseph's life as an example of how the will of God works, bringing good out of bad. Cyril of Jerusalem[17] comments, God "took the un-brotherly

---

[15] Muhammad Asad (1900–92), b. Leopold Weiss, Austrian Jewish parents, fluent in Hebrew and Aramaic. In 1920s traveled to Jerusalem, stayed with an uncle. Worked for *Frankfurter Zeitung* showing sympathetic understanding of Arab fears of Zionism; converted to Islam 1926 in Berlin. In 1932 moved to British India, involved with independent Pakistan, imprisoned for three years during the war. In 1947 given Pakistani citizenship and appointed Director of the Department of Islamic Reconstruction; 1949 joined Ministry of Foreign Affairs, head of the Middle East Division; 1952 Minister Plenipotentiary to the UN in New York. Well known for two books: *The Road to Mecca*, a biography up to the age of thirty-two, and *The Message of the Qur³an*. Died in Spain.

[16] Muhammad Asad, trans., *The Message of the Qur³an* (Bristol: Book Foundation, 2003), 816, surah 40, note 24.

[17] Cyril of Jerusalem (ca. 315–86). Bishop of Jerusalem from 349. In 357 Acacius, an Arian, bishop of Caesarea, claimed authority over Jerusalem

purpose of Joseph's brethren for a groundwork of His own dispensation, and, by permitting them to sell their brother from hatred, took occasion to make him king";[18] from a wicked plan came a way to salvation, in Gregory of Nyssa's[19] words, Joseph had "no reason to grieve at the envy of his brethren inasmuch as the malice of his own kith and kin became to him the road to empire."[20] Chrysostom describes Jacob, though "now an old man, bowed himself to Joseph, showing the obeisance of the whole people which was to be [directed] to him."[21]

Clearly Joseph's life was part of the divine plan; he was especially gifted as shown by his big-hearted forgiveness following his brothers' repentance. Chrysostom comments on Joseph's words, " 'God did send me hither,' that is, He made use of their wickedness for a good end . . . Thus he contracts the time, acknowledges the offence and turns it all to a providence."[22] Joseph gave glory to his Master and was himself glorified, in Chrysostom's words; this was "very great proof of his intimacy with God. There is no one thing so good as to be the intimate friend

---

and had Cyril banished; restored in 359. Two further banishments, then Gregory of Nyssa sent to report: he found the church corrupt in morals but orthodox in faith. Cyril is best known for his *Catechetical Instructions* given during Lent and Easter, stressing the importance of baptism and the Real Presence in the Eucharist.

[18] Cyril of Jerusalem, *Catechetical Instruction 8*, in NPNF 2, vol. 7, p. 49, para. 4.

[19] Gregory of Nyssa (ca. 330–ca. 395), younger brother of Basil, joined his monastic community. Bishop of Nyssa ca. 371. Preached the faith of Nicaea, deposed by Arians in 376, reinstalled 378. Attended Council of Antioch in 379, championed Nicaea at Council of Constantinople 381, later in demand as a preacher. Treatises against Eunomius and Apollinarius with his Catechetical Orations are his most notable writings.

[20] Gregory of Nyssa, *Letter 12: On His Work against Eunomius*, in NPNF 2, vol. 5, p. 535.

[21] John Chrysostom, *Homily XXVI on Hebrews*, xi:20-22, in NPNF 1, vol. 14, p. 482, sec. 2.

[22] John Chrysostom, *Homily II on Philemon 1:4-6*, in NPNF 1, vol. 13, p. 552, vv. 15-16.

of God."[23] In all his dealings, Joseph's behavior was exemplary, as Cassian eulogises:

> In prosperity he was very dear to his father, affectionate to his brethren, acceptable to God; and, in adversity, was chaste and faithful to the Lord, in prison most kind to the prisoners, forgetful of wrongs, generous to his enemies; and to his brethren, who were envious of him, and as far as lay in their powers, his murderers, he proved not only affectionate but actually munificent.[24]

Joseph was inspired by God and trusted by family and people. Christians can learn from him how to live within the parameters of God's will, perplexing as it so often is.

A Muslim Perspective. The story of Joseph is offered as an ideal to be imitated by the committed Muslim. Maneri writes that as a young man he "was without fault yet his brothers threw him into a well. His father, a venerated messenger, suffered for years on account of his separation from him. Joseph was taken out of the well and sold into slavery. Then he was sorely tried and taken in hand by chastity. Thereafter he was raised from slavery to rule over Egypt and his brothers were raised from sin to greatness."[25] The mix of good and bad, of virtue and vice, show there is "a lesson in the stories of such people for those who understand. This revelation is no fabrication: it is a confirmation of the truth of what was sent before it; an explanation of everything; a guide and a blessing for those who believe" (Qur'an, 12:111). There can

---

[23] John Chrysostom, *Homily V on Philippians ii:1-4*, in NPNF 1, vol. 13, p. 204.

[24] John Cassian, *VI Conference of Theodore: On the Death of Saints*, in NPNF 2, vol. 11, chap. 10, p. 257. John Cassian (360–435), joined a monastery in Bethlehem, then to Egypt to study monastic life: influenced by Evagrius Pontus. Later a deacon in Constantinople sent by John Chrysostom to Pope Innocent I in Rome. Moved to establish two monasteries in the Marseilles area of France. Wrote the "Institutes" and the "Conferences"—guidance for living the monastic life.

[25] Sharafuddin Maneri, *In Quest of God*, letter 60, 131.

never be an exaggerated application of this story, for, as Maneri states, "if a thousand volumes were written concerning the wonders of that story, it would be but a drop in the ocean or a ray of the sun";[26] the triumph of virtue is at the heart of this revelation. This encourages those who "become the laughing stock of people and taste derision"[27] but remain faithful to God. The story also highlights how daily efforts at transformation can be the clearest way to God: "Reject this rubbish heap! Go to the rose garden! Abandon the manner of a beggar! Since kingship awaits you in Egypt, why, like Joseph, do you remain in a well?"[28]

Joseph suffered abandonment but found God for "in one hour Joseph experienced Your love in the well, though intellects had missed it for a hundred years!"[29] The deeper truth is that "the wonders of the world of love are not comprehensible to the intellect. . . . When the messenger Joseph went away, the eyesight of the messenger Jacob was also lost. As long as he did not see him, neither did his brothers see him. When the messenger Joseph returned, so did his eyesight."[30] In the life of faith there is loss, absence and doubt, but a revealing God will show that the final solution is within the will of God, as the Joseph story shows. Indeed these are signs of growing maturity, for "whoever has not experienced the loss of Joseph, even though he believes, hasn't really believed."[31] In this way the story of Joseph exemplifies the challenge for all who seek ever greater intimacy with God.

Joseph's Moral Integrity as Manager Dealing with His Brothers

A Christian Perspective. The guilt of Joseph's brothers is a favorite theme of Christian commentators. Chrysostom writes, when

---

[26] Sharafuddin Maneri, *The Hundred Letters*, letter 49, 197.

[27] Ibid.

[28] Sharafuddin Maneri, *In Quest of God*, letter 58, 237, with a quotation from Kwaja Attar.

[29] Sharafuddin Maneri, *The Hundred Letters*, letter 68, 284.

[30] Sharafuddin Maneri, *In Quest of God*, letter 140, 272.

[31] Ibid., letter 140, 272.

they "had sold the just man, and thirteen years had passed away, suspecting they had fallen into punishment, and fearing for their lives, they remembered their sin, and said one to another, 'we are verily guilty concerning our brother Joseph.' "[32] By jealousy they tried to enslave Joseph, only later did they realize Joseph "was a slave but not a slave to men: wherefore, even in slavery he was freer than all that are free."[33] This freedom is also illustrated in these words of Clement of Alexandria: "since Joseph's master's wife was not able to seduce him from his steadfastness; but as she violently held his coat, divested himself of it—becoming bare of sin, but clothed with seemliness of character."[34] Theodoret of Cyrus[35] used Joseph, specifically, as a model of chaste behavior. Joseph, "suffering under a calumnious charge, imprisoned and fettered for invading another man's bed, and spending a long time in a dungeon, his pain is lighted by the remedy that the story furnishes,"[36] an illustration of the truth that innocent

[32] John Chrysostom, *Instructions to Catechumens Homily III* in NPNF 1, vol. 11, p. 80, para. 20.

[33] John Chrysostom, *Homilies on 1 Corinthians*[7:1-2] in NPNF 1, vol. 12, homily 14, p. 109, sec. 5.

[34] Clement of Alexandria, *Stromata*, book 7 in the *Ante-Nicene Christian Library: Translations of the Writings of the Fathers*, vol. 2, chap. 11, 540. All subsequent references to the *Ante-Nicene Christian Library*, trans. Alexander Roberts and James Donaldson (Edinburgh: T&T Clark, 1890–97), hereafter ANF, are from this series. Clement of Alexandria (ca. 150–ca. 215), theologian, head of the Catechetical School at Alexandria. In 202 forced to flee persecution. In the time of Gnosticism he taught true "gnosis" is the faith of the Church, based on Divine Revelation. Saw Greek philosophy as a gift. Christ the Logos, source of human reason and interpreter of God to humanity: ignorance of Christ a greater evil than sin.

[35] Theodoret of Cyrus (ca. 393–ca. 466) entered monastery and at thirty was appointed bishop of Cyrus. Involved in the christological controversies of Nestorius and Cyril of Alexandria. An admirer of Nestorius and the Antiochene school. Opposed Cyril at Council of Antioch (431), but controversial. Took part in Council of Chalcedon (451) and accepted its formula, then returned peacefully to his diocese.

[36] Theodoret of Cyrus, *Letter LXXXVIII of Theodoretus, Bishop of Cyrus, to Dioscorus, Archbishop of Alexandria* in the NPNF 2, vol. 3, p. 278.

victims are strengthened by God shown by their courage in defending their virtue.

In his management of the food distribution, Joseph wanted to ensure that all received a portion so he opened the storehouses, as Ambrose describes "that all might buy their corn supply, lest if they received it for nothing, they should give up cultivating the ground. For he who has the use of what is another's often neglects his own."[37] Joseph's wise provision enabled farmers to help themselves; by making them pay for the seed, he encouraged them to farm.

At the same time, "by his watchfulness, when so high an office was given him, he gathered together such vast supplies; and through his justice he treated all alike."[38] Joseph was a manager of insight and integrity, who understood that by helping all his conduct would be approved by all.

A Muslim Perspective. Maneri stresses that self-will is a form of slavery because self-will focuses on the self and becomes a habit, as shown by Zulaikha, who "following her unbridled desires changed from a noble lady to a prisoner, while the renowned Joseph told her to abandon her desires. He, though a captive, became a great man."[39] Living the virtuous life is a sign of an inner freedom, more powerful than physical imprisonment.

The celibacy of Joseph has wider relevance: al-Hujwiri writes, "when God ordains celibacy unto a man, his celibacy should be like that of Joseph, who, although he was able to satisfy his desire for Zulaykha, turned away from her and busied himself with subduing his passion and considering the vices of his lower

[37] Ambrose, *Duties of the Clergy*, book 2, in NPNF 2, vol. 10, chap. 16, pp. 55–56, para. 79. Ambrose (ca. 334–97), b. Trier, son of Roman official, prefect in Gaul. Lawyer in Rome. Circa 370 appointed governor of Liguria and Emilia, capital Milan then, in 374 Ambrose was acclaimed bishop, though only a catechumen. As bishop, countered Arianism and paganism, brought peace to Milan. In 386 converted Augustine. Ambrose known for preaching and teaching. One of the four Latin Doctors of the Church.

[38] Ibid., p. 56, para. 84.

[39] Sharafuddin Maneri, *The Hundred Letters*, letter 82, 336.

soul."[40] By facing his emotions, he gained the moral strength to resist their "attractions."

His brothers thought they had solved the Joseph problem, but the brothers were shortsighted, raising the question, expressed by Maneri, "Grief in this world stems from the lack of grieving over the life to come. It would cause grief, so why did you sell Joseph?"[41] A short-term solution based on injustice will lead to a long-term problem with a God dedicated to virtue.

Some have challenged the view that prophets are sinless, but Maneri explains, "the story of Joseph's brothers who, like him, were prophets, and yet committed great sins,"[42] is explained by recognizing that "whatever emanated from the brothers of the prophet Joseph occurred before revelation descended upon them and this, in turn, resulted in repentance and correction."[43] Repentance for sin committed is more powerful than the sin itself: it results in forgiveness and rebuilds friendship.

Joseph's Journey of Faith

A Christian Perspective. Chrysostom has presented Joseph's time in prison as the most difficult part of his journey of faith, for there he "was in the extreme of poverty, being not merely a slave."[44] But in the loneliness of prison, Joseph remained steadfast. As Ambrose states, he "certainly had a longing for freedom, and yet endured the bonds of servitude. How meek he was in slavery, how unchanging in virtue, how kindly in prison! Wise, too, in interpreting and self-restrained in exercising his power!"[45] He was careful with his power, fair in dealing with

---

[40] Ali Bin Uthaman Al-Hujwiri, *The Kashf Al-Mahjub*, trans. Reynold A. Nicholson (New Delhi: Adam Publishers & Distributors, 2009), 365.

[41] Sharafuddin Maneri, *In Quest of God*, letter 86, 185.

[42] Sharafuddin Maneri, *The Hundred Letters*, letter 21, 87.

[43] Ibid.

[44] John Chrysostom, *Homilies on John*, homily 76 on John 14:31, 15:1, in NPNF 1, vol. 14, p. 281, sec. 3.

[45] Ambrose, *Duties of the Clergy*, book 1, chap. 24, p. 18, para. 112.

the people during the famine, and committed to justice being done. Throughout, Joseph, inspired by God, chose the way of moral integrity, lived his ethical values, having learned from the injustices he had suffered.

A Muslim Perspective. Joseph is a wise man, because, as the Prophet said, he "supervises his soul and acts with a view to his death."[46] Others justify themselves, saying "that they took note of what Joseph said, even though he was a prophet: 'I do not call myself sinless, for myself still urges me to sin!' "[47] Weakness is part of the human condition that even prophets cannot avoid, but Joseph provided an example of moral behavior, recalling his progress from sale into slavery to high office in Egypt. Maneri reflects on this change, "O world of the soul, all are astonished by you: a hundred thousand intellects have been confused by You."[48]

When Joseph was sold, "his price exceeded the treasuries of kings."[49] This valuation comes from an old man with a few kilograms of cotton, which he took to market, saying, " 'I shall buy this slave.' People said; 'Old man, you have become mad. His price exceeds the treasuries of kings. How can you purchase him with this cotton?' He replied: 'I know this, but I have brought it in order to be numbered among those who wanted to purchase him.' Whoever is not colored by this love is considered sticks or stones by God."[50] The value of Joseph is not in owning or copying but in a willingness to give all to buy, an echo of Jesus' story of the pearl of great price; only the enthusiast will sell all to buy it. The journey of faith cannot be compromised.

---

[46] Sharafuddin Maneri, *The Hundred Letters*, letter 67, 277.
[47] Ibid., quoting Qurʾan 12:53, Maneri translation.
[48] Sharafuddin Maneri, *In Quest of God*, letter 51, 115.
[49] Ibid., letter 150, 288.
[50] Ibid.

Christ and Joseph in Christian Writing

Joseph has been used as a forerunner of Jesus Christ. The former is persecuted by his brothers, as Tertullian[51] put it, "sold into Egypt, on account of the favor of God; just as Christ was sold by Israel . . . when he was betrayed by Judas."[52] Ambrose highlights the contrast: "Joseph was sold Jesus Christ was bought, the one to slavery, the other to death."[53] Augustine repeats the theme, "Christ appears to me in Joseph, who was persecuted and sold by his brethren, and after his troubles obtained honor in Egypt,"[54] and "Joseph sold into Egypt is Christ passing over to the Gentiles. There Joseph, after tribulations, was exalted, and here Christ, after the suffering of the Martyrs, was glorified."[55] In this respect the life of Joseph became a model not only for Christ and his redemptive death but also for all Christians, confirming the faith that their lives are in the hands of God.

[51] Tertullian (160–220), b. Carthage in Roman North Africa and had fine education, became a lawyer, wrote in Greek as well as Latin. Became Christian about 197 and ten years later a Montanist. Some thirty-one works extant, from both periods of his Christian life. He is the first theologian to use the word "Trinity."

[52] Tertullian, *An Answer to the Jews*, in ANF, vol. 18, chap. 10, pp. 236–37.

[53] Ambrose, *Of the Holy Spirit*, in NPNF 2, vol. 10, book 3, chap. 17, pp. 152–53, para. 123.

[54] Augustine, *Reply to Faustus: The Manichaean*, in NPNF 1, vol. 4, book 12, p. 192, para. 28. Augustine of Hippo (354–430), b. North Africa, son of pagan father and Christian mother (Monica). In 370 studying in Carthage, then taught philosophy, later attracted to Manichaeism. In 383 to Rome to teach, then to Milan where he came under the influence of Bishop Ambrose, who baptized him in 387. Returned to Africa, set up a religious community. In 391 ordained. In 396 bishop of Hippo. Lived with his community till his death, working tirelessly for the pastoral needs of his people. Wrote 113 books and treatises, 200 letters, and 500 sermons, best known: *Confessions* and the *City of God*. Latin Doctor of the Church.

[55] Augustine, *Homilies on the Psalms*, in NPNF 1, vol. 8, p. 392, para. 8.

A Muslim Description: The Beautiful Joseph

Perhaps the most significant element in the Muslim Joseph is his physical beauty. Al-Hujwiri writes, "Human nature prevailed in the women of Egypt as they gazed, enraptured, on the wondrous beauty of Yusuf [Joseph], on whom be peace! But afterwards the preponderance was reversed, until at last they beheld him with their human nature annihilated and cried: 'This is no human being.' "[56] They were dazzled by his masculine beauty, which transcended their deepest emotions. Al-Hujwiri continues, "Purity is not one of the qualities of Man, for Man is clay, and clay involves impurity, and Man cannot escape from impurity."[57] But purity "is the attribute of those who love and the lover is he that is dead in his own attributes and living in the attributes of his Beloved and their 'states resemble the clear sun in the opinion of mystics,' "[58] a reference to the particular purity found in the mystical union with God.

Context for Dialogue

Abdel Haleem comments that the Genesis account of Joseph "shows him as appearing rough, accusing them [his brothers] of spying, and keeping Simeon in prison as security for their return with Benjamin."[59] This contrasts with Qur'an's gentler Joseph, who appears "as a pleasant, gentle and kind man, different from the picture given in Genesis of Joseph distributing corn in Egypt."[60] One might suggest he overstates the case. The Joseph of Genesis is full of subtlety. On the one hand, an innocent victim of a dysfunctional family, on the other, patronized and spoiled by a doting father. As victim he was subject to his employer's wife's

---

[56] Ali Bin Uthaman Al-Hujwiri, *The Kashf Al-Mahjub*, 32, quoting Qur'an 12:31.

[57] Ibid.

[58] Ibid.

[59] Muhammad Abdel Haleem, *Understanding the Qur'an*, 151.

[60] Ibid.

sexual desires; when he resisted he was given a significant prison sentence. There he is trusted enough to have some responsibility. By interpreting dreams accurately, he gained no favors; the one who lived *forgot* Joseph. But when the emergency came and Pharaoh needed an interpreter, Joseph was *remembered*. After succeeding in interpretation he became manager of the country's farmers. In that context the appearance of his brothers, not unexpected, was a particular challenge. Might one say that Haleem's Joseph would not have gotten to where the Genesis Joseph did?

The two versions of the Joseph story clearly focus on the same person. Their role in the respective Inspired Scriptures shows differences. But both present Joseph as one who trusted the guidance of God and was deemed trustworthy by Egyptian authorities. The Genesis version includes another role: to show how the Chosen People reached Egypt.

In the Qur'an, the story shows how, by putting one's trust in God, believers, being faithful in impossible difficulties, will be justified.

These are complementary interpretations enabling fruitful but demanding reflection in a dialogue of spirituality.

Chapter 21

Affirming the Positive Echoes in the Understanding of God as the One Who Knows All

Muslims and Christians believe in an all-knowing God, simultaneously aware of past, present, and future, but their respective presentations differ. In the Qurᵓan, God has "the keys to the unseen; no one knows them but Him. He knows all that is in the land and sea. No leaf falls without His knowledge" (Qurᵓan 6:59), and "everything before us, everything behind us, everything in between, all belongs to Him" (Qurᵓan 19:64). No part of human history is hidden from God, for "whatever good you may do, God is well aware of it" (Qurᵓan 2:197), and "remember that God knows what is in your souls, so be mindful of Him. Remember that God is most forgiving and forbearing" (Qurᵓan 2:235), and at the end God knows "what state you are in—on the day when all are returned to Him, He will tell them everything they have done" (Qurᵓan 24:64). These sentences emphasize a relationship developed at some distance. The knowledge may be intimate, but the verbal description displays the power of full knowledge.

The Christian Scriptures offer an alternative approach: "His [the Lord's] eyes are on those who fear him, and he knows every human action" (Sir 15:19). The God who knows is also a God who cares: "Do not keep striving for what you are to eat and what you are to drink, and do not keep worrying. For it is the nations of the world that strive after all these things, and your Father knows that you need them" (Luke 12:29-30). God not only provides but also uses words that would echo more deeply in the ears of the listeners, "for we are the temple of the living God; as God said: 'I will live in them and walk among them, and I will be their God, and they shall be my people" (2 Cor 6:16).

The all-knowing and all-powerful God is, for Muslim and Christian alike, more a comfort than a threat. Behind the pain and suffering of the present moment there is a future, for the all-knowing God has offered a fulfillment more permanent than the pain of the present, however long it has to be endured. By forgetting God, not only does the person turn on him- or herself, but also puts little value in a life fulfilled after death.

Al-Ghazālī highlights watchfulness as "praiseworthy in man if his watchfulness is directed to his Lord and his heart. And that will be the case when he knows that God the Most High observes him and sees him in every situation,"[1] and, therefore, knows all.

The Catholic Catechism offers the same teaching: "God created everything for man, but man in turn was created to serve and love God and to offer all creation back to him: 'What is it that is about to be created, that enjoys such honor? It is man—that great and wonderful living creature, more precious in the eyes of God than all other creatures' ";[2] human beings alone in the created world are capable of a personal response to the invitation to believe in lasting fulfillment after death.

Both Christian and Muslim Inspired Scriptures reveal a divine infatuation with the people about whom God knows everything. The human response tries to ensure openness, honesty,

---

[1] Al-Ghazālī, *The Ninety-Nine Beautiful Names of God*, 114.
[2] *Catechism of the Catholic Church*, 81–82, no. 358, quoting from St. John Chrysostom, *Sermones in Genesim* 2, 1 PG 54, 587D–588A.

and transparency because what is concealed disfigures the goodness of God's creating act. To forget God is to exclude oneself from the divine presence. For believers, given that God has full knowledge, it is in their best interest to accept what cannot be changed and trust in the all-knowing God who will ensure, ultimately, an outcome beyond dreams.

22

Noah: Believed in the All-Knowing God and Faced an Impossible Task with Confidence

Noah: The Story as Revealed

The Christian Story

God affirms that Noah (see Gen 5:28–9:29) was "blameless in his generation. . . . [He] walked with God" (Gen 6:9). Noah is hailed as the "the Flood hero."[1] He was responsible for the tiny remnant who survived the destructive storms, a punishment from God determined to "make an end of all flesh" (Gen 6:13). Noah is instructed to make a boat big enough and strong enough to withstand storms and floods, to take himself, his family, and two of every species of animal, these alone destined to survive. "Noah did this; he did all that God commanded him" (Gen 6:22). When the ark was complete all entered, ready for the moment

---

[1] Lloyd R. Bailey, in *The Anchor Bible Dictionary*, ed. David Noel Freedman, s.v. "Noah and the Ark."

God's words became reality. "I will send rain on the earth for forty days and forty nights; and every living thing that I have made I will blot out from the face of the ground" (Gen 7:4). The Lord closed the door of the ark; forty days of rain and the water covered the mountains; no living being survived. It lasted for a hundred and fifty days, then the water began to subside and, eventually, the ark came to earth again. Noah tested the situation, sending, first, a raven, which returned soon enough, finding nothing to eat, then a dove, which also returned, and then a dove again, who returned with a new green shoot, the sign of new life on dry land. God commanded Noah to come out of the ark, and Noah immediately built an altar and offered a sacrifice, which so pleased God that he said in his heart, "I will never again curse the ground because of humankind, for the inclination of the human heart is evil from youth; nor will I ever again destroy every living creature as I have done" (Gen 8:21). A new covenant was made between God and Noah, and "this is the sign of the covenant that I make between me and you and every living creature that is with you, for all future generations: I have set my bow in the clouds, and it shall be a sign of the covenant between me and the earth" (Gen 9:12-13). When the sign appears God will remember this covenant; there will never be "a flood to destroy all flesh" (Gen 9:15). Noah is saved; he received the new covenant and became the father of a new generation; "Noah is an epoch divider figure as well as a bridge between the quasi-mythological history and a more humanly accountable history."[2]

Having landed, Noah started to cultivate the new land, planting a vineyard that later produced wine. On one occasion Noah, overcome with wine, was found asleep, naked. His son took the initiative and put a cover over him to prevent further embarrassment. On waking, a sober Noah reduced his inheritance.

God's struggle with human beings continued; this covenant did not last, but it elicited an assurance from God that this form of punishment would not be repeated.

[2] Ibid.

The Muslim Story

The Noah story in the Qurʾan is significant because of its multiple repetitions, occurring in twenty-six surahs, one of which carries his name.[3]

Noah was sent by God to warn his people that there is only one God. So to worship other gods now will mean a guilty verdict on Judgment Day. They refused to listen, saying, "'We believe you are far astray.' He replied, 'my people, there is nothing astray about me! On the contrary, I am a messenger from the Lord of all the Worlds. I am delivering my Lord's messages to you and giving you sincere advice. I know things from God that you do not'" (Qurʾan 7:60-62).[4] Noah stood firm; his people remained skeptical. He challenged them again, "Do you find it so strange that a message should come from your Lord—through a man in your midst—to warn you and make you aware of God so that you may be given mercy? But they called him a liar" (Qurʾan 7:64). God saved Noah and his family in the ark and the rest were drowned in the flood for "they were wilfully blind" (Qurʾan 7:64), a message for those who continue to reject the revelation of God. Noah in his clashes with unbelievers is seen "as the prototype of the prophet Muhammad, suffering the same hatred and threats of physical harm that the Prophet was later to experience from his Meccan compatriots."[5]

Noah had total trust in God, received no reward for his work, even enduring rejection by his son who refused his invitation to join him in the ark, because he thought he would be safer on the highest mountain. He was drowned; he failed to realize the flood was not extreme weather conditions but divine punishment. Later, God, with ruthless divine logic, told the enquiring Noah "he was not one of your family. What he did was not right" (Qurʾan 11:46); disobedience to God meant exclusion from the family.

[3] Surah 71, Noah, Nuh.

[4] See also 10:71-73; 11:25-48; 21:76-77; 23:23-30; 25:37; 26:105-22; 29:14-15; 37:75-82; 54:9-17; 71:1-28.

[5] William M. Brinner, in *Encyclopaedia of the Qurʾān*, ed. Jane Dammen McAuliffe, s.v. "Noah."

Noah's courageous denunciation of idol worshipers and those who disobeyed God earned him the status of Prophet. He remains popular in Islam because "he was truly a thankful servant" (Qurʾan 17:3), who lived nearly a thousand years:[6] a "sign for all people" (Qurʾan 29:15).

Cyril Glassé writes, the "flood symbolizes the submerging of the awareness of God as God by the overpowering experience of the *world* as God . . . When the 'Flood was over'—the dawn of history—and the waters gone down, awareness of the Divine Unity—preserved in the ark, the 'conscience,' the 'inner observer'—re-emerged."[7]

The end of the flood marked an important moment for the human family, a day the remnant of that family came out of the ark, becoming "a day of fasting for both humans and animals who had been in the ark for six months."[8]

This summarizes the importance of Noah, a bridge between those who forgot God and those who remembered God: the memory of the latter now enriched with this story of power, wonder, courage, and faith.

Noah: The Man of Weakness

A Christian Perspective

Several of the church fathers comment on Noah's drunkenness, with different views of his nakedness.[9] Clement of Alexandria writes, "With the clear and written description of his transgression before us, we might guard with all our might against drunkenness. For which cause they who covered the shame of his

---

[6] The figure corresponds to that in Genesis 9:29.

[7] Cyril Glassé, ed., *The New Encyclopaedia of Islam*, s.v. "Noah." The italics are the author's.

[8] William M. Brinner, in *Encyclopaedia of the Qurʾān*, ed. Jane Dammen McAuliffe, s.v. "Noah."

[9] See Genesis 9:20-21.

drunkenness are blessed by the Lord."[10] John Chrysostom asked, "How many shall I enumerate who have suffered evils from in-dulgence? Noah was drunken, and was exposed in his nakedness, and see what evils came of this,"[11] but for Jerome,[12] Noah became intoxicated, "living as he did in the rude age after the flood, when the vine was first planted, perhaps he did not know its power of inebriation,"[13] while for Augustine the event was "pregnant with prophetic meanings, and veiled in mysteries,"[14] then, linking it to the passion of Christ and the sacramental life, he states, "The garment signifies the sacrament, their backs the memory of things past,"[15] adding, since Noah was "foreshadowing the future real-ity, [he] drank, not water, but wine, and thus showed forth our Lord's passion."[16] From these comments it is clear that Christian commentators focused more on its meaning in the context of Jesus' redemptive work than on Noah's weaknesses.

A Muslim Perspective

One important question for Muslims was how Iblis survived the flood. The answer was linked to the order of entry into the ark; the smallest (the ant) first and the largest (the donkey) last.

---

[10] Clement of Alexandria, *The Instructor (Paedagogus)*, book 2, in the ANF, vol. 4, chap. 2, p. 210.

[11] John Chrysostom, *Homily XXVII on Acts XII:18-19* in NPNF 1, vol. 11, p. 177.

[12] Jerome (ca. 342–ca. 420), early life in Dalmatia, baptized at eighteen, studied in Rome for eight years. In 374 living eremitical life and learning Hebrew in Syria. From 382 to 385 secretary to Pope Damasus in Rome; commissioned new Latin translation of the Bible, from Hebrew and Greek; "Vulgate" completed 404. Spiritual adviser to a group of pious women, settled in Bethlehem from 386, where he died in 420. One of the four great Latin fathers of the Church.

[13] Jerome, *Letters: Letter XXII to Eustochium*, in NPNF, vol. 6, p. 25, para. 8.

[14] Augustine of Hippo, *City of God*, book 16, in NPNF 1, vol. 2, book 1, chap. 1, 309.

[15] Ibid., chap. 2.

[16] Augustine of Hippo, *On Christian Doctrine*, in NPNF 1, vol. 2, book 4, chap. 21, p. 590, para. 45.

When the donkey was loading, Brannon Wheeler[17] records, when "only its chest was inside, Iblis attached himself to its tail so that it was unable to lift its legs. . . . Finally, Noah said, 'Get going even if Satan is with you!' The words he said were a slip of the tongue but when Noah said it, Satan let the donkey proceed. The donkey went in and Satan with him";[18] an imaginative answer!

Noah: The Exemplar

A Christian Perspective

Many of the church fathers see Noah as a man of virtue because, as Gregory Nazianzen[19] expressed it, "he was pleasing to God; he who was entrusted with the saving of the whole world from the waters, or rather of the seeds of the world, escaped the Deluge in a small Ark."[20] To achieve this he needed not just faith but also courage to face the opposition and the skill to build an ark: accurate in dimensions, seaworthy in flood waters, and habitable for the survivors. He was to be the only survivor of previous

[17] Brannon Wheeler, associate professor of Islamic studies and comparative religion at the University of Washington, Seattle, specializing in Islamic Law and Quranic studies, PhD in Near Eastern languages and civilizations from the University of Chicago, 1993. From 2004, senior Fulbright Research Fellow for Jordan, Egypt, and Saudi Arabia for 2004.

[18] Brannon M. Wheeler, *Prophets in the Qur'an* (London and New York: Continuum, 2002), 57, quoting Ibn Abbas, cousin and companion of the prophet Muhammad.

[19] Gregory of Nazianzen (329–89). Studied in Athens where he met Basil, became a monk, suiting his contemplative spirit. Under pressure, ordained priest by his bishop-father, ca. 362; ten years later ordained bishop for the see of Sasima, Cappadocia, but remained assistant to his father. In 379 summoned to Constantinople to the church of Anastasis, where his preaching restored the Nicene faith, finally approved at the Council of Constantinople 381. During the Council appointed bishop of the city but resigned within a year. Died in 389. One of the four Greek Doctors of the Church.

[20] Gregory Nazianzen, *Oration 28: The Second Theological Oration*, in NPNF 2, vol. 7, p. 295, para. 18.

generations and, as Ambrose writes, "the author of one to come; he was born, too, rather for the world and the universe than for himself. How brave he was to overcome the flood!"[21] Noah trusted God and completed the task given him, even though, as Chrysostom puts it, "there were many hindrances, since many others shone after him, yet will he have nothing less than they; for in his own time he was perfect."[22] The people would not listen. They, Chrysostom's words, "chose this soft and dissolute life."[23] For the "the Universe was not made by chance, Hell is a proof,"[24] and "if in the time of Noah they had feared the deluge, they would not have been drowned,"[25] but "in the midst of their playing, eating, marrying, doing all the things to which they were used, even so they were overtaken by that fearful judgment,"[26] having "lived on in senseless mirth, foreseeing nought of what was coming. For this cause also the flood came and swept them all away, and wrought, in that instant, the common shipwreck of the world."[27] The story of Noah has been used by preachers to draw important lessons for Christians, encouraging them to be faithful to the command of God, to show moral courage in face of opposition, and be alert enough to discern good from bad.

A Muslim Perspective

Muslims see Noah also as a role model in ways similar to Christians. The Prophet advised that anyone who wished to see

[21] Ambrose, *Duties of the Clergy*, book 1, chap. 25, p. 21, para. 121.

[22] John Chrysostom, *Homilies on St. John's Gospel*, homily 71 on John 13, in NPNF 1, vol. 14, sec. 3, 262.

[23] John Chrysostom, *Homilies on the Letter to the Hebrews*, homily 29 on Hebrews 12:4-6, in NPNF 1, vol. 14, sec. 4, 501.

[24] John Chrysostom, *Homilies on the Letter to the Colossians*, homily 5 on Colossians 1:26-28, in NPNF 1, vol. 13, p. 283.

[25] John Chrysostom, *Homilies on the Second Letter to the Thessalonians*, homily 2 on 2 Thessalonians 1:1-2, in NPNF 1, vol. 13, p. 383.

[26] John Chrysostom, *Homilies on Matthew*, homily 20 on Matthew 6:16, in NPNF 1, vol. 10, sec. 6, 146.

[27] Ibid., homily 6 on Matthew 2:1-2, p. 42, para. 9.

the virtues of the former prophets should look to Noah for "his obedience," in the words of Mahmoud Ayoub.[28] Some filled out the Noah story to make it more effective as this comment shows: "Noah's people used to grab him and choke him until he was unconscious, so he said: 'Oh God, forgive my people for they do not understand.'"[29] Continuing disobedience and rebellion compounded sin, which, as time passed, got worse and worse. When God saw the situation was impossible, work on the ark began. Even then the people ridiculed him, saying, "Noah, you have become a carpenter after being a prophet! So God made the wombs of women infertile and they bore no children."[30] Finally, "God revealed that he would never send a Flood to the earth again"[31] because of the courageous virtues displayed by Noah.

Noah: The Man of Faith

A Christian Perspective

Following the courageous obedience of Noah, God, in Chrysostom's words, "showed forth anew great miracles,"[32] made a new Covenant with Noah, whose terms limited the divine options to punish human sinfulness. Noah showed such great faith, obeying God without question, never doubting how the great rescue would turn out.

A Muslim Perspective

Noah is important for Muslims because he warned people of the punishment if they did not repent and change their lives—an

---

[28] Brannon M. Wheeler, "Ibn Ishaq," in *Prophets in the Qurʾan*, 56–57.

[29] Ibid.

[30] Ibid., 57.

[31] Ibid., "Tabari," 61.

[32] John Chrysostom, *Homilies on St. Matthew's Gospel*, homily 14 on Matthew 4:12, in NPNF 1, vol. 10, p. 88, sec. 4.

early model of the prophet Muhammad. Cook[33] writes, for "Noah, the doom was temporal, the physical destruction of mankind in this world. In the case of the Prophet the predicted doom is that of the Judgment Day, and the punishment of souls rather than bodies, as well as the social disaster that irreligion breeds in this world."[34]

Five signs illustrate Noah's importance: first, he is "father of humankind,"[35] for only his family survived; second, "God blessed Noah with long life, for it is said, 'blessed is he whose life is long and whose deeds are good' ";[36] third, God answered his prayers for "the people of faith, as well as the rejecters of faith";[37] fourth, God saved him and his family; and, fifth, Noah was the first to abrogate laws of consanguinity, "for before his time marriage with maternal and paternal aunts was not prohibited."[38] Then he was blessed as the "the second father of humanity. God . . . saying 'Peace be upon Noah among all beings.' "[39]

---

[33] Jay R. Crook (Md. Nur), born and brought up in New York. Interest in Islamic culture and civilization led to his conversion. Studies in East Pakistan (now Bangladesh) for a few years then to the Middle East for most of his working life; Iran and Saudi Arabia with the Peace Corps until 1971. Enrolled in the doctoral program of Persian Literature for Foreigners at Tehran University, PhD in 1978 (later, *The Old and New Testaments: An Islamic Perspective*). Left Iran in 1980, worked as English teacher in the United States and Saudi Arabia before retiring in 1997.

[34] Jay R. Cook, *The Old Testament: An Islamic Perspective*, vol. 1, 2nd ed. (Chicago: ABC International Group, 2007), 207.

[35] Mahmoud M. Ayoub, *The Qurʾan and Its Interpreters: The House of 'Imran*, vol. 2 (New York: State University of New York Press, 1992), 87. Mahmoud M. Ayoub, b. South Lebanon, BA American University of Beirut (philosophy 1964), MA University of Pennsylvania (religious thought 1966), PhD Harvard University (history of religion 1975). From 1988–2008 professor and director of Islamic Studies, Temple University, Philadelphia. Has written *Redemptive Suffering in Islam: The Qurʾan and Its Interpreters*.

[36] Ibid.

[37] Ibid.

[38] Ibid.

[39] Ibid., 91. Quoting Qurʾan 37:79.

Noah: Pointing to the Future

A Christian Perspective

Noah witnessed the destruction of his world. The drama of the flood revealed the fragility of all life, natural and human. Christian writers have used the story as an image of baptism. As the earth was cleansed by the flood, so human beings are cleansed by the water of baptism. As Ambrose wrote, "The outer man is destroyed but the inner is renewed."[40] Later, asked why the Spirit descended as a dove, he replied, "In order that . . . you might acknowledge, that that dove also, which just Noah sent forth from the ark, was a likeness of this dove that you might recognize [in it] the type of the sacrament."[41] Augustine interprets the story of Noah as "a figure of the city of God sojourning in this world";[42] that is, the Church rescued by a different sort of wood, the wood on which Jesus was crucified. Put another way, "the ark is the Church, it is there the dove baptizeth; for the ark was borne on the water, the incorruptible timbers were baptized within,"[43] an imaginative link to Christian baptism: Noah becomes a forerunner of Christ.

Noah's role was to focus on the destruction of a world terminally ill with sin. Christ, on the other hand, by his death and resurrection offered a universal cure, made available through the water of baptism.

A Muslim Perspective

Sufis, dedicated to a life of simplicity and asceticism, are encouraged by the example of Noah for all he required "of the

[40] Ambrose, *Duties of the Clergy*, book 3, chap. 18, para. 108, 85.

[41] Ambrose, *The Book Concerning the Mysteries*, in NPNF 2, vol. 10, chap. 4, p. 320, para. 24.

[42] Augustine, *City of God*, book 15, chap. 26.

[43] Augustine, *Homilies on St. John's Gospel*, tractate 6 on chap. 1:32, 33, p. 46, para. 19.

world was a blanket."[44] This somewhat simplified interpretation of the account provided inspiration. Maneri writes, "O brother, the commands of God are beyond the power of the human mind to comprehend! Canaan was a son of Noah. He was not allowed to proceed into the ark, yet there was a passage for the accursed one, Satan."[45] His message: when the divine eye focuses, it is on "His own pure knowledge, not at the value of your stained works."[46] Spirituality, Muslim or Christian, starts from the divine gift, available to transform the believer. Noah's obedience offers one example of how the divine gift works.

Context for Dialogue

Behind these stories, which make up Noah's life in both Inspired Scriptures, there is faith in the all-knowing God who can be trusted even when asking the impossible, becoming in Genesis a boatbuilder and in the Qurʾan a courageous preacher. But there are other elements.

Noah had weaknesses; in Genesis his drunken state was commented on by church fathers, while Muslim scholars interpreted both Iblis' ability to enter the ark and his anger at losing his son as momentary lapses of concentration. For these mistakes Noah repented and becomes a role model for believers.

His virtue outshone these weaknesses. God thought him worthy enough to be saved. With his vocation clarified, his skill as boatbuilder came into its own; still, most ignored his words and failed to understand his actions. Saddened by their rejection, he courageously resisted their taunts and patiently continued this extraordinary task until the rain started. His critics did not survive long enough to repent their behavior.

Noah's faith was confirmed after the deluge; he and his family survived and became the first of a new generation of human

---

[44] Sharafuddin Maneri, *The Hundred Letters*, letter 22, 91.

[45] Ibid., letter 71, 296.

[46] Ibid.

beings. God answered his prayers. In this respect he became, for Christians, a type of the Christ to come and, for Muslims, a prototype of the Prophet.

It is significant that the Noah of the Qur'an is more vocal than his Genesis equivalent—necessarily so, as his principal role was to argue for God's cause, challenging his people to listen. He failed because their moral sensitivities had been dulled by the comforts of daily life. Even the gathering clouds visible in the distance raised no questions in the minds of his people. In contrast the Noah of Genesis is a symbol of the divine commitment to virtue, the first of a series of "redeemers" culminating, for Christians, in the life and work of Jesus.

23

Affirming the Positive Echoes in the Understanding of the God Who Guides

God Guides to Eternal Life

We have seen that the fundamental truth revealed in both the Christian and Muslim Inspired Scriptures is the promise of life after death, offered, after certain conditions have been fulfilled. It is for those who "believe, and do righteous deeds, there will be Gardens of bliss where they will stay: that is God's true promise" (Qurᵓan 31:8). Spelled out more clearly, "those who recite God's scripture, keep up the prayer, give secretly and openly from what We have provided for them, may hope for a trade that will never decline. He will repay them in full, and give them extra from His bounty" (Qurᵓan 35:29-30). Such is the person of principle and self-discipline; neither ambitious nor self-centered.

Jesus offers a dramatic story to illustrate his preferred way of gaining eternal life. He was asked by a rich man what he needed to do to reach eternal life. Jesus replied, "Go, sell what you own, and give the money to the poor, and you will have treasure in heaven" (Mark 10:21). Again, self-centered living is a pathway to failure; it increases forgetfulness of God. In the teachings of both Islam and Christianity believers are obliged to reach out to those less fortunate than themselves.

In ways not always clear, God offers guidance on how to face temptations to self-centeredness: "Put on the armor of God, so that you may be able to stand against the wiles of the devil. For our struggle is not against the enemies of blood and flesh, but against the rulers, against the authorities, against the cosmic powers of this present darkness, against the spiritual forces of evil in the heavenly places" (Eph 6:11-12). Truly, using cosmic images, the Word of God challenges human selfishness.

The Inspired Scriptures also underline the importance of choice, often set against a framework in which the divine will appears dominant. Cyril Glassé affirms every believer "has the gift of free will in that he does make choices and decisions. Resignation to the Will of God is a concomitant to striving in the Path of God. Above all, man is completely free in what is essential, that is, he can accept the Absolute and surrender himself to God, or reject God and pay the price. In this he has absolute free will."[1] Said Nursi develops this Muslim understanding of conscience first by describing the Qurʾan as the formator of the Muslim conscience by enshrining the freedom of the decision maker. Many strive to seek the right decision with heart and mind considering the options, fully aware of their responsibility both to their faith and to the integrity of their free choice. In Nursi's words, the conscience is asked "to testify to its truth and securing its submission. In its inside is the pure guidance of the All-Merciful One, and on its outside is the light of belief."[2] In this way he affirms free choice emerging from an informed

---

[1] Cyril Glassé, "Maktūb" in *The New Encyclopedia of Islam* (1989; repr. London: Stacey International, 2002), 282.

[2] Bediüzzaman Said Nursi, "The Twenty-Second Word," in *The Words: The Reconstruction of Islamic Belief and Thought*, trans. Huseyin Akarsu (New Jersey: Light, 2005), 321.

conscience, the guardian of personal freedom and responsibility. This view is echoed for Christians most clearly in this statement from the Second Vatican Council:

> Deep within their consciences men and women discover a law which they have not laid upon themselves and which they must obey. Its voice, ever calling them to love and to do what is good and to avoid evil, tells them inwardly at the right moment: do this, shun that. For they have in their hearts a law inscribed by God. Their dignity rests in observing this law, and by it they will be judged. Their conscience is people's most secret core, and their sanctuary. There they are alone with God whose voice echoes in their depths. By conscience, in a wonderful way, that law is made known which is fulfilled in the love of God and of one's neighbor.[3]

Christians see the pursuit of the good as the best means to protect freedom, "the more one does what is good the freer one becomes. There is no true freedom except in the service of what is good and just."[4] Sadly, this often becomes distorted by the overpowering priority given to self-interest. Both Muslim and Christian affirm that true freedom can only come from within, where choices are made with knowledge and without compulsion.

God Who Guides with Teachings

Many chapters in the Inspired Scriptures are devoted to behavior: promoting the good and making people aware of evil, as in the Qur'an, "you knew neither the Scripture nor the faith, but We made it a light, guiding with it whoever We will of Our servants. You give guidance to the straight path" (Qur'an 42:52).

---

[3] "Pastoral Constitution on the Church in the Modern World" (*Gaudium et Spes*) in Austin Flannery, ed., *Vatican Council II: The Basic Sixteen Documents* (Northport, NY: Costello, 1996), 178.

[4] *Catechism of the Catholic Church*, 389, no. 1733.

God has always offered guidance to people, as shown in many accounts, Muslim and Christian, as was seen in the story of Adam and Eve. The divine intention is clear, as the Qurʾan expresses it, "God does not wish to place any burden on you: He only wishes to cleanse you and perfect His blessing on you, so that you may be thankful" (Qurʾan 5:6). If God's intention is designed for people's benefit, then the human response should be to "have faith in God and His Messenger and struggle for His cause with your possessions and your persons" (Qurʾan 61:10-14).

In the Beatitudes, Jesus offers a more challenging teaching. He turned contemporary interpretations upside down. He called "blessed" those whom human assessment would classify as deprived, "the poor in spirit . . . those who mourn . . . the meek . . . those who hunger and thirst for righteousness . . . the merciful . . . the pure in heart . . . the peacemakers . . . those who are persecuted for righteousness' sake" (Matt 5:3-10). This accolade was given because many faced personal suffering that could not be alleviated or were inspired to give themselves to help people in need. Toward the end of his life, Jesus gave a practical example of the service he expected. During his last meal he washed the feet of his friends. Afterward he said, "If I, your Lord and Teacher, have washed your feet, you also ought to wash one another's feet. For I have set you an example, that you also should do as I have done to you. Very truly, I tell you, servants are not greater than their master, nor are messengers greater than the one who sent them (John 13:14-16). Jesus' example becomes a priority for his followers. To be dedicated to service enables growth in humility.

Al-Ghazālī offers another way of assessment: it is good to desire for one's neighbor what one desires for oneself; it is better to offer what one desires for oneself to one's neighbor first before providing it for oneself; but best of all is what one believer said: "I would like to be a bridge over the fire [hell], so that creatures might pass over me and not be harmed by it."[5] Virtue is

---

[5] Al-Ghazālī, *The Ninety-Nine Beautiful Names of God*, 119.

perfected when neither anger, nor hatred, nor harm to oneself prevent the desire to do good for another. Christian and Muslim take the unnamed neighbor so seriously that he or she is seen as God. Further, both support the principle that one would like to treat others in the way one would like to be treated oneself: the sure way to build a culture of mutual respect.

The Catholic Catechism presents this as a challenge: "The beatitude we are promised confronts us with decisive moral choices. It invites us to purify our hearts of bad instincts and to seek the love of God above all else."[6] Echoing Muslim teaching, the Catechism emphasizes that human happiness is not found in amassing wealth or possessions but in God alone.

Both Muslims and Christians challenge the unbalanced distribution of wealth. The disproportionate amount held by few very rich people is especially scandalous alongside the billions who live in utter poverty. Muslims are obliged to be generous, hospitable, pay the annual tax, and at all times show concern for those in particular need. This is most clearly expressed after Friday prayers or during Ramadan, an example that Christians might imitate.

God Who Guides with Practical Suggestions

Both Muslim and Christians are given practical advice as to how to put these teachings into effect. Believers should "give food to the poor, the orphan and the captive, though they love it themselves, saying, 'We feed you for the sake of God alone. We seek neither recompense nor thanks from you'" (Qurʾan 76:8-9) and again those who "give away some of their wealth, however much they cherish it, to their relatives, to orphans, the needy, travelers and beggars, and to liberate those in bondage; those who keep up the prayer and pay the prescribed alms" (Qurʾan 2:177). This primacy of service to those in need is replicated in Christian teaching—"You shall love your neighbor as yourself"

---

[6] *Catechism of the Catholic Church*, 387, no. 1723.

(Mark 12:31)—and its practical consequences can be summarized as "Love righteousness, you rulers of the earth" (Wis 1:1), and "Seek good and not evil" (Amos 5:14). To know the Love-Who-Is-God requires a focus on the other present in the community, especially the despised, poor, abused, sick, bereaved, imprisoned, lonely, and forgotten.

Chapter 24

Abraham: An Example of One Obedient to the Guidance of God, Even When It Does Not Seem to Make Sense

Abraham in the Sacred Texts

Introduction

Abraham, a key figure in the Inspired Scriptures of Christianity and Islam, plays an important role in their respective spiritual traditions down to the present day because of his unquestioning obedience to God. As the founder, in different ways of both faiths, he provides a rich subject for dialogue.

The Christian Bible

For Christians, "Abraham's favor with God is made clear in the famous verse, 'Abraham believed the Lord; and the Lord reckoned it to him as righteousness.'"[1] Once he left Haran,

---

[1] A. R. Millard, in *The Anchor Bible Dictionary*, vol. 1, ed. David Noel Freedman, s.v. "Abraham," quoting Genesis 15:6.

Abraham never returned. Later, he ensured that Isaac married a girl from the family home and, in consequence, was able to inherit his father's land. A. R. Millard summarizes this, saying, "Abraham believed his God to be just, hence his concern for any righteous in Sodom. Even so, he attempted to preempt God's actions by taking Hagar when Sarah was barren and by pretending Sarah was not his wife."[2] But, in each incident, it was the will of God that had the final say.

Stories That Overlap in the Qurʾan and the Christian Bible

Surprisingly, in only three key moments do these Inspired Scriptures overlap: the visit of the heavenly visitors to Abraham, the obedience to God's command to sacrifice his son, and the incident where Abraham conceals the truth about Sarah being his wife when visiting a local king. The first two are of particular importance.

In the surprise appearance of heavenly visitors, "without recognizing their unusual nature or mission, Abraham provided generous hospitality for his visitors. But the purpose of the divine mission was made known when Yahweh promised 'I will surely return to you in the spring and Sarah your wife shall have a son.'"[3] God's presence, uninvited and unrecognized, promising a son, when both knew Sarah was beyond the age of childbearing, caused Sarah to laugh. She failed to recognize the voice: it was more than human with an authority not limited by the rules of human biology. When they asked, "Is anything too wonderful for the Lord?" (Gen 18:14a) Abraham knew these were no ordinary visitors.

In the Qurʾan the messengers caused Abraham to worry; they did not eat anything.[4] Abraham concluded they must be of heavenly origin, only angels would have no need of food. "Abra-

---

[2] Ibid.

[3] L. Hicks, in *Interpreter's Dictionary of the Bible*, vol. 1, ed. G. A. Buttrick (Abingdon: Abingdon Press, 1981), s.v. "Abraham."

[4] Compare Qurʾan 11:70 with Genesis 18:8.

ham therefore interprets their refusal to eat as a sign of hostility, causing him to fear for his safety until he is assured by them that they have come to announce the happy news of a future son."[5] As in Genesis, the wife, here unnamed, laughs. Throughout the Qur'an, the first son, Ishmael, born to Hagar, is given the rights of the firstborn, not Sarah's son Isaac.

The second instance is the testing of faith. In the Genesis account, Abraham was called to sacrifice his only son and heir Isaac on one of the mountains of Moriah. Abraham responded without question, but to Isaac's inquiry "he gave an answer calculated to inspire in his son a like measure of faith: 'God will provide himself the lamb . . . my son.'"[6] Abraham shows extraordinary obedience to this illogical and frightening request. In response he received an equally extraordinary divine commitment; God not only confirmed the promise of a multitude of descendants and a new land but then by "bringing the whole Abrahamic tradition to its climax, [God] roots Israel's universal mission in the faith of Abraham: 'By your descendants shall all the nations of the earth bless themselves, because you have obeyed my voice,'"[7] a promise interpreted differently by Muslims.

In the Qur'an Abraham is commanded to sacrifice his unnamed son, a fact that subsequently caused some debate though the majority identify him with Ishmael.[8] In the event, the boy asks his father first to tie him tightly so he will not squirm and then "to draw back his clothes so they will not be soiled by his blood and to return his shirt to his mother so as to offer her comfort. Abraham kisses his son and they soak the ground with their tears."[9] When Abraham tries to carry out the command,

---

[5] Reuven Firestone, in *Encyclopaedia of the Qur'ān*, ed. Jane Dammen McAuliffe, s.v. "Abraham—'Abraham in the Qur'an.'"

[6] L. Hicks, in *Interpreter's Dictionary of the Bible*, s.v. "Abraham," quoting Genesis 22:8.

[7] Ibid.

[8] See Reuven Firestone in *Encyclopaedia of the Qur'ān*, ed. Jane Dammen McAuliffe, s.v. "Abraham—'Abraham in the Qur'ān.'"

[9] Ibid., s.v. "Abraham—'The Narrative Abraham Cycle.'"

the knife fails to cut, according to tradition it turned in his hand; the blunt side caused no injury.

Other References in the Qurʾan

The most significant of the other references to Abraham are the titles: "man of truth" (Qurʾan 19:41), "tender-hearted and forbearing" (Qurʾan 9:114), one who "fulfilled his duty" (Qurʾan 53:37), and, most significant of all, "God took Abraham as a friend" (Qurʾan 4:125). Eight times Abraham is called "*hanif*," usually translated as "true in faith."[10]

Three other stories in the Qurʾan have an echo in Genesis. First, Abraham leaves his family and goes to a new land in obedience to God to raise his family.[11] There he established a sacred shrine, the House of God.[12] Second, Abraham questions God about life. God instructs him to cut open or divide birds. Later they miraculously come back to life.[13] A similar story in Genesis confirmed Abraham's faith in God and led to the new covenant.[14] Third, Abraham tried to persuade God not to be so hard on the people of Lot without using the bargaining technique described in Genesis.[15] He failed, and they were all punished.[16]

But many stories about Abraham recorded in the Qurʾan have no biblical echo. Abraham's enthusiastic monotheism was the result of careful thinking and resulted in "the most oft-repeated Abrahamic narrative in the Qurʾān, the story of his smashing the pagan idols."[17] Though his father disapproved, he continued to preach faith in One God, even to the sentence of execution by

[10] Ibid.

[11] See Qurʾan 19:48-9; 21:71; 37:83-101; cf. Gen 12:1-5.

[12] See Qurʾan 2:125-7; cf. Gen 12:6-8, 13:18.

[13] See Qurʾan 2:260; cf. Gen 15:1-10.

[14] See Qurʾan 2:124-125; cf. Gen 17:1-14.

[15] See Gen 18:22ff.

[16] See Qurʾan 11:69-76; 15:51-59; 29:31; 51:24-30; cf. Gen 18:1-33.

[17] Reuven Firestone, "Abraham—'*Abraham in the Qurʾān*,'" in *Encyclopaedia of the Qurʾān*, ed. Jane Dammen McAuliffe, para. 5. See also Qurʾan 6:74-84; 19:41-50; 21:51-73; 26:69-86; 29:16-27; 37:83-98; 43:26-7; 60:4.

burning: "They said, 'burn him and avenge your gods, if you are going to do the right thing.' But We said, 'fire, be cool and safe for Abraham'" (Qur'an 21:68). Later, Abraham asked forgiveness for his father because of an earlier promise, "but once he realized that his father was an enemy of God, he washed his hands of him" (Qur'an 9:114). Such stories offered important reassurance to the Prophet whose own forebears were idol worshipers.[18]

Abraham played an important role in founding the center for prayer and pilgrimage at Mecca. Together with Ishmael, they laid the foundations for the new buildings and together prayed, "Our Lord, accept [this] from us. You are the All Hearing, the All Knowing. Our Lord, make us devoted to You; make our descendants into a community devoted to You. Show us how to worship and accept our repentance, for You are the Ever Relenting, the Most Merciful" (Qur'an 2:127-128). Abraham was shown the site for the House and instructed: "Do not assign partners to Me. Purify My House for those who circle around it, those who stand to pray, and those who bow and prostrate themselves" (Qur'an 22:26). Abraham brought Hagar and Ishmael to Mecca, leaving them in the shade of a thorn tree, entrusted to God's mercy. There is no water, distressing for her, and more so for baby Ishmael. Hagar "leaves him and desperately searches for water by running between the nearby hills of al-Safa and al-Marwa, an action that set the precedent for the 'running ritual' of the pilgrimage."[19] When all seemed lost, they were rescued by an angel, who scratched the ground to allow water to flow, today the famous Zamzam spring in Mecca. These references to the story of Abraham remain powerful in Muslim memory, especially during the Hajj.

Question: Are There Two Abrahams?

The difference in these two accounts alongside narratives particular to each has raised the question of whether they refer

---

[18] Ibid., "Abraham—'The Narrative Abraham Cycle.'"
[19] Ibid.

to the same Abraham. The main argument against this is that the accounts of Ishmael coincide in so many details. He is the elder son, he spent time in the desert with his mother, and promises are made about his future in the Bible. Taken together they suggest two versions of the same Abraham. This is important because Muslims and Christians can "share in a vision of him, jointly to refer to him as 'Our father in Faith,' notwithstanding the different theologies, the different hermeneutic in which each situates its reverence for him."[20]

The question leads to a more difficult one: Does salvation occur by one or two ways? "Can common ground be found beneath the theological and cultural clothing with which the two traditions invest Abraham?"[21]

Once it is accepted that the God of Islam and the God of Judaeo-Christianity is the One, all-powerful, creating, and Merciful God, then it can be accepted that there are two ways to salvation according to the will of the One God; both Christianity and Islam give Abraham a central role as guide to salvation, while allowing significant differences.

These issues could become important topics in a community of dialogue, where the aim is not to sharpen differences but to see them in a fuller, more accurate light. With greater mutual understanding difference can become less divisive.

Abraham in Later Writings, Christian and Muslim

Abraham Leaving Home

A Christian Perspective. Abraham's vocation started when he heard the call of God to leave his family so that, as Clement of Rome[22] expresses it, "by forsaking a small territory, and a weak

---

[20] Tony Johns, "Abraham—Our Father in Faith?," 18.

[21] Ibid.

[22] Clement of Rome, third successor to St. Peter, little known about him, but his letter to the Corinthian Christians, sent to bring peace to a divided

family and an insignificant house, he might inherit the promises of God."[23] The image of leaving home is central in the Christian spiritual journey. It is, in Clement of Alexandria's words, "by Abraham that he who follows God must despise country and relations and possessions and all wealth, by making him a stranger."[24] A break with family required courage, as Ambrose wrote, "Abraham, once bidden to go to foreign lands, and not being held back either by the danger to his wife's modesty, nor by the fear of death before him, preserved both his own life and his wife's chastity."[25] Jerome encouraged his readers to "go out with Abraham from your country and from your kindred, and go whither you know not,"[26] because it is the start of a love affair, initiated by the call from a God who wishes to take possession of the seeker's heart. The divine call, even when we are asleep, as Cassian expressed it, "stirs in us a desire for eternal life and salvation, and bids us follow God and cleave to His commandments with life-giving contrition, as we read in Holy Scripture that Abraham was called by the voice of the Lord from his native country."[27] Faith in God requires a journey from self-interest to a firm commitment to obey.

A Muslim Perspective. Abraham's departure from his home came when he challenged his family, "How can you choose false gods instead of the true God? So what is your opinion about the Lord of all the Worlds?" (Qurʾan 37:86-87). Not receiving an appropriate answer, he said, " 'I am sick,' so [his people] turned away from him and left" (Qurʾan 37:89-90). Abraham spoke to

---

community, is a model of pastoral care and earned him the title, First of the Apostolic Fathers.

[23] Clement of Rome, *First Letter to the Corinthians*, in the ANF, vol. 1, chap. 10, p. 14.

[24] Clement of Alexandria, *The Instructor*, book 3, chap. 2, 281.

[25] Ambrose of Milan, *On the Holy Spirit*, book 3, in NPNF 2, vol. 10, p. 141, chap. 6, para. 42.

[26] Jerome, *To Rusticus Letter 125*, in NPNF 2, vol. 6, p. 252, para. 20.

[27] Cassian, *Conferences: III Conferences of Abbot Paphnutius, On Three Sorts of Renunciation*, in NPNF 2, vol. 11, chap. 6, p. 320.

the family idols, " 'Do you not eat?' 'Why do you not speak?' then he turned and struck them with his right arm" (Qurʾan 37:92-93). To his angry family he replied, "How can you worship things you carve with your own hands, when it is God who has created you and all your handwork?" (Qurʾan 37:95-96). Their anger spilled over into revenge. He was arrested, summarily tried, and handed over to execution by burning. God intervened: "They wanted to harm him, but We humiliated them. He said, 'I will go to my Lord: He is sure to guide me" (Qurʾan 37:98-99). On this journey, God told Abraham to take Hagar and Ishmael "to a barren valley and committed them to God. . . . [I]nstead of making wife and child [his] . . . chief care, [he] fixed [his] heart on God. . . . [T]he heart that is so enriched is not made poor by having no worldly goods, nor glad by having them."[28]

The Muslim story of Abraham's separation from his family differs markedly from the Christian. The Qurʾan focuses on the false gods of the family in contrast to Abraham's single-minded faith in God, which made him a courageous promoter of the One God at the expense of his family.

In the Christian Scriptures, Abraham left his family to found a new people at the request of God. Little information is provided about the family religion. The stories are recognizably similar in outline but differ in tone and detail.

Abraham Using Common Sense in Difficult Situations

A Christian Perspective. Ambrose pondered Abraham's "lie" to the Egyptian Pharaoh and justified it, for he "feared for the chastity of his wife, he feared for his own safety, he had his suspicions about the lust of the Egyptians, and yet the reasonableness of performing his duty to God prevailed with him."[29] Abraham was confident that God would look after him even in conflicts with secular authorities. The important point: he

---

[28] Ali Bin Uthaman Al-Hujwiri, "The Caliph 'Ali B. Abí Tálib," in *The Kashf Al-Mahjub*, 74, chap. 7, sec. 4.

[29] Ambrose, *Duties of the Clergy*, chap. 24, para. 108, 19.

thought it through and "reason conquered passion, and brought it into subjection to itself."[30]

Others might see this as a husband protecting himself by deceiving the authorities about his relationship with Sarah. However, Augustine's solution is probably the most accurate: Abraham had a double relationship with Sarah. He did not say, " 'She is not my wife,' but he said, 'she is my sister,' because she was in truth so near akin that she might without a lie be called a sister."[31]

A Muslim Perspective. Abraham's move to foreign lands caused him to trust God in order to preserve his wife's virtue; a tyrannical king seeing this "most charming woman"[32] asked Abraham about her. He was told, "She is my sister (i.e. in religion)."[33] Invited to the king's quarters, and following her ablutions, she prayed: "O Allah! If I have believed in You and Your Apostle and saved my private parts from everybody except my husband, then please do not let this pagan overpower me."[34] The king became agitated. She prayed: "O Allah! If he should die, the people will say that I have killed him."[35] The king recovered and approached her. She prayed, and the cycle was repeated. The king returned her to Abraham to whom she said, "Allah humiliated the pagan and gave us a slave-girl for service."[36] Another version has the king's hand stiffening when extended to take her; "he was confounded"[37] and asked her to "pray to Allah for me and I shall not harm you."[38] She did, and he was cured. On this second occasion, the king said to one of his guards, "You have not brought me a human being but have brought me a devil."[39]

[30] Ibid.
[31] Augustine, *Against Lying*, in NPNF 1, vol. 3, sec. 23, 491.
[32] *Sahih al-Bukhari*, vol. 3, book 34, no. 420.
[33] Ibid.
[34] Ibid.
[35] Ibid.
[36] Ibid., vol. 3, book 47, no. 803.
[37] Ibid., vol. 4, book 55, no. 578.
[38] Ibid.
[39] Ibid.

God's presence protected her against sin. A prophet cannot be tempted beyond his or her means.

These versions provide different interpretations, one relying on the intervention of God, the other on an accident of daily life; both sought to promote the greater good.

Abraham: Living Detached from Worldly Attractions

A Christian Perspective. Abraham looked to the future and received promises. Basil wrote that he "was a sojourner who did not possess even so much land as to set his foot on, and when he needed a tomb, bought one for money."[40] As a human being he lived as a temporary resident, but after his death he "rests in his own home."[41] Like Abraham, the Christian, too, is a traveler, encouraged to let go of the things of this world and, in Jerome's words, "you, too, must leave your home as he [Abraham] did, and must take for your parents, brothers, and relations only those who are linked to you in Christ,"[42] for the "spiritual attractions are for this all the greater."[43] To achieve this, Abraham had, according to Cassian, to do three things: first, "make light of all the wealth and goods of this world"; second, "reject the fashions and vices and former affections of soul and flesh"; and third, "detach our soul from all present and visible things, and contemplate only things to come, and set our heart on what is invisible."[44] In this way Abraham's desire for total dedication

[40] Basil of Caesarea, *On Psalm 14/15,* in NPNF 2, vol. 8, p. 46. Basil (330–79), brother of Gregory of Nyssa and Macrina, both saints. Educated in Cappadocia, Constantinople, and Athens, then became a monk. In 370 made bishop of Caesarea, defended orthodoxy against the Arians. Renowned as eloquent, learned, and holy, with a talent for organization; played an important part in establishment of a community on the outskirts of Caesarea for Christians. Writings include "On the Holy Spirit" and three books against Eunomius, the Arian; one of the four Greek Doctors of the Church.

[41] Ibid.

[42] Jerome, *Letter LXXI to Lucinius,* in NPNF 2, vol. 6, pp. 152–53, para. 2.

[43] Jerome, *Letter XLVI to Paula,* in NPNF 2, vol. 6, p. 61, para. 2.

[44] Cassian, *Conferences,* chap. 6.

to God is realized. This prepared him to receive unannounced guests, by which he, as Ambrose put it, "in looking for guests, received God Himself to entertain."[45] To this Chrysostom commended the one "who entertains a great man is not so worthy of praise, as he who receives the wretched and miserable,"[46] and continuing, Abraham "was rich, but he was not covetous. . . . going forth he looked around wherever there chanced to be a stranger, or a poor man, in order that he might succor poverty and hospitably entertain the traveler."[47]

Jerome identified Abraham's hospitality to the three visitors as a sign of his special friendship with God. "Never turning any man away from his door, he was accounted worthy at last to entertain God himself. He was not satisfied with giving orders to his servant and hand-maids to attend to his guest, nor did he lessen the favor he conferred by leaving others to care for them; but as though he had found a prize, he and Sarah his wife gave themselves to the duties of hospitality. With his own hands he washed the feet of his guests, upon his own shoulders he brought home a fat calf from the herd."[48]

In this story, Christians are reminded of the unique value of every person, whatever their religion or status or nationality. Each represents the presence of God—a view firmly held by Muslims.

A Muslim Perspective. Using another story, Islam focuses on God's protection of Abraham because he was before Judaism and Christianity and worshiped the One God. Sahih Bukhari recorded these words of the Prophet: "O Allah! I make You my Witness that I am of the religion of Abraham."[49] He endured

---

[45] Ambrose, *Duties of the Clergy*, book 2, chap. 21, paras. 104 and 107.

[46] John Chrysostom, *Homilies on John*, homily 60 on John 5:14-15.

[47] John Chrysostom, *Address to the People of Antioch, Concerning Statues*, in NPNF 1, vol. 9, homily 2, para. 15, 349.

[48] Jerome, *Letter LXVI to Pammachius*, in NPNF 2, vol. 6, p. 139, para. 11.

[49] *Sahih al-Bukhari*, vol. 5, book 58, no. 169.

persecution from his family and was persecuted by the evil Nimrod. Once he found himself:

> In a raw hide to be thrown into the fire, he [Abraham] said: "God suffices for me." When he was placed in the catapult and hurled towards the fire, then, while he was still in the air, Gabriel arrived and said: "Is there anything you need?" He replied: "Nothing from you." Gabriel answered: "Ask your Lord." He said: "God suffices for me. I ask for full knowledge of Him."[50]

This story highlights both God's love for Abraham and Abraham's total trust in God. There was nothing anyone could do to break that trust; God honored him for it. The importance of this incident is confirmed by Maneri: "The true seeker should weigh himself on the scale of religion to see how far he has abandoned prohibited things. Then will it be fitting to repeat this saying of the father of the community, Abraham, the Friend of God, I desire 'the One who, I hope, will forgive my sins on Judgment Day."[51] There is only one way to judge: " 'Give the reins of your heart into the hands of right intention!' Hence religious scholars in Islam have noted: 'Intention is the activity of the heart.' "[52] When Abraham destroyed the family idols, Maneri comments, "You have set out along the road of lovers: can you be less vigilant than a dog on that road?"[53]

Abraham's desire for God resulted in a life of strong commitment and courage—a view shared by Christian and Muslim.

Abraham: The Special Relationship with God

A Christian Perspective. As already mentioned, Abraham's obedience to God's command to sacrifice Isaac was a terrifying test of loyalty. It deepened his relationship with God. Abraham proved, writes Ambrose, that his "movings of fatherly affection"

---

[50] Sharafuddin Maneri, *In Quest of God*, letter 4, 14.

[51] Sharafuddin Maneri, *The Hundred Letters*, letter 73, 301–2, quoting the Qurʾan 26:82.

[52] Ibid., 302.

[53] Ibid., letter 58, 237.

were subordinated to "the work of submission" that "hastened his obedience," to "set God before all those whom we love."[54] This total commitment to God may provide its own pressures. As Jerome advised parents, "Too great affection towards one's children is disaffection towards God."[55] To this awesome command, Abraham could never believe, as Augustine put it, that "God delighted in human sacrifices; yet when the divine commandment thundered, it was to be obeyed, not disputed,"[56] and, in that way, became an example for us, as Cyprian[57] wrote, "Abraham, the friend of God, who did not delay to offer his son as a victim with his own hands, obeying God with a faith of devotion."[58] Nor did he delay. As Cyprian put it, Abraham "obeys the commands of God with all the patience of devotion,"[59] opening the door to something more important; in Hilary's[60] words, "Abraham . . . was, upon his proving himself faithful to the Lord, admitted to intimacy with God. . . . Now I know that thou fearest the Lord thy God, and for My sake thou hast not spared thy dearly loved son. . . . Abraham the faithful . . . worthy . . . of being known

---

[54] Ambrose, *On Belief in the Resurrection*, book 2, in NPNF 2, vol. 10, p. 190, para. 97. All four quotations.

[55] Jerome, *Letter XXXIX to Paula*, in NPNF 2, vol. 6, p. 53, para. 6.

[56] Augustine, *City of God*, book 16, chap. 32.

[57] Cyprian (d. 258), convert to Christianity ca. 246. Two years later elected bishop of Carthage. Decian persecution (249) forced him to flee, but administered diocese from exile. Returned in 251, many had lapsed during the persecution; he opposed easy readmission, supported by two local councils (251, 252). Readmission should come after penance and suitable delay. Hard-liners went into schism. In a second persecution, he was martyred in 258. Best known for his treatise "Unity of the Church."

[58] Cyprian, *Epistle LV*, in the ANF, vol. 8, p. 183.

[59] Cyprian, *Treatise IX*, in the ANF, vol. 8, p. 28, para. 10.

[60] Hilary of Poitiers (ca. 315–67), from pagan family, well educated, became Christian later. Aged thirty-five, with his wife still living, he was elected bishop of Poitiers ca. 353. Most outstanding opponent of Arianism in the West. In 356 condemned at Synod of Biterrae (356) and spent four years in Phrygia. Most important writing—*On the Trinity*—used hymns to teach doctrine. Doctor of the Church in 1851.

by God."[61] True obedience brings intimacy; commitment liberates, especially when it is realized that once God receives the vow, guidance and support is offered without limit.

A Muslim Perspective. As mentioned before, in the Qurᵓan Abraham is Allah's *khalil,* "special, dearest, most sincere friend who has no rival in the love and reliance placed upon him and is without disorder and defect,"[62] superior to Allah's prophet, shown by Abraham's prayer in the fire, mentioned earlier, "Allah is sufficient for us, and He Is the Best Disposer of affairs."[63] When "Allah took Abraham as a *'khalil,'*" one present replied, "How glad the mother of Abraham is!"[64] Abraham in prayer, as Maneri puts it, says, "Look at me! I cannot take any rest except with You; nor do I see anything but You; nor do I hope in anyone except You; nor do I fear anyone except You!"[65] Such intimacy brings perspective; it also brings trials, shown by his willingness "to slaughter his beloved son: 'the eternal goal is our surrender' ":[66] to grow in intimacy with God requires total surrender.

Abraham: Life in the Resurrection

A Christian Perspective. Jesus used Abraham as model of how difficult it is for the rich to enter heaven. A questioner asked him, "Why do sinners have abundance of wealth and riches and fare sumptuously and have no grief or sorrow whilst the upright are in want?"[67] Jesus replied by telling the story of the rich man and

---

[61] Hilary, *Homily on Psalms,* Psalm 1, in NPNF 2, vol. 9, pp. 242–43, para. 24.

[62] ʿAbdul Mannân ʿOmar, *The Dictionary of the Holy Qurᵓân* (2003; repr. Hockessin: NOOR Foundation, 2005), s.v. "Khalla."

[63] *Sahih al-Bukhari,* vol. 6, book 60, no. 87.

[64] Ibid., vol. 5, book 59, no. 635.

[65] Sharafuddin Maneri, *The Hundred Letters,* letter 21, 86.

[66] Annemarie Schimmel, *The Mystical Dimensions of Islam,* 321, quoting Jalāluddīn Rūmī, *Mathnawī-ī maʿnawī,* ed. Reynold A. Nicholson, vol. 3, line 4258.

[67] Ambrose, *Duties of the Clergy,* book 1, chap. 15, para. 57.

Lazarus, in which the rich man goes to turmoil and Lazarus to the presence of Abraham in heaven. Jesus concluded that the rich man is punished for his selfishness while the poor man is rewarded for his patience under trial.

Ambrose challenged: "Is it not plain from this that rewards and punishments according to deserts await one after death?"[68] Chrysostom explained the rich man was punished, "not because he was rich, but because he was cruel and inhuman. And that poor man who rested in the bosom of Abraham was praised, not because he was poor, but because he had borne his poverty with thankfulness."[69] Abraham was a wealthy man but always served God first. Such behavior required a conscious choice, for, as Jerome wrote, "It is difficult, nay impossible, for a man to enjoy both the good things of the present and those of the future, to satisfy his belly here and his mind yonder, to pass from the pleasures of this life to the pleasures of that, to be first in both worlds, and to be held in honor both on earth and in heaven."[70] For the rich, "although they were rich, [they] entered the kingdom of heaven; for, by spending their riches on good works, they ceased to be rich; nay, rather, inasmuch as they were rich, not for themselves, but for others, they ought to be called God's stewards rather than rich men."[71] The rich man had a grand funeral, Augustine commented, "but far more handsome did that poor man who was full of sores obtain the ministry of Angels: who bore him not out into a marble tomb, but into Abraham's bosom bore him on high."[72] Patristic writers would use the memory of Abraham so people could appreciate that divine judgment looked to the inner heart and its priorities, not simply at outward appearances.

---

[68] Ibid.

[69] John Chrysostom, *Homily against Publishing the Errors of the Brethren*, in NPNF 1, vol. 9, p. 236, para. 2.

[70] Jerome, *Letter CXVIII to Julian*, in NPNF 2, vol. 6, p. 223, para. 6.

[71] Jerome, *Against the Pelagians*, in NPNF 2, vol. 6, p. 453, book 1, para. 10, quoting Atticus the Catholic in dialogue with Critobulus, a heretic.

[72] Augustine: *On Care to Be Had for the Dead*, in NPNF 1, vol. 3, p. 541, sec. 4.

A Muslim Perspective. Islam, too, highlights Abraham's role in heaven, identifying "the old man sitting at the base of the tree"[73] as Abraham caring for the children of those suffering. He will be "the first to be dressed on the Day of Resurrection."[74] But on the Day of Resurrection Abraham will be challenged by meeting his pagan father Azar, "whose face will be dark and covered with dust. Abraham will say to him: 'Didn't I tell you not to disobey me?' His Father will reply: 'Today I will not disobey you.' Abraham will say: 'O Lord! You promised me not to disgrace me on the Day of Resurrection: and what will be more disgraceful to me than cursing and dishonoring my father?' Then Allah will say to him: 'I have forbidden Paradise for the disbelievers,' "[75] a poignant picture of filial love, spiked by hardness of heart and refusal to repent.

Abraham, as the *khalil*,[76] has influence but is not without limits for "they will go to Abraham and say, 'O Abraham! You are Allah's Apostle and His *"khalil"* from among the people of the earth, so please intercede for us with your Lord. Don't you see in what state we are?' "[77] He will refuse, because God is angry with him for telling lies. Maneri offers another view: Abraham has the power to secure forgiveness; he writes, "Look at Abraham, the Friend, emerging from the idol-temple of Azar! 'He brings forth the living from the dead.' "[78] Confirmation comes from the Prophet's journey through heaven, "I passed by Abraham and he said, 'Welcome! O pious Prophet and pious son.' I asked Gabriel 'Who is he?' Gabriel replied: 'He is Abraham.' "[79] This picture of heavenly life encourages believers that the resurrection is real: there the friends of God will find peace and fulfillment, like Abraham, in spite of their weaknesses.

[73] *Sahih al-Bukhari*, vol. 2, book 23, no. 468.

[74] Ibid., vol. 4, book 55, no. 568.

[75] Ibid., no. 569.

[76] Ibid., vol. 6, book 60, no. 3.

[77] Ibid., no. 236.

[78] Sharafuddin Maneri, *The Hundred Letters*, letter 77, 317.

[79] *Sahih al-Bukhari*, vol. 1, book 8, no. 345.

The Religion of Abraham:
The Starting Point of Christian-Muslim Dialogue?

Within Muslim tradition the religion of Abraham is the description of the earliest confession of faith, the formation of a religion happening before Judaism, Christianity, or Islam. Sidney Griffith sees this as particularly significant: it "somehow also scripturally unites them."[80] Hints of this are found in the canonized scriptures, for example, "And he [Abraham] believed the LORD; and the LORD reckoned it to him as righteousness" (Gen 15:6). "God took Abraham as a friend" (Qurʾan 4:125), and "Abraham was neither a Jew nor a Christian. He was upright and devoted to God" (Qurʾan 3:67). These texts show Abraham's special intimacy with God, the foundation of religion. Muslims would suggest that this religion defines the word *muslim* (one who has surrendered to God).[81] The Qurʾan affirms this: "Say[s the Prophet], 'No, [ours is] the religion of Abraham, the upright, who did not worship any god besides God'" (Qurʾan 2:135).

The fundamental questions are, first, whether this is the Jewish understanding of Abraham's faith and, second, whether the Christian understanding of Abraham as a man of faith is "compatible with the Islamic idea of the 'religion of Abraham' as we find it in the Qurʾān."[82] The answer of Sidney Griffith is clear: "Strictly speaking, the Qurʾān's 'religion of Abraham' is not that of the Jews or Christians."[83] But at a more fundamental level, all three are monotheist, Abraham is of good faith and from both sons, Isaac and Ishmael, primacy has been claimed: both received the sign of God's covenant, were circumcised,

---

[80] Sidney Griffith, *The Church in the Shadow of the Mosque* (Princeton and Oxford: Princeton University Press, 2008), 162.

[81] There is no upper or lower case in Arabic, which has caused confusion among Muslims who think Abraham was truly a Muslim in the restricted sense of the word. See Sidney Griffith, *The Church in the Shadow of the Mosque*, 162.

[82] Sidney Griffith, *The Church in the Shadow of the Mosque*, 163.

[83] Ibid.

survived with God's protection (either in a desert or on a mountain), were promised numerous descendants, and were present at Abraham's burial.[84] But for Jews and Christians, Abraham's greatness comes from the truth that in the Hebrew Bible "faith . . . is never understood as acceptance of a truth which has been laid down, as holding the un-provable to be true, but as unshakeable trust in a promise which cannot be realized in human terms: as faithfulness, as confidence, as saying 'Amen.' "[85] On the other hand, in the Qurʾan "Muslims stand closest to Abraham: in the descent from Abraham they are not the only worshippers of God but they are the only true worshippers. They owe much to Abraham: their 'name' (Muslim), their faith, their rites in Mecca, their theocentricity and their universalism."[86] These different interpretations suggest Abraham might be a good starting point for dialogue, as Hans Küng comments: "Abraham does not necessarily appear to be an ideal starting point. . . . However, he is a real starting point."[87]

Put another way, Islam seeks its truth about God by looking back to Abraham. Christianity seeks its truth about God by looking forward to Christ.

There is confusion about the meaning of *primacy*; for one, it refers to the first in line (Islam through Ishmael), for he is the first recipient of revealed truth (the Jewish Covenant), and another sees primacy as completed in God becoming man in Jesus Christ (Christianity), the realization of the promises first made to Abraham, reinforced by Moses, and fulfilled in Jesus' statement,"Before Abraham was, I am" (John 8:58).

---

[84] K-J Kuschel, *Abraham: A Symbol of Hope for Jews, Christians and Muslims* (New York and London, 1995), quoted in Hans Küng, *Islam: Past, Present and Future* (Oxford: One World, 2007), 47. Full treatment 45–56.

[85] Hans Küng, *Islam, Past, Present and Future*, 48.

[86] Ibid., 51.

[87] Ibid.

Context for Dialogue

For Christians, the story of Abraham is fundamental: a man specially guided by God, able to debate with God but obedient to divine commands, even the most destructive and perplexing, while being worldly wise, protecting his wife, respecting the visitors, and negotiating a burial ground. With faith, Abraham was able to move when commanded, to be available for consultation, and to trust the promises. He is the starting point of a process of revelation, taken up by others and fulfilled in Jesus Christ, God made Man.

For Islam, Abraham is the prophet, specially loved for his obedience to faith in the one God and his courage in standing against idolatry and traditional religions. He is the one who transformed the Kaaba into a place for prayer and began the tradition of pilgrimage. Such was his intimacy with God that his life was protected from the murderous actions of idolaters, the suspicions of kings, and the understated sacrifice of a son. As a special friend of God he was chosen as the preacher of the One God whose revelation was completed in the revelations to Muhammad, the last prophet, whose special relationship with God came through the Revealing Voice.

The story of Abraham in both Christianity and Islam provides an example of God's guidance and the inspired response of obedience without question, a sound basis for dialogue.

25

Affirming the Positive Echoes in the Understanding of God as a God of Mercy, Compassion, and Forgiveness

Affirming God's Mercy

The divine desire to forgive the repentant sinner is the most consistent theme in both the Qurʾan and the Bible. The Divine Mercy brings reassurance and hope to sinners, expressed with identical words by both Muslims and Christians, but the "economies of forgiveness" differ.

Muslims, remembering the words of the Qurʾan, "do not despair of God's mercy—only disbelievers despair of God's mercy" (Qurʾan 12:87); they can confidently plead, "Grant us Your forgiveness, our Lord. To You we all return" (Qurʾan 2:286). This strong teaching about forgiveness enables repentant Muslims to be affirmed by God, "For those who say, 'Our lord is God,' and then follow the straight path there is no fear, nor shall they grieve: they are the people of Paradise, there to remain as a reward for what they were doing" (Qurʾan 46:13-14). The response to the repentant sinner is immediate forgiveness. Those forgiven are reaffirmed as part of the divine promise.

Christians use the same model, and their teaching, frequently illustrated by powerful stories, gives the same message: the forgiveness of God knows no limits to the repentant sinner. This story illustrates the point: Jesus was invited to dine with Simon. A woman whose sins were publicly known came to wash Jesus' feet, kissed them, and wiped them with her hair. Simon, puzzled, was challenged by Jesus, who outlined to Simon the normal customs of hospitality: water to soothe tired feet, a friendly greeting with a kiss, and so on. Then, Jesus turned to the woman and said, "Her sins, which were many, have been forgiven; hence she has shown great love. But the one to whom little is forgiven, loves little" (Luke 7:47, full story 44–48): serious sins can be forgiven by loving service to one in need.

When immoral behavior becomes part of the culture of family or community, the sense of personal guilt is diminished. So consistent and dramatic is the availability of divine forgiveness that those who need it have only to repent to secure it.

Forgiveness: God's Initiative

For Muslims, the creating God is merciful and forgiving, God "will give you a double share of His mercy; He will provide a light to help you walk; He will forgive you" (Qur'an 57:28), and again, "God forgives whoever He will" (Qur'an 48:10-15).

To Christians God speaks directly, "I have swept away your transgression like a cloud, and your sins like mist: return to me, for I have redeemed you" (Isa 44:22). Later, Jesus is even clearer, "I tell you, people will be forgiven for every sin and blasphemy . . . Whoever speaks a word against the Son of Man will be forgiven, but whoever speaks against the Holy Spirit will not be forgiven, either in this age or in the age to come" (Matt 12:31-32). The sin against the Holy Spirit indicates a refusal to see the need for forgiveness, also described as the pride of self-righteousness.

In contrast, God's mercy is important enough for Paul to emphasize that he saved us, "not because of any works of righteousness that we had done, but according to his mercy" (Titus 3:5).

No repentant sinner can demand forgiveness from God: God has already made the commitment to forgive the repentant before the words are uttered.

Muslims and Christians are at one in understanding that God took the initiative, making mercy available. In the words of Al-Ghazālī, God "who is full of forgiveness—is the one who makes manifest what is beautiful and conceals what is ugly. Sins are among the ugly things which He conceals, by letting a cover fall over them in this world. . . . So forgiving is concealing,"[1] a teaching echoed in the Catholic Catechism: "Out of love for his Father and for men, whom the Father wants to save, Jesus freely accepted his Passion and death: 'No one takes (my life) from me, but I lay it down of my own accord.'"[2] For Christians, the death of Jesus was an offering he alone could make: repairing the damage caused by the first sin. Without that first sin, no offering by the Innocent One would have been needed.

Christians and Muslims both acknowledge that the sinner, however wicked, who repents sincerely, is treated to a most generous level of forgiveness, through God's unlimited mercy, in ways that the rational human mind finds difficult to understand. This article of faith, accepted by Muslims and Christians, enlightens the believer's mind.

Encouraging Repentance

It has been shown that God the Word invites sinners to repent, but sometimes the most effective encouragement comes from forgiven sinners themselves. Muslims are encouraged to "race for your Lord's forgiveness" (Qurʾan 57:21), and hear the plea of God: "My servants who have harmed yourselves by your own excess, do not despair of God's mercy. God forgives all sins" (Qurʾan 39:53), adding, "If you make a generous loan to God He will multiply it for you and forgive you" (Qurʾan 64:17), and

---

[1] Al-Ghazālī, *The Ninety-Nine Beautiful Names of God*, 73.
[2] *Catechism of the Catholic Church*, p. 139, no. 609, quoting John 10:18.

to believers: "Be mindful of God, speak in a direct fashion and to good purpose, and He will put your deeds right for you and forgive you your sins. Whoever obeys God and His Messenger will truly achieve a great triumph" (Qurʾan 33:70-71). Repentance is made especially easier for longtime sinners by the immediate availability of forgiveness.

The Hebrew Scriptures are no less convincing: "The one whose service is pleasing to the Lord will be accepted, and his prayer will reach to the clouds. The prayer of the humble pierces the clouds" (Sir 35:20), and the believer is assured that "the LORD is gracious and merciful, slow to anger and abounding in steadfast love" (Ps 145:8), later reaffirmed, "God, who is rich in mercy, out of the great love with which he loved us even when we were dead through our trespasses, made us alive together with Christ" (Eph 2:4-5). Here again God takes the initiative, guarantees forgiveness to the repentant, developed by Pope John Paul II: "Mercy in itself, as a perfection of the infinite God, is also infinite. Also infinite therefore and inexhaustible is the Father's readiness to receive the prodigal children who returned to his home. . . . No human sin can prevail over this power or even limit it";[3] this is echoed also by al-Ghazālī: "The Effacer of Sins is the one who erases sins and overlooks acts of disobedience. . . . [Since] the one who repents of wrongdoing becomes like the one who did no wrong, and this is the utmost point of erasing crime."[4] The strong emphasis in both texts is the divine desire to forgive, which might be called a divine addiction to forgive at the slightest sign of regret.

A further point, God is not angered by sin, for the freedom to choose and take responsibility is a divinely given gift. The use and abuse of freedom, on the one hand, enhances the value of good choices but, on the other, allows those who choose to sin to become aware of the corruption caused and come to see repentance as the best way out. God's reaction to sin is more akin

---

[3] John Paul II, *Dives in Misericordia* (On the Mercy of God), encyclical letter (Vatican City: Vatican, 1980), chap. 7, para. 13.

[4] Al-Ghazālī, *The Ninety-Nine Beautiful Names of God*, 138–39.

to the human sense of disappointment. Muslims and Christians suggest that sin brings a cloud of forgetfulness over the divine face, dissipated only when God hears "I am sorry," the trigger for divine forgiveness. This powerful echo of agreement around human sin and divine forgiveness ensures a fertile topic for dialogue.

26

Moses: The One Who Led the People away from Slavery and Then Persuaded God to Show Mercy, Compassion, and Forgiveness

Introduction to Christian and Muslim Perspectives

It is the intimacy of Moses with God that provides the loudest echo between the Bible and the Qurʾan. Meeting God in the burning bush, obedience to God's command to dialogue with Pharaoh, the divine appointment to lead his people from Egypt, and his discussions with God on Mount Sinai provided rich memories of a pivotal leader in the founding events of the Hebrew people. They are recorded in both Inspired Scriptures.

Moses dominates the Pentateuch and is equally prominent in the Qurʾan where over five hundred verses refer to him (twice that of Abraham).[1] At the same time, the contrast in

---

[1] See A. H. Johns, "Moses in the Qurʾan," in Robert B. Crotty, ed., *The Charles Strong Lectures 1972–1984* (Leiden: Brill, 1987), 123.

interpretation of the Exodus is but one element of difference. A. H. Johns writes, "For Christians, the crossing of the Red Sea represents the passage from death to life, signifying dying to sin and rising to grace, and an image of the resurrection,"[2] while, for Muslims, Moses is an example of God's power "in overwhelming those who reject his messengers. He chose Moses to be the great law-giver and ruler of his people and spoke to him, establishing a covenant that was to endure until the time of the final revelation to be made to Muhammad."[3]

Alongside these views, Christians see Moses as a type of Christ. Before the incarnation, as Origen[4] writes, "Christ the Word of God was in Moses . . . [Who] spake and performed all [he] did through being filled with the Spirit of Christ."[5] The "signs" worked by Moses were echoed and enhanced by Jesus. Cyril of Jerusalem makes the comparison: first, "Moses changed the river into blood; and Jesus at the last gave forth from His side water with blood";[6] second, there "we have Moses sent from God to Egypt; here, Christ, sent forth from His Father into the world";[7] third, "there Moses might lead forth an afflicted people out of Egypt; here, that Christ might rescue those who are oppressed in the world under sin";[8] fourth, there "the blood of a

[2] Ibid.

[3] Ibid.

[4] Origen (ca. 185–ca. 254), b. Alexandria, biblical scholar, theologian, and spiritual writer. After persecution of 202, appointed head of the Alexandrian Catechetical School where he led a strict life of fasting, vigils, poverty. Visited Rome, Arabia, and Palestine, where he was asked to preach, though only a layman. From 218 to 230 research and writing. In 230 back to Palestine, ordained priest, but Demetrius of Alexandria disapproved, so dismissed him from his teaching job and priesthood; sent into exile in Caesarea (231) where he established a school. Persecution of 250 imprisoned, survived only a few years. Many of his works were destroyed.

[5] Origen, *De Principiis*, in the ANF, vol. 1, p. 1, para. 1.

[6] Cyril of Jerusalem, *Catechetical Lectures, Instruction*, in NPNF 2, vol. 7, lecture 13, para. 21.

[7] Ibid., lecture 19, para. 3.

[8] Ibid.

lamb was the spell against the destroyer; here, the blood of the Lamb without blemish Jesus Christ is made the charm to scare evil spirits."[9] Such comparisons helped the early Christians to see the strong link between the work of Moses and that of Jesus; the second completed the work of the first.

A similar comparison has been made by Muslim scholars: Moses as a prototype of Muhammad, by which, as Cornelia Schöck states, "the biography of Moses is seen in the light of the biography of Muhammad."[10] The Qurʾan describes the deeds of Moses and links them to "circumstances in Muhammad's life."[11] Moses is strictly monotheist and the messenger from God. He endures abuse, hostility, violence, and, as Schöck expresses it, "just as God 'separated' Muhammad and the polytheists, so he 'separated' Moses and Pharaoh, proceeding in the case of the former as he had with the latter."[12]

One of the biblical Moses' qualities is perseverance; McKenzie writes,

> The various traditions represent him as the one man who sustains the purpose of the journey from Egypt to Canaan, against the opposition at one time or another of almost the entire group which he leads. . . . That Moses did not live to see the final success of his leadership must, in Israelite thinking, have been a punishment for some fault and this is alluded to more than once.[13]

Moses is the founder of Israel, for "no lesser designation does justice to the place he occupies. . . . [H]e is the founder of Yahwism, the worship of Yahweh as the God of Israel."[14] Moses presented Israel's God as one "with an irresistible moral

---

[9] Ibid.

[10] Cornelia Schöck, in *Encyclopaedia of the Qurʾān*, ed. Jane Dammen McAuliffe, s.v. "Moses."

[11] Ibid.

[12] Ibid., sec. 9, "Kitāandfurqān."

[13] John L. McKenzie, *Dictionary of the Bible*, s.v. "Moses" at "The Person of Moses."

[14] Ibid., at "The Work of Moses."

will, who imposes His standards of conduct on the people. He presents Yahweh also as the Lord of history, who moves events so as to bring His people to their destiny."[15] His life was sustained by the "immediacy and intimacy of Moses' knowledge of Yahweh"[16]—a privilege not granted to anyone else—sustained him.

Moses' infancy in Egypt is echoed in the Qurʾan, where there is also mention of his murder of the Egyptian; the flight to Midian; the burning bush; Moses' mission to Pharaoh, which resulted in the escape from Egypt; the destruction of Pharaoh's army; the journey through the desert; and the meeting with God on Sinai.

From these, the most significant are the "splendidly dramatic accounts of two great encounters with God: in the burning bush where Moses receives his commission to warn Pharaoh, and on Mt. Sinai, when he is given the Law."[17] Later, Moses' difficulties with his followers are used "as a model for Muhammad's own debates with the Jews who refused to accept his message, his role, or his authority."[18] The echo of one in the other is much greater than in the case of Abraham but similar to those of Adam, Noah, and Joseph.

Moses' Spiritual Journey

A Christian View

Moses, educated within Egyptian religion and culture, found no satisfaction in it. He turned away, and, in Ambrose's words, he "sought God with all the desire of his heart."[19] God gifted Moses, but, as Clement of Alexandria states, "it was really the Lord that was the instructor of the ancient people by Moses. . . . The law was given through Moses, not by Moses, but by the

---

[15] Ibid.
[16] Ibid.
[17] A. H. Johns, "Moses in the Qurʾan," 124.
[18] Ibid.
[19] Ambrose, *Duties of the Clergy*, book 1, chap. 26, para. 123.

Word, and through Moses his servant."[20] Moses, the channel for God's communication, remained unchanged, for, as Augustine expresses it, "with great wisdom and entire absence of jealous pride, [he] accepted the plan of his father-in-law, a man of an alien race, for ruling and administering the affairs of the great nation entrusted to him,"[21] because Moses knew that this inspiration came from the God Who is Truth. Accepting the unpredictability of God's ways and the challenges of journeying in a harsh environment, Moses guided his people. He, in the words of Origen, "spake and God answered him by a voice: and as God answered Moses, so also does every saint answer God."[22] The desire may be present, but not everyone can draw near to God. As Gregory Nazianzen writes, "Only one who, like Moses, can bear the glory of God,"[23] and in Ephraim's[24] words, "Moses saw and saw not. He saw, that he might be exalted; he saw not, that he might not be injured."[25]

God revealed his inner being to Moses by setting him, as expressed by John of the Cross,[26] "in the cleft of the rock, and covered him, with His right hand to protect him from death when

[20] Clement of Alexandria, *The Instructor*, book 1, chap. 7.

[21] Augustine, *On Christian Doctrine*, preface, para. 7.

[22] Origen, *de Principiis*, book 3, chap. 1, para. 21.

[23] Gregory Nazianzen, *Oration II*, in NPNF 2, vol. 7, p. 223, para. 92.

[24] Ephraim of Syria (ca. 306–73), Syrian biblical scholar and poet from Nisibis, Mesopotamia. In 363 migrated to the theological school at Edessa (Urfa, Iraq). Renowned for his metrical homilies and his hymns, designed for popular use. Wrote commentaries on Bible. His works were translated into Greek, Armenian, and Latin.

[25] Ephraim, *Homily on our Lord*, in NPNF 2, vol. 13, p. 317, para. 29.

[26] John of the Cross (1542–91). Entered Carmelite monastery of Medina del Campo in 1563, studied theology at Salamanca. Disturbed by laxity. Met Teresa of Avila, joined her reform movement. Antireform movement decided to imprison him in Toledo for nine months, from which he escaped to Andalusia where he worked for Discalced Carmelites, becoming prior in Granada then Segovia, later to Andalusia, where he died. *Spiritual Canticle* composed in 1578 while in prison and *The Ascent of Mount Carmel* soon afterward.

the divine glory passed by."[27] The splendor of God is a foretaste of resurrection. As Irenaeus writes, "Through the wisdom of God, man shall see Him in the last times, in the depth of a rock, that is, in His coming as a man."[28] Moses, though naturally meek, was still able to be intimate with God as "a man speaketh unto his friend."[29]

When Moses needed time for prayer, he would visit the tabernacle of God, where he could talk to God, while outside he was occupied, in the words of Gregory the Great,[30] "with the affairs of those who are subject to infirmity. Within he considers the secret things of God; without he carries the burdens of the carnal."[31]

For prayer, Moses climbed the mountain to be alone in God's presence described by Clement of Alexandria, " 'Moses entered into the thick darkness where God was,' this shows to those capable of understanding, that God is invisible and beyond expression by words,"[32] but, in Dionysius'[33] words, Moses hears

[27] John of the Cross, *The Collected Works of St John of the Cross*, trans. Kieran Kavanaugh and Otilio Rodriguez (Washington, DC: Institute of Carmelite Studies, 1991); *The Ascent of Mount Carmel*, 241, book 2, chap. 24, para. 3.

[28] Irenaeus, *Against the Heresies*, in ANF, vol. 1, book 4, chap. 20, p. 490, para. 9.

[29] Tertullian, *Against Praxeas*, in ANF, vol. 3, chap. 14, p. 609.

[30] Gregory the Great (540–604), born noble Roman family, well educated, became a monk on the family estate of Caelian Hill in Rome. Sent by Pope Pelagius II in 579 as ambassador to Constantinople to seek help against the Lombards, he failed but made many friends. First monk to be elected pope (in 590), encouraged mission work in England and northern Europe, revised Christian worship, gave his name to Gregorian Chant, wrote some 850 letters as pope and best known for his advice to pastors, commentary on Job, and the details of the life of Benedict in the Dialogues.

[31] Gregory the Great, *Of the Life of the Pastor*, in NPNF 2, vol. 12, chap. 5, p. 13.

[32] Clement of Alexandria, *Stromata*, book 5, chap. 12.

[33] Dionysius the Areopagite (ca. 500), mystical theologian (not the Dionysius mentioned in Acts), probably from Syria; mystical writing focuses on gradual deification by a process of "unknowing" in which the soul abandons ideas from the senses and the mind. In the darkness of the soul

"the many-voiced trumpets and sees many lights flash forth with pure and diverse-streaming rays, and then stands separate from the multitudes. . . . He meets not with God Himself, yet he beholds—not Him indeed (for He is invisible)—but the place wherein He dwells."[34] Dionysius considered this as the "highest of the things perceived by the eyes of the body or the mind [and they] are but the symbolic language of things subordinate to Him who Himself transcendeth them all."[35] After this, the divine "breaks forth, even from the things that are beheld and from those that behold them, and plunges the true initiate unto the Darkness of Unknowing."[36]

In these ways Moses is seen as a model for the contemplative life, where the image of darkness is a favorite way of describing those moments when senses are numbed and the subject remains still without any assurance that progress is being made.

From intimacy with God, Moses was successful in softening the divine anger, aroused by the people's disobedience, urging God to show mercy, compassion, and forgiveness.

Muslim View

Maneri describes five stages by which Moses was taught leadership: first, "submission of servanthood common to our servants"; second, "an aptitude to receive truth directly from God"; third, "submission distinguishable from the first submission by a very special grace"; fourth, "the honor of receiving divine knowledge of God without any intermediary"; and fifth, "the riches of receiving infused knowledge."[37] These parallel the

---

illumination comes by the "ray of divine darkness"; knowledge of God is achieved through purgation, illumination into union. Influenced mystical writers of later centuries like Eckhart, the author of *The Cloud of Unknowing*, and Tauler.

[34] Dionysius, the Areopagite, *On the Divine Names and the Mystical Theology*, trans. C. E. Rolt (London: SPCK, 1920), chap. 1.

[35] Ibid.

[36] Ibid.

[37] Sharafuddin Maneri, *The Hundred Letters*, letter 6, 30.

stages described above both of Moses' experience and of the contemplative's journey into darkness; starting with submission then moving to an ever-deeper intimacy, an experience offered to few. Schimmel contrasts Moses' experience with that of the Prophet: "Moses was the prophet who heard God—heard his voice speaking in him and through him; but Muhammad was blessed with the vision of God during his ascension,"[38] both shared the gift of intimacy with God and arising from it an insight into the immeasurable scale of divine mercy and compassion.

In discussion with God, Moses asked where he should search and was given the answer, expressed by Maneri, " 'in that heart which has been broken as a result of a wound inflicted by Me!' He said: 'O God, there is no heart that is more hopeless or broken than mine is!' He said, 'I am where you are!' "[39] United in this way to God, Maneri suggests "Moses himself ceased to exist, absorbed as he was with such a total listening. Every time that he became 'clever,' this wound was inflicted on his heart: 'O Moses, you killed an Egyptian. Without My revelation you were doomed' "[40]—a timely reminder that whatever the intimacy, there remains an immeasurable gulf between the Uncreated God and the created seeker.

For Moses there was no turning back because, as God said to him, "You can't do without Me. There is an escape from everything else, but not from Me."[41] Maneri interprets God's message to the Chosen People by putting these words into God's mouth: "You have fallen into My net, and have put My name on your heart, and have set out on the way to Me, your heart should become acquainted with grief and your soul with danger!"[42] The lesson concludes, "one must keep in mind that 'God Almighty does not look at your faces and your works: He looks at your heart and your intentions.' Do you think there is only one Mt.

---

[38] Annemarie Schimmel, *The Mystical Dimensions of Islam*, 41.

[39] Sharafuddin Maneri, *The Hundred Letters*, letter 77, 318.

[40] Ibid., letter 63, 257, quoting Qurʾan 20:40.

[41] Sharafuddin Maneri, *In Quest of God*, letter 23, 65.

[42] Sharafuddin Maneri, *The Hundred Letters*, letter 79, 327.

Sinai in the world? Or only one Moses? Your body is Mt. Sinai. Your heart is Moses! The strength of both lies in this: 'Surely I am God!' "[43]—a description of the union with God through love that echoes strongly with the Christian mystical experiences.

Moses and the Burning Bush

A Christian View

The Church Fathers offer many interpretations of Moses' meeting with God at the burning bush. Augustine writes, "Moses spake with the Lord face to face, as a friend with his friend,"[44] and to his question God did not say: "I am God; or, I am the framer of the world; or, I am the creator of all things; or, I am the multiplier of the very people to be delivered; but only this, 'I am who am.' "[45] The directness of this description surprised Moses but within it was the divine call, for God added, "I am the God of Abraham, and the God of Isaac, and the God of Jacob, Who appeared to Moses in the bush, concerning Whom Moses saith 'He Who Is hath sent me.' "

Ambrose, writing about this, states the bush was not destroyed. It represents a mystery for "the Lord was showing that He would come to illuminate the thorns of our body, and not to consume those who were in misery, but to alleviate their misery."[46] Origen takes a different line: for Moses, God was "not beholding Him with the bodily eye, but understanding Him with the vision of the heart and the perception of the mind, and that only in some degree."[47] Such a revelation may begin with the mind, be fed by the sight, but is only fully understood

[43] Ibid., letter 28, 115.

[44] Augustine, *Tractates on St. John's Gospel*, in NPNF 1, vol. 7, tractate 3, p. 23, para. 17.

[45] Ibid., tractate 38, para. 8.

[46] Ambrose of Milan, *On the Holy Spirit*, book 1, chap. 14, para. 164.

[47] Origen, *de Principiis*, book 2, chap. 4, para. 3.

in the loving intimacy of the heart. Eusebius[48] uses the vision to encourage people to devote "themselves persistently to the worship of God."[49]

For some, a new revelation, for others, an example of how to move from the intellect to the heart, for still others, a way of marking the distance between the divine and human—taken together they show the many ways this story has been interpreted by Christians.

A Muslim View

Muslim commentators also expand on the "fire." The Prophet "saw a tree, green from its base to its summit as though it were a white fire. He stood in wonder at the brilliant light of the fire, and the brilliant green of the tree. The fire has no effect on the green, and the abundant sap of the tree has no effect on the brightness of the fire, then he heard the praises of angels, and saw a mighty light."[50] Moses, stunned by the experience, heard his name called, so responded, and added that he heard the voice but could see no one and asked, as quoted by Johns, " 'Where are you?' He replied: 'I am with you, in front of you, behind you and totally encompass you. I am closer to you than your very self,' "[51] a vivid presentation of the intimacy God had with Moses. This is especially important for the faithful as it affirms their accessibility to the divine presence: Moses in a mystical relationship. "Of the burning bush, Muqatil says that

---

[48] Eusebius (ca. 260–ca. 340), "Father of Church History," pupil of Pamphilus. In 315 bishop of Caesarea, leader of the moderate party during Arian controversy. Later summoned by Constantine to advise on Athanasius. Active until his death. Known for his "Ecclesiastical History," main source of history from apostolic times to his own.

[49] Eusebius, *Church History*, in NPNF 2, vol. 1, book 1, chap. 2, p. 84, para. 22.

[50] A. H. Johns, "Moses in the Qur'an," 129, quoting al-Razi *al-Tafsir*, 22, 15–16.

[51] Ibid.

the fire Moses saw was the light of his Lord."[52] He was told to remove his shoes because he was in a holy place. Terrifying as the experience was, Johns states it was "followed by a deep interior peace."[53] Finally Moses leaves his own to walk the path to "mystical union, and al·Hallaj explains: 'Cast far from your created nature in order that in Reality you become He, and He becomes you.'"[54] The burning bush is not a symbol for the select few called to contemplative prayer but for every believer who seeks to magnify the Word of God.

These mystical interpretations of the burning bush, shared by Muslim and Christian, provide a strong echo of the affirmation given to those seeking to penetrate the mystery of God.

Moses' Behavior

A Christian View

Moses' teaching flowed from his dialogues with God, but, as Chrysostom writes, "one would not be wrong in calling Moses both a teacher, and a nursing father . . . the man's wisdom was great."[55] Ephraim encourages the faithful to "let the love of Moses abide in thee, for his love was a discerning love, his zeal a discreet zeal."[56]

On descending the mountain, writes Jerome, "Moses boldly broke the tables: for he knew that drunkards cannot hear the word of God."[57] Though the commandments were rewritten, there was another motive: to show Christians the law of love

---

[52] Ibid., 131, quoting Paul Nwyia, "*Exeges Coranique et Langage Mystique*," *Recherches* 49 (Beirut, 1970): 83.

[53] Ibid., 131, quoting al-Thaʾlabī, *Qisas*, 124.

[54] Ibid., 132, quoting G. C .Anawati and Louis Gardet, *Mystique Musulmane Aspects et Tendances—Expériences et Techniques* (Paris: 1961), 263.

[55] John Chrysostom, *Homilies on Colossians*, in NPNF 1, vol. 13, homily 4 on Colossians 1:21-22, 279.

[56] Ephraim, *Nisibene Hymns*, in NPNF 2, vol. 13, p. 189, no. 19, para. 7.

[57] Jerome, *Against Jovininanus*, in NPNF, vol. 6, book 2, p. 399, para. 15.

was not written on tablets of stone but, as Gregory Nazianzen expresses it, on "the tables of your heart; I will be your Moses . . . I will write on them with the finger of God a new Decalogue. I will write on them a shorter method of salvation,"[58] referring to law as a commitment of the heart, not simply of observable behavior. Failure to obey the law of love requires a skilled healer who, aware of the increase in sin, is able to speak in such a way that, in Augustine's words, "the proud might be humbled, the humbled might confess, the confessing might be healed; these are the hidden ways, which He made known to Moses, through whom He gave the Law, by which sin should abound, that grace might more abound."[59] So, those who desire to be perfect will be judged not only by reference to outward behavior as shown in attitudes to parents, houses, riches, and pleasure but by looking within, to see if selfishness has been removed from the heart. All will then be stronger, in Cassian's words, never to "be drawn back by any desires to those things which we have forsaken, as those who were led up by Moses, though they did not literally go back, are yet said to have returned in heart to Egypt."[60] In these ways Moses' teaching aimed to transform the heart: not just conformity to rules, but commitment to the deepest values. Believers, praying with faith, living by love, ever-mindful of God's presence, will show, in their outward behavior, the way of selfless love revealed to Moses in the Covenant God made through him with his people.

A Muslim View

Among Sufis, Moses is held in high honor, because he repented his sins. Maneri writes, "Moses said 'I have repented before You.' That is to say I turned from myself to You because of my passionate desire to see Your Face,"[61] knowing that sin

---

[58] Gregory Nazianzen, *Orations*, oration 40 on baptism, in NPNF 2 , vol. 7, p. 376, para. 45.

[59] Augustine, *Homilies on the Psalms*, homily on Ps 103, p. 507, para. 12.

[60] Cassian, *Conferences*, chap. 7, 323.

[61] Sharafuddin Maneri, *The Hundred Letters*, letter 2, 16, quoting Qur'an 7:143.

would be like a cloud between us. He adds that Moses inspired the comment since sinners have to repent of their sins so also "do the righteous have to repent of their righteousness."[62] This extraordinary statement is interpreted by Maneri, not as a suggestion that righteousness is sinful but that, by its nature, it tempts believers to self-glorification. They think they have mastered their hearts and are proud of their ability to obey the Law. In this way they lose their awareness that righteousness is a gift from God, not a virtue earned by self-discipline.

In another letter, Maneri writes of a revelation in which Moses is asked to find the worst sinner. He found the most austere and dedicated person and asked him to seek out the worst sinner. Four days later he returned with a rope round his neck saying I have found that I am the worst sinner. "Moses said: 'You are the most devoted ascetic from among them all. How can you of all people say such a thing?' He replied: 'because I am certain about my own sins, but in doubt about those of others. And anyone who is certain about his own sins is certainly worse than anyone whose sins are doubtful"[63]—a powerful reminder that the judgment of others is inevitably partial. All should convict themselves of sin first: this echoes strongly with Benedict's chapter on humility (RB 7).

Moses and Prayer

A Christian View

The most significant moment in Moses' life was his ascent of Mount Sinai, there, alone, he heard God speak to him. John of the Cross shows how this can be applied to ascending the mount of perfection. For each "must not only renounce all things by leaving them at the bottom, but also restrict their appetites (the beasts) from pasturing on the mountainside, on things that are not purely God."[64] When arriving at this intimacy with God, all

---

[62] Ibid., letter 63, 255.
[63] Ibid., letter 98, 416–17.
[64] John of the Cross, *Ascent of Mount Carmel*, book 1, chap. 5, para. 6.

that is not God is a distraction. But Moses sees God not "through likenesses and figures,"[65] but by standing in the divine presence where God is communicated "mouth to mouth; the pure and naked essence of God (the mouth of God in love) with the pure and naked essence of the soul (the mouth of the soul in love of God)."[66] Moses' experience led him to an understanding of the depth of this union that God seeks with those who love and are ready to be loved. Many seek this intimacy, but few attain it. Moses entered the cloud of God's presence and was magnified by the experience; it was beyond verbal description.

A Muslim View

Muslims know that effective prayer requires humility and use Moses as their model. In prayer he asked, " 'O God, where should I seek You?' The reply came: 'Where you find a broken heart which is terrified about its own salvation.' "[67] The brokenness of the human spirit is the place most in need of the healing love of God, the fruit of prayer. Maneri writes, "No matter how much knowledge, dedication and witness there may be, still 'the more broken, the more valuable.' "[68] It is through humility and emptiness that the power of God's love can flood the soul: a strong echo of Christian teaching.

Moses and Resurrection: A Christian View

Through the law Moses was a forerunner of resurrection. Even though it was, as Augustine writes, unable to "liberate any man from the dominion of death, there were, even then, too, at the time of the law, men of God who were not living under the terror and conviction and punishment of the law, but under the delight and

---

[65] Ibid., book 2, chap. 16, para. 9.
[66] Ibid.
[67] Sharafuddin Maneri, *In Quest of God*, letter 7, 23.
[68] Ibid.

healing and liberation of grace."[69] In the Hebrew Scriptures, there are many examples of men and women of virtue. Their lives were not lived in vain, though only toward the end of this period did there appear hints of a life after death, an issue of dispute between Sadducees and Pharisees, as shown in the gospels.

Moses offered one hint. He was ordered to make a bronze serpent and then hold it high. The people were instructed, "When any had been bitten by a serpent, he should look to that serpent raised up on the pole,"[70] and he would be healed. Augustine interpreted the serpents as "sins from the mortality of the flesh. What is the serpent lifted up? The Lord's death on the cross; for as death came by the serpent, it was figured by the image of a serpent. The serpent's bite was deadly; the Lord's death is life-giving."[71] Following the success of this life-giving bronze serpent, Augustine encouraged his listeners, "Brethren, that we may be healed from sin, let us now gaze on Christ crucified; for 'as Moses,' saith he, 'lifted up the serpent in the wilderness, so must the Son of man be lifted up; that whosoever believeth on Him may not perish, but have everlasting life.' "[72] Moses' bronze serpent enabled earthly men, injured and dying, to look and be healed; a miracle of life, opening up the possibility of life after death.

The Mystical Journey

The description of Moses' mystical journey is only found in the Qur'an (18:60-82). Moses set out with his servant to a place "where the two seas meet, even if it takes me years" (Qur'an 18:60). Getting hungry Moses asked for his lunch. At this point his servant admits he left the fish behind, the fault of Satan.

[69] Augustine, *Treatise on the Grace of Christ and Original Sin*, in NPNF 1, vol. 5, book 2, p. 247, para. 29.

[70] Augustine, *Homilies on St. John's Gospel*, vol. 7, tractate 12 on John 3:6-21, p. 85, para. 11.

[71] Ibid.

[72] Ibid.

Moses thought this odd but decided that they should go back and look for it. On the way they met "one of Our servants—a man to whom We had granted Our mercy and whom We had given knowledge of Our own" (Qur'an 18:65). Moses asked him, "May I follow you so that you can teach me some of the right guidance you have been taught?" (Qur'an 18:66). The reply was not enthusiastic: Moses would be incapable of obeying the rules, for example, "How could you be patient in matters beyond your knowledge?" (Qur'an 18:68). But Moses committed himself to being patient and obedient. The servant's single rule was that no questions should be asked concerning his words or actions during the journey. They walked along and arrived at a jetty where there was a boat. They got into it: immediately the man started to drill a hole. Moses could not restrain himself, "How could you make a hole in it? Do you want to drown its passengers? What a strange thing to do!" (Qur'an 18:71). The man reminded him of the agreement, and Moses apologized. They continued and next met a young boy. The man killed him. Moses again asked, "How could you kill an innocent person? He has not killed anyone! What a terrible thing to do!" (Qur'an 18:74). Again, the man rebuked Moses, and again he apologized. They traveled on and came to a town where they were refused hospitality. They saw a wall about to fall down. The man repaired it but took no payment for his work. Moses challenged him for not seeking payment. The man did not answer. Later, before they parted, he interpreted for Moses the meaning of his actions:

> The boat belonged to some needy people who made their living from the sea and I damaged it because I knew that coming after them was a king who was seizing every [serviceable] boat by force. The young boy had parents who were people of faith, and so, fearing he would trouble them through wickedness and disbelief, we wished that their Lord should give them another child—purer and more compassionate—in his place. The wall belonged to two young orphans in the town and had treasure buried beneath it which belonged to them. Their father had been a righteous man so your Lord intended them to reach

maturity and then dig up their treasure as a mercy from your Lord. (Qur'an 18:79-82)

These interpretations were beyond Moses' understanding. He realized God's ways are not limited by human reasoning—ways different even from one who has come closer than anyone to the mind of God. Later "the servant of God who was endowed with knowledge is identified as 'al-Khidr,' 'the green man, and the green.' "[73] Green here, according to Muhammad Asad, "is an epithet rather than a name, implying (according to popular legend) that his wisdom was ever-fresh and imperishable: a notion which bears out the assumption that we have here an allegoric figure symbolizing the utmost depth of mystical insight accessible to man,"[74] one superior, even to Moses, indicating, as Maulana Muhammad Ali puts it,[75] "the beneficent hand of Allah that works in nature, is always directing humanity to the goal of great good, though that goal must necessarily be reached with apparent loss."[76]

Maneri writes, "When men of insight see this, they remove their selves and their inheritance entirely from their awareness and say: 'We are slaves. What business does a slave have with possessions, portion and control?' This is because 'a slave and whatever he possesses belongs to his master.' "[77]

---

[73] Cornelia Schöck, in *Encyclopaedia of the Qur'ān*, ed. Jane Dammen McAuliffe, s.v. "Moses," sec. 12, "Moses and the servant of God whom God had taught of his knowledge." See also Ian Richard Netton, *Islam, Christianity and the Mystic Journey: A Comparative Exploration* (Edinburgh: Edinburgh University Press, 2011), on al-Khidr, 31ff.

[74] Muhammad Asad, trans., *The Message of the Qur'an*, surah 18:65, note 73.

[75] Maulana Muhammad Ali (1874–1951), b. in Punjab, obtained MA English and LLB in Law in 1899. Joined the Ahmadiyya Movement in 1897, lifelong commitment to restore the purity of Islam. In 1914 movement split, Ali led a group to Lahore, the *Lahori Party*, and organized its activities. Translated the Qur'an and wrote texts, other writings include *The Religion of Islam*, *Muhammad the Prophet*, and *A Manual of Hadith*.

[76] Maulana Muhammad Ali, *The Holy Qur'an* (1917; repr. Ohio: Ahmadiyya Anjuman Isha'at Islam Lahore Inc., 2002), note 78a, on Qur'an 18:78.

[77] Sharafuddin Maneri, *In Quest of God*, letter 24, 68.

The story illustrates not just the limitation of human perception and the precociousness of those who claim insight but also the unfathomable logic of the divine plan. Through revelation believers know life is fulfilled in resurrection; but their journeys are rarely straightforward. Strong faith gives greater appreciation that human life, with its multiple skills, can always seek a clearer understanding of divine revelation. But revelation shows this can be deceptive; the nearer humans get to God, the greater the mystery, the lesser the certainty, which inevitably ends in an overpowering sense of the majesty of God. From divine majesty, the believer reaffirms the importance of faith in the unique goodness of the One God, revealed through Moses so powerfully presented in the Inspired Scriptures of Christianity and Islam.

The Context for Dialogue

The many elements in the story of Moses defy easy classification. A dialogue of spirituality will roam widely round these issues but will always come back to focus on Moses as the one who was intimate with God and yet able both to repent his own sins and seek the mercy, compassion, and forgiveness of God: a good starting point.

Chapter **27**

Affirming the Positive Echoes in the Understanding of God Who Gives Life after Death

Reward

The disciplined life of prayer and good works is rewarded, according to Muslim teaching, in an afterlife where the wrongs of the present are put right. The Qurʾan confirms that "any who direct themselves wholly to God and do good will have their reward with their Lord: no fear for them, nor will they grieve" (Qurʾan 2:112). Billions are forced to accept their situation of exploitation, poverty, violence, abuse. No human rescue is available. Some put their trust in God, the one who "give[s] those who believe and do good the news that they will have Gardens graced with flowing streams" (Qurʾan 2:25). So "men who are not distracted, either by commerce or profit, from remembering God, God will reward such people according to the best of their actions and will give them more of His bounty" (Qurʾan 24:35-40). It is those who trust God, keep the faith, obey the rules, and endure the pain that have a guaranteed reward.

Christians express the same truth but in a different way. Jesus preached that those who serve will be rewarded: "All who exalt themselves will be humbled, but all who humble themselves will be exalted" (Luke 18:14). On another occasion, he challenged the motive of donors to the Temple; observing a poor widow, he said, "This poor widow has put in more than all of them; for all of them have contributed out of their abundance, but she out of her poverty has put in all she had to live on" (Luke 21:3-4). On another occasion Jesus challenged his listeners: "If your enemies are hungry, feed them; if they are thirsty, give them something to drink; for by doing this you will heap burning coals on their heads" (Rom 12:20-21). Christians, who want to be rewarded after death, should be givers during their lives.

Christians and Muslims are encouraged by their respective Inspired Scriptures to lead morally upright lives. In that way they enhance the possibility, after death, of life in the presence of God. Faithful in prayer, generous in hospitality, virtuous in daily living, supportive of the most vulnerable in the community are all signs of one living under the eye of God, whose life will be rewarded.

Final Judgment

Before final fulfillment there is judgment, a moment for divine justice and decision. There are, according to both the Qurʾan and the Bible, no exceptions. The Christian Scriptures contain a remarkable account of how this judgment will work. Jesus, Son of Man, in glory with angels alongside, will face all the people who have ever lived. First the saved, who served their neighbor with selfless love, will be admitted to heaven, and second, the damned, the self-centered, who put their own interests ahead of their neighbor, will hear the words, "For I was hungry and you gave me no food: I was thirsty and you gave me nothing to drink, I was a stranger and you did not welcome me, naked and you did not give me clothing, sick and in prison and you did not visit me" (Matt 25:42-44). Asked when this happened, Jesus will reply, "Just as you did not do it to one of the least of these, you did not do it to me" (Matt 25:45).

These are the priorities to be used at the Last Judgment, at a moment decided by God. Millions of people live that teaching in small ways, known only to God and the recipients of their kindnesses. By contrast, the self-centered are condemned; they have been blind to the presence of God in their neighbor.

A similar judgment is described in the Qurʾan, where "the good will live in bliss and the wicked will burn in the Fire. They will enter it on the Day of Judgment and they will find no escape" (Qurʾan 82:10-15). The will of God cannot be changed, "Neither their possessions nor their children will be any use to the disbelievers against God. The disbelievers will be fuel for the Fire. . . . God is severe in punishing" (Qurʾan 3:5-10). Cyril Glassé describes this day as the moment when

> the world is rolled up like a scroll, and the dead issue from their graves and are reunited with their bodies; the limbs testify to reveal the owner's good or evil deeds. On the scales of God's judgment nothing is overlooked: an atom's weight of good is manifest, and an atom's weight of evil. According to their deeds and their belief, men are judged and their real nature revealed.[1]

These pictures, Muslim and Christian, offer the same message. Islam and Christianity require their followers to remember that the divine judgment will assess the quality of life lived, the motives behind decisions made, and the degree to which each was aware of the presence of God in the neighbor. The echo is strong. In the moment after death the evaluation is made. No one, Christian or Muslim, should presume its outcome; better to be continually reforming one's lifestyle now. One difference: for Christians, Jesus is Judge, for Muslims, God is.

Resurrection

For Muslims the resurrection brings renewal to the whole earth, God "brings the living out of the dead and the dead out

---

[1] Cyril Glassé, in *The New Encyclopedia of Islam*, s.v. "Yawm ad Dīn."

of the living. He gives life to the earth after death, and you will be brought out in the same way" (Qurʾan 30:19); there the hopes of the just will be fulfilled, for "this is for everyone who turned often to God and kept Him in mind, who held the Most Gracious in awe, though He is unseen, who comes before Him with a heart turned to him in devotion—so enter it in peace. This is the Day of everlasting Life. They will have all that they wish for there, and We have more for them" (Qurʾan 50:32-35). This is the privileged entry into paradise for those "who are killed for His cause" (Qurʾan 47:4). Here, there is a special place for martyrs. With pain and suffering over, the sense of happiness will be beyond earthly imagination. Life in paradise will be one of complete fulfillment and perpetual peace.

In the Christian Inspired Scriptures, Paul gives a more dramatic description of the moment of resurrection: "We will not all die, but we will all be changed, in a moment, in the twinkling of an eye, at the last trumpet. For the trumpet will sound, and the dead will be raised imperishable, and we will be changed" (1 Cor 15:51-52). The focus is on a change beyond description in earthly terms. The change will be accompanied by the sound of the trumpet, but, as with the Muslim description, the detail of the risen life is beyond imagination.

Al-Ghazālī shows the concept of resurrection as the way to overcome ignorance, for "whoever lifts another out of ignorance to knowledge has already created him anew and revivified him to a blessed life."[2] This powerful idea offers a new perspective: all knowledge is found in God. But humans constantly seek more understanding of the world, themselves, and the meaning of life. It takes time for many to realize this can only be found through deeper union with God, finally completed in resurrection.

The Catholic Catechism takes a different view: resurrection is something to which a person's lifestyle now acts as witness and, as such, is an appropriate preparation for life after death. The risen Christ shows the way to his followers: they should "become a witness with us to his resurrection" (Acts 1:22) and

---

[2] Al-Ghazālī, *The Ninety-Nine Beautiful Names of God*, 123.

for the apostles, chosen precisely because they "ate and drank with him after he rose from the dead" (Acts 10:41). It was the reported evidence of Jesus' resurrection that molded "the Christian hope of resurrection. We shall rise like Christ, with him, and through him."[3] The Christian understanding of resurrection will be founded on the historical fact of the risen Jesus.

These authors say the same thing from different starting points. The Muslim eternity emphasizes there are no boundaries to knowledge, while the Christian proposes no boundaries to life. The one understands the reality of ignorance now, while the other focuses on the reality of death now. In resurrection, a life without boundaries is a life without end, and a life without end is one that is knowledge fulfilled, which both translate into love without limit either in expression or in understanding. Revealed knowledge is available both through the revelations to the Prophet in the Qurʾan and through the recorded reflections of the risen Jesus in the New Testament. They are only fragments of the reality that is resurrection. They strengthen faith in a future of fulfillment and are not mutually exclusive.

Resurrection itself is not disputed; it is the role of Jesus that marks the difference. For Christians, Christ introduces the way to live the risen life, partially now, later fulfilled. For Muslims, resurrection is future reward for a life lived now in fidelity to God. The same message, with different antecedents, creates an opportunity for a shared memory from a dialogue that focuses on resurrection's influence on daily lives.

[3] *Catechism of the Catholic Church*, 227, no. 995.

28

Jesus Christ: Muslim Prophet Raised to Heaven by God without Dying and Christian God-Made-Man Who Rose from the Dead

Muslim and Christian in Dialogue

Jesus is the crucial figure in the dialogue between Islam and Christianity. He is highly respected by both, in different ways, for different reasons, with different effects. This makes for a challenging dialogue, but one worth the effort. The focus is on the Jesus as presented in the Inspired Scriptures, where the language of doctrine, being language of difference, is less important. The stories of Jesus offer a better approach to a dialogue of spirituality because they provide immediate comparison with many echoes and some counter-echoes.

As the dialogue about Jesus progresses, there may be moments when words are no longer helpful: better to struggle with difference in silence, allowing the power of the Word to work in the heart of each, encouraging a journey to a greater depth of mutual understanding in the hope of finding appropriate words to move the reflection forward. At this point the silent affirmation of difference may create a new form of communication in which the unique inspiration of Jesus can be held in a way that is enriching for both without denying a central tenet of either. This opportunity arises from the hospitality of silence, which allows space for God's inspiration through stillness.

Jesus Christ in the Inspired Scriptures: Muslim and Christian

Jesus in the New Testament

Many Christians will refer to two key texts, the prologue of John's gospel (John 1:1-14) and the hymn in Paul's Letter to the Philippians (Phil 2:5-11),[1] as particularly important in describing the truth of Jesus, recognized by them as God made Man.

In Hebrew, the name *Jesus* means "God saves." So "in Jesus, God recapitulates all of his history of salvation on behalf of men."[2] Further, "Jesus Christ is true God and true man in the

---

[1] "In the beginning was the Word; the Word was with God and the Word was God. He was with God in the beginning. Through him all things came to be, not one thing had its being but through him. All that came to be had life in him and that life was the light of men, a light that shines in the dark, a light that darkness could not overpower. . . . [He] was born not out of human stock or urge of the flesh or will of man, but of God himself. The Word was made flesh, he lived among us, and we saw his glory, the glory that is his, the only Son of the Father, full of grace and truth" (John 1:1-5, 13-14, JB).

"In your minds you must be the same as Christ Jesus: his state was divine, yet he did not cling to his equality with God but emptied himself to assume the condition of a slave, and became as men are: and being as all men are, he was humbler yet, even to accepting death, death on a cross. But God raised him high and gave him the name which is above all other names so that all beings in the heavens, on earth and in the underworld, should bend the knee at the name of Jesus and that every tongue should acclaim Jesus Christ as Lord, to the glory of God the Father" (Phil 2:5-11, JB).

[2] *Catechism of the Catholic Church*, 96, no. 430.

unity of his divine person; for this reason he is the one and only mediator between God and men."[3] Christian spirituality is founded on the belief that intimacy with God comes uniquely through the life and work of Jesus Christ, continued each day through Word and Sacrament.

Jesus in the Qurʾan

The Word of God, spoken and recorded in the Qurʾan, is the Muslim way into the mystery of the One all-powerful and all-merciful God. Like the Christian, it is a mystery without limit and beyond definition. It is God speaking, as directly to Muslims as Jesus does to Christians.

As a Prophet. The Qurʾan's version of the birth of Jesus and his mother is, in some respects, more detailed than that in the gospels. In the Qurʾan Jesus is named as a prophet, along with Adam, Noah, Abraham, Joseph, and Moses, but is distinctive because he "came with a scripture."[4] His qurʾanic name (mentioned twenty-five times) is Isa, usually with the addition, "son of Mary. The Qurʾān asserts that he was a prophet and gives him the unique title 'the Messiah.' "[5] This "is derived ultimately from the Hebrew Māshīah, 'anointed' or 'Messiah.' "[6]

Jesus and Mary. Jesus was born to Mary, whose own birth was exceptional: "I name her Mary and I commend her and her offspring to Your protection from the rejected Satan" (Qurʾan 3:36). Accepted by God, she grew in goodness and was cared for by Zachariah who noted that she always seemed to have provisions. Mary's reply, "They are from God: God provides limitlessly for whoever He will" (Qurʾan 3:37). "Mary, God has chosen you

[3] Ibid., 108, no. 480.

[4] Neal Robinson, in *Encyclopaedia of the Qurʾān*, ed. Jane Dammen McAuliffe, s.v. "Jesus."

[5] Ibid.

[6] Ibid., at "References to Jesus as 'the Son of Mary' and 'the Messiah.' "

and made you pure: He has truly chosen you above all women. Mary, be devout to your Lord, prostrate yourself in worship, bow down with those who pray" (Qur'an 3:42-43). Later she hears "of a Word from Him, whose name will be the Messiah, Jesus, son of Mary, who will be held in honor in this world and the next" (Qur'an 3:45), a child, near to God, speaking in his infancy, righteous, born to Mary, a virgin. When Mary protested, the angel said, "This is how God creates what He will: when He has ordained something, He only says, 'Be' and it is" (Qur'an 3:47).

Birth of Jesus. Mary withdrew to a distant place.

> When the pains of childbirth drove her to [cling] to the trunk of a palm tree, she exclaimed, "I wish I had been dead and forgotten long before all this!" But a voice cried to her from below, "Do not worry: your Lord has provided a stream at your feet and, if you shake the trunk of the palm tree towards you, it will deliver fresh ripe dates for you, so eat, drink, be glad and say to any you may see: 'I have vowed to the Lord of Mercy to abstain from conversation and I will not talk to anyone today.'" (Qur'an 19:23-26)

Mary went back to her people with her child; they thought something immoral had happened. Her only reply was to let the child speak for himself. He said, "I am a servant of God. He has granted me the Scripture: made me a prophet; made me blessed wherever I may be. He commanded me to pray, to give alms as long as I live, to cherish my mother. He did not make me domineering or graceless. Peace was on me the day I was born, and will be on me the day I die and the day I am raised to life again" (Qur'an 19:30-33). Distinct from the language of the gospels, but any confusion over Jesus' real nature is soon clarified, "People of the Book, do not go to excess in your religion, and do not say anything about God except the truth: the Messiah, Jesus, son of Mary, was nothing more than a messenger of God, His word, directed to Mary, a spirit from Him" (Qur'an 4:171). Jesus is not divine, in the Christian sense, and "the Qur'an attaches no salvific importance to his death,"[7] because Adam repented and was forgiven. There is no "original sin" in Islam, so no need of a savior in the Christian sense as was shown above.

Jesus, Origins, Life, and Ministry. In Muslim thought, Jesus is just a human being, a specially chosen one nonetheless: "In God's eyes Jesus is just like Adam: He created him from dust, said to him, 'Be,' and he was" (Qurʾan 3:59). So, "those who say, 'God is the Messiah, son of Mary' have defied God" (Qurʾan 5:72). It is impossible for the Messiah to be God and God to remain one. Muslims were commanded to serve only one God: there is no god but Him: He is far above whatever they set up as His partners.

Jesus' public ministry. An angel tells Mary how God will care for Jesus:

> He will teach him the Scripture and wisdom, the Torah and the Gospel. He will send him as a messenger to the Children of Israel: "I have come to you with a sign from your Lord: I will make the shape of a bird for you out of clay, then breathe into it, and, with God's permission, it will become a real bird; I will heal the blind and the leper, and bring the dead back to life with God's permission." (Qurʾan 3:48-49)

Jesus' life was filled with teaching and miracle working, undertaken with God's permission: "We gave Jesus, son of Mary, clear signs and strengthened him with the Holy Spirit. . . . So how is it that, whenever a messenger brings you something you do not like, you become arrogant, calling some impostors and killing others?" (Qurʾan 2:87, 253). Jesus' signs point to God, One, True, Holy, Merciful, and All Powerful, encouraging people to obey the Torah. To help him, he is given disciples.

---

[7] Ibid., at "The Plot to Kill Him: His Exaltation and Future Descent."

Death of Jesus. A tradition in Islam holds Jesus did not die. "It is easy for Me—We shall make him a sign to all people, a blessing from Us" (Qur'an 19:21). When the Jews decided to kill Jesus, God intervened and another, looking like Jesus, took his place and was crucified. God saved Jesus, but the Jews continued to hold they had killed him. The Qur'an states: "They [the Jews] did not kill him, nor did they crucify him, though it was made to appear like that to them: those that disagreed about him are full of doubt, with no knowledge to follow, only supposition; they certainly did not kill him—God raised him up to Himself. God is almighty and wise" (Qur'an 4:157-158). There is, however, still some confusion about what the Qur'an means: "It does not mention his resurrection on the third day, and has no need of it as proof of God's power to raise the dead."[8] Muslims accept that the Jews killed Jesus but then affirm that, from God's point of view, they neither crucified nor killed him.

Jesus is taken to heaven, where he lives. Looking to the future, Jesus "will return to kill the Antichrist, and after a forty-year reign of peace he will eventually die and be buried in Medina. On the day of resurrection, he will be a witness against the unbelieving People of the Book."[9] Jesus has a unique role after his death: he has power, but he is not a divine being.

Jesus' Resurrection? With regard to the Last Day, "this [Qur'an] gives knowledge of the Hour" (Qur'an 43:61). Muslim commentators offer three interpretations of Jesus' function. First, Jesus' return will be a signal that the final judgment is approaching; second, the Qur'an provides information about the resurrection and how the final judgment will be conducted; and third, Jesus, acting with power from God, will raise the dead.[10]

At this moment, God will remind all present of his special favors to Jesus, Son of Mary, which include the gift of the Holy Spirit, a power demonstrated from his earliest years, speaking

---

[8] Ibid.
[9] Ibid.
[10] Ibid.

with clarity and lucidity, teaching the Scriptures persuasively, working miracles such as raising the dead, healing the sick, and offering other signs, all of which were accepted by believers destined to be saved. Unbelievers and idolaters rejected these signs and will be punished with great pain.

On Judgment Day, God will challenge Jesus:

> Did you say to people, "Take me and my mother as two gods alongside God?" He will say, "may You be exalted! I would never say what I had no right to say—if I had said such a thing You would have known it: You know all that is within me, though I do not know what is within You, You alone have full knowledge of things unseen—I told them only what You commanded me to: "Worship God, my Lord and your Lord." (Qurʾan 5:116-117)

This reaffirms Jesus' complete identity as a human being, drawing a line between the Jesus of the New Testament and the Jesus of the Qurʾan.

Jesus and Muhammad

Both are messengers; Jesus prepared the way for Muhammad, illustrated by three points: First, "Jesus and Muhammad are depicted as having had similar experiences. For instance, both were sent as a 'mercy,' both needed to eat food, both had 'helpers' and both were suspected of sorcery."[11]

Second, God tells Muhammad he is inspired with the same faith as Noah, Abraham, Moses, and Jesus. "Uphold the faith and do not divide into factions within it" (Qurʾan 42:13).

Third, Jesus predicted the coming of an envoy "bringing good news of a messenger to follow me whose name will be Ahmad" (Qurʾan 61:6), "the heavenly name of Muhammad."[12] These

---

[11] Ibid., at "His Status and Mission."
[12] Ibid.

functions show that Jesus has a specific role within the Muslim prophetic tradition, the line of holy people inspired by God to proclaim the Truth (that God is One, Merciful, and Forgiving) and foretell the good news of a future envoy.

Two Contrasting Positions:
Muslim and Christian about Jesus Christ

With these differences and similarities in mind, it is possible to look more closely at the way selected Christian and Muslim theologians articulate their respective beliefs about Jesus and try to offer a way into a deeper understanding of the differences. These are two selected opinions to provide an example useful for a dialogue of spirituality.

The Significance of Jesus in the Life of Christians and Muslims: Catholic Catechism and Seyyed Nasr

For Roman Catholics, their catechism explains, "Jesus himself affirms that God is 'the one Lord,' whom you must love 'with all your heart, and with all your soul, and with all your mind and with all your strength.' At the same time, Jesus reveals himself as 'the Lord.' To confess that Jesus is Lord is distinctive of Christian faith and not contrary to belief in the One God,"[13] and is made explicit in the confession of faith, with states, "We believe and confess that Jesus of Nazareth, born a Jew of a daughter of Israel at Bethlehem at the time of Herod the Great and the emperor Caesar Augustus, a carpenter by trade, who died crucified in Jerusalem under the Procurator Pontius Pilate during the reign of the emperor Tiberius, is the eternal Son of God made man."[14] Ultimately the Christian defense is that infinite freedom lies within the gift of the all-powerful Creator. The mystery of

---

[13] *Catechism of the Catholic Church*, 49, no. 202.
[14] Ibid., 94, no. 423.

God becoming man can be described but not analyzed. The gift is greater than the human mind can comprehend.

For Muslims, Seyyed Nasr presents this view:

> Christ did not bring a new revealed law, or sharī'ah, but a way based on the love of God. Islam recognized the particular function of Christ, which thus differed from that of other prophets who usually brought a law or reformed a previous one, by acknowledging his particular nature as the "Spirit of God" and his "supernatural birth" connected with the virginity of Mary.[15]

Jesus had a particular mandate: to reveal God's deep relationship with the people of the world, expressed as an ongoing act of love, an appeal to the heart of all. The Muslim Jesus fits the Muslim definition of "prophet," but it is not "an incarnation."[16] Islam draws a clear distinction between the Absolute God and the divine manifestations or "descents" of God. The being of God cannot cross that boundary without compromising Divinity.[17] Nasr expresses the difference between them: the Christ for Christians is unique in his divine-human being. He has crossed the line between uncreated Divinity and created humanity and cannot be copied. The Prophet for Muslims is a holy man, specially chosen by God to be emulated.[18]

For Muslims, the function of savior or redeemer is not so dramatic as the Christian. It falls within the definition of *emulation* as defined by Nasr: a disciplined life, remembering God, transforms the believer into one who becomes ever more in tune with God now and fulfilled in resurrection.

Christians, by contrast, believe it is the very life of God made man in Jesus, which is the cause of the transformation of the believer into Christ, enabling the faithful to live the risen life now and confident

---

[15] Seyyed Hossein Nasr, *Ideals and Realities of Islam*, 34.
[16] Ibid.
[17] Ibid., 75.
[18] Ibid.

it will be fulfilled in resurrection after death. This dramatic conversion was needed to dissolve the effects of original sin.

Keith Ward[19] and Joseph Lumbard[20]

These two theologians challenge traditional attitudes to the theology of Jesus. Each seeks to find a way of bridging the gap. Their work is particularly interesting for those engaged in a dialogue of spirituality.

Keith Ward, a Christian theologian, starts with a quotation taken from Nicholas of Cusa: "God alone is infinite and the being of God cannot be mixed with or united to any finite and limited being at all."[21] He uses it to unlock the meaning of the qurʾanic verse, "Do not call out to any other god beside God, for there is no god but Him. Everything will perish except His Face" (Qurʾan 28:88). This emphasizes that God alone is real because God is independent of the act of creation, which is a reflection of God providing the energy that causes creation.

For Ward, all human beings have a specific origin. They are "expressions of God's will, as they live directly in the conscious experience of the immanent reality of God, the only truly Real."[22]

---

[19] Keith Ward (1938–) 1962 BA, 1964–69 lecturer in logic at Glasgow University, 1968 BLitt Oxford. Lecturer in philosophy at St. Andrew's University, 1969–71. In 1972 ordained priest in the Church of England, 1971–75 lecturer in philosophy of religion at London University, 1975–83 dean of Trinity Hall, Cambridge, 1982–91 professor of moral and social theology, then of history and philosophy of religion at King's College, London, 1991–2004 Regius Professor of Divinity, Oxford.

[20] Joseph Lumbard, b. Washington, DC, brought up Episcopalian, introduced to Islam while at George Washington University, converted eighteen months later. PhD and MPhil in Islamic studies from Yale University, MA and BA in religious studies, George Washington University. Studied Qurʾan, Sufism, Hadith, and Islamic philosophy in Morocco, Egypt, Yemen, and Iran, and worked as assistant professor of Islamic studies at the American University in Cairo. Founder and director of the Islamic Research Institute.

[21] Keith Ward, "Islam and Christianity—Is a Clash of Civilizations Inevitable?" (lecture, Gresham College, January 24, 2007), para. 1, subpoint 5.

[22] Ibid., para. 2.5.

Muslims will accept that statement. Differences then "are more like differences of emphasis and attachment to different key metaphors, than they are like straightforward contradictions."[23]

To support this view he offers six similarities:

1. Jesus and Muhammad are both called "Word of God," a finite expression of the will of God.

2. Both Christianity and Islam believe there is an intimacy simply by *being*. This intimacy arises because of the relationship between the God Who Is Existence and each recipient of limited existence.

3. The Qurʾan for Muslims and Jesus Christ for Christians are both tangible expressions of the revealing God.

4. When the Qurʾan asserts God has no son, Christians agree Jesus is not a person separate from God.

5. Christians worship one God and qualify it by saying, "Some finite things—and especially the person of Jesus—can be such perfect expressions of God, that God can be worshipped in and through them,"[24] while Muslims say the Qurʾan is a public recital of the One God speaking.

6. Each in different ways, the Christian (through Sacrament) and the Muslim (through Word) are able to share in the divine being.

These six similarities bring the two views closer. Ward concludes, "As Christians receive the life of Christ, the eternal Word of God in eating consecrated bread and wine, so Muslims internalize and feed upon the Qurʾan, the eternal Word of God, in reciting the Chapters of the Book,"[25] for both a life enduring beyond death.

[23] Ibid., para. 2.6.
[24] Ibid., para. 2.9.
[25] Ibid., para. 3.2.

For Ward, Christianity and Islam come close especially in the way each expresses its deep involvement in the One God,[26] creating a space for a dialogue of spirituality.

Lumbard approaches the subject from another direction. He reiterates what was said earlier that an important Muslim belief is that the Qur'an is uncreated, so close to the being of God that it existed before creation. Muslims differ about this, but "both sides are agreed on the existence of this heavenly prototype, but are in disagreement as to whether it is co-eternal with God or contingent upon the will of God, and thus created and existing within a limited sphere of time."[27]

Allowing for this difference, Lumbard suggests that this opens a new avenue for dialogue. Some Muslim theologians are "uncomfortable with their own doctrine of the uncreated Qur'an, because they understand that admitting to an uncreated Word of God lends more credence to the understanding of Jesus as the Word who is coeternal with the Father."[28]

The prologue of John presents this problem clearly. If they maintain "that the Qur'an is itself eternal and uncreated, the Word 'inlibrate,'"[29] then how do they reply to this question: if God's Word can be revealed in an uncreated book, why is it impossible for God's Word to be revealed as an uncreated man?

Al-Ghazzālī presented the case for the uncreated Qur'an by saying it "is read by tongues, written in books, and remembered in the heart, yet it is, nevertheless, ancient, subsisting in the Essence of God, not subject to division or separation through its transmission to the heart and paper."[30] So coming directly

---

[26] Joseph E. B. Lumbard, "Discernment, Dialogue and the Word of God," in *Criteria of Discernment in Interreligious Dialogue*, ed. Catherine Cornille (Eugene: Cascade Books, 2009), 143–52.

[27] Richard C. Martin, in *Encyclopaedia of the Qur'ān*, ed. Jane Dammen McAuliffe, s.v. "Createdness of the Qur'ān."

[28] Joseph E. B. Lumbard, "Discernment, Dialogue and the Word of God," 145.

[29] Ibid., 146.

[30] Ibid., 147, quoting from Abū ʿāmid al-Ghazzālī, *Qawāʾid al-ʿaqāʾid fi l-tawhīd*, in *Rasāʾil al-Ghazālī* (Beirut: Dār al-Fikr, 1996), 162.

from the *essence of God* without any intermediary, it can only be uncreated, before time.[31]

Jesus, God and man, could be understood "within an Islamic context as someone who derives from the nature of revelation itself."[32] In the Qur'an God reveals, "We sent Jesus, son of Mary, in their footsteps, to confirm the Torah that had been sent before him: We gave him the Gospel with guidance, light and confirmation of the Torah already revealed—a guide and lesson for those who take heed of God. So let the followers of the Gospel judge according to what God has sent down in it" (Qur'an 5:46-47).

So the revelations of the Word of God through the Qur'an, the gospels, and the Jewish Scriptures are so closely linked that "even the person of Jesus is understood as an extension of the eternal, uncreated Word of God."[33] So when "our texts are read in relation to one another in a spirit of faith seeking understanding. . . . Perhaps we can find elements of our traditions that help us to view the divine Word in a manner that transcends the bounds of one particular tradition."[34]

In this way the uncreated Book and the uncreated Jesus create a new opportunity for a dialogue of spirituality. What is owned by one could magnify the understanding of the other. Ward and Lumbard offer two ways of bringing the Muslim-Christian dialogue closer, hoping that the respective understandings of Jesus would be less polemical. Differences will remain; more

---

[31] The three key qur'anic texts: "This is truly a noble Qur'an, in a protected Record that only the purified can touch, sent down from the Lord of all being" (Qur'an 56:77-80). "This is truly a glorious Qur'an (written) on a preserved Tablet" (Qur'an 85:21-22). "By the Scripture that makes things clear, We have made it a Qur'an in Arabic so that you [people] may understand. It is truly exalted in the Source of Scripture kept with Us, and full of wisdom. Should We ignore you and turn this revelation away from you because you are insolent people? We have sent many a prophet to earlier people" (Qur'an 43:2-6). All Abdel Haleem translation.

[32] Joseph E. B. Lumbard, "Discernment, Dialogue and the Word of God," 147.

[33] Ibid., 149.

[34] Ibid., 152.

accurately understood they should provide stronger threads between the two faiths, bringing new insights into the mystery underlying Jesus.

Jesus in the Religious Life of Islam

Submission to God

Seyyed Nasr writes,

> Every practicing Muslim, which includes the vast majority of the population of the Islamic world, could not but agree that his or her highest wish is none other than the prayer uttered by Christ, "Thy Will be done on earth as it is in Heaven." No matter what the aberrations that cloud the horizons today, the Islamic tradition remains and must remain witness to God's Oneness and dedicated to the effort to carry out His Will here on earth.[35]

Such a statement would be enthusiastically endorsed by Christians, who are also committed to living the will of God, as Benedict recommends, "not to love having our own way nor to delight in our own desires. Instead we should take as our model for imitation the Lord himself when he says: I have come not to indulge my own desires but to do the will of him who sent me" (RB 7:31-32, NPB). Particularly important for Sufis is that Jesus gives an example of true submission to God. "He lived in God's presence, free from all attachments to this world and its vain pleasure. He is a source of hope and solace for the poor and oppressed, and a stern reproach for the rich and greedy oppressors."[36] The Jesus of the Qur'an is especially important for those seeking greater intimacy with God.

---

[35] Seyyed Hossein Nasr, *The Heart of Islam*, 305–6.
[36] Irfan A. Omar, ed., *A Muslim View of Christianity: Essays on Dialogue by Mahmoud Ayoub* (New York: Orbis Books, 2007), 117.

Jesus: An Example of Holiness

Many Muslim mystics find in Jesus not only "the example of piety, love, and asceticism which they sought to emulate, but also the Christ who exemplifies fulfilled humanity, a humanity illumined by the light of God."[37] Jesus, as a prophet, or one informed "by the divine Word,"[38] is also life-giving in the "spiritual 'blowing' of which he, as a channel, transmits the divine Command."[39] This special power arose from the unique manner of his conception, enabling him "to communicate the divine Spirit not only verbally, but also vitally, since the Spirit enlivens at every level. Thus, Jesus was, in a special way, what every man is potentially, that is to say, a spirit enshrined within natural form."[40]

The Spirit enabled Jesus to raise the dead to life for "he was a divine spirit. In this the quickening was of God, while the blowing itself came from Jesus, just as the blowing was from Gabriel, while the Word was of God."[41] This put Jesus on a higher level, defined by Maneri as unique in three ways: first, he lived in remembrance of God, in which he was able to keep meditative silence and when meeting others was able by a glance to give a warning;[42] second, he was a man of spiritual authority, deeply united to God, but hardly different from the Prophet, shown by Maneri's appeal to Jesus' ability to bestow "new life upon a dead youth."[43] And, third, Maneri encouraged all to use concrete imagery as Jesus did, quoting an example, "smash the oyster and extract the pearl!"[44]

In addition, Maneri proposed, in line with Jesus' spiritual teaching, that all should focus on the third day: "The first is the

---

[37] Ibid., 152.

[38] Ibn Al 'Arabi, *The Bezels of Wisdom* (The Classics of Western Spirituality), trans. and intro. R. W. J. Austin (Mahwah, NJ: Paulist Press, 1980), 174.

[39] Ibid.

[40] Ibid.

[41] Ibid., 176.

[42] See Sharafuddin Maneri, *The Hundred Letters*, 245.

[43] Sharafuddin Maneri, *In Quest of God*, letter 42, 96.

[44] Sharafuddin Maneri, *The Hundred Letters*, letter 90, 372, quoting Khwaja Attar.

day that has passed—you can expect nothing from it now! As for tomorrow, you do not even know if you will survive until it comes. You are now in the third day—do not expect anything more than that!"[45] Focused on the present moment, Jesus further counseled, "Nothing comes from the light of the eyes of the head: it is the light of the eye of heart that is needed,"[46] adding, "Be content with a modicum of the world yet with your faith intact,"[47] rather than a faith weakened by worldly concerns. Schimmel presents Jesus as a model for the spiritual life of Muslims, "the ideal ascetic and also as the pure lover of God. A homeless pilgrim, wandering without knowing where to put his head, he instructs the devout about the importance of modesty, peace and charity, for 'just as the seed does not grow but from dust so the seed of wisdom does not grow but from a heart like dust.'"[48] It is not learning that matters but humble desire, openness to gift, and the patience to wait, ready for the divine moment of revelation.

Jesus and His Mother

With his virgin mother, Jesus' words became, as Schimmel states, "exalted symbolic figures—the woman unspoiled by worldly concern, the pure receptacle of the divine spirit, and the prophet born out of the divine command, surnamed 'Spirit of God.'"[49]

Taken together these show the importance of Jesus and Mary in the spirituality of some Muslims.

---

[45] Ibid., letter 83, 341.

[46] Ibid., letter 53, 216.

[47] Sharafuddin Maneri, *In Quest of God*, letter 85, 182.

[48] Annemarie Schimmel, *The Mystical Dimensions of Islam*, 34–35, quoting Abū Ṭālib al-Makkī.

[49] Ibid., 35.

Is This the Encouragement to Do It Now?

These six qualities of the One God, along with the divinely inspired stories of Adam, Noah, Abraham, Joseph, Moses, and Jesus, revealed in the Inspired Scriptures of Islam and Christianity, provide a framework within which a dialogue of spirituality becomes possible.

This provides an agenda, enabling the participants in dialogue to engage with each other, listening and learning, in both challenging and life-giving ways. From this dialogue new insights will emerge, enriching their faith in the One God and giving richer understandings of the other, strengthening the community of dialogue, and opening up the opportunity for the creation of a new shared memory.

Part 6

*Experience and Support for
a Community in a Dialogue of
Spirituality: Do They Encourage
a Decision to Go Ahead?*

Part 6 offers six themes relevant for a new community dedicated to a dialogue of spirituality:

1. the Benedictine experience of living alongside a Muslim community in Algeria

2. proven guidelines for dialogue

3. insights into a dialogue of Scriptures from Scriptural Reasoning

4. the role of a spiritual guide for those in dialogue

5. the convergence of Muslim and Benedictine understandings of prayer during the day

6. relevant insights from contemporary ways of living the Rule of Benedict

The Benedictine Experience in Algeria: The Example of the Trappist Community of Tibhirine

The first Trappist monastery (they follow the Rule of Benedict) in Algeria was founded in 1843 at Staouéli on coastal lowlands to the west of Algiers.

> The Trappists from Aiguebelle, France, were recruited to apply their well-known agricultural skills to fertile land French settlers were taming with difficulty. The monks, known as tireless workers, were devoted to peace and contemplation, without the proselytizing instincts of missionaries. Through their piety and hard work, it was thought, they would be excellent ambassadors to carry out France's civilizing mission.[1]

Their 2,200 acre farm established a good reputation with the local Muslim population whose leader, Abdelkader, told the abbot,

---

[1] John W. Kiser, *The Monks of Tibhirine: Faith, Love, and Terror in Algeria* (New York: St. Martin's Press, 2002), 36.

"I had heard about you a long time ago because my men spoke of your monks. You always received them as though they were your own brothers."[2] They were helped, too, by the similarity of the monastic habit to the Arab *abya* (long-hooded robe), and their shared view of the sacredness of hospitality to every visitor. The community survived until 1904, when the rise of anticlericalism in France forced them to leave.

The Story of Tibhirine

The Trappists returned in 1938 to make a new foundation at Tibhirine, about an hour-and-a-half drive inland from Algiers near the town of Médéa. The buildings are still there, silent in their emptiness, situated on a ledge facing north with the village of Tibhirine below. The spring continues to provide water for several acres of land on which fruit and vegetables are grown by Muslim workers from the village, the produce sold to pay their wages.

In the monastic cemetery lie the remains of the seven monks martyred in May 1996, among them Christian de Chergé, the prior, who arrived in the monastery in 1972, having completed his studies at the Pontifical Institute for the Study of Arabic and Islam in Rome. Before his arrival, the community had been struggling. Three factors caused this: first, life was harsher inland; second, political changes following Algeria's independence caused uncertainty; and third, the community was still struggling with the changes following the Second Vatican Council. In addition the community had to cope with civil unrest, often targeted at Europeans.

The monks strengthened their relationship with the local Muslim community by developing a strong sense of mutual affection based on their commitment to God, mutual help for each other, and hospitality.

[2] Ibid., 37.

Christian de Chergé

Christian de Chergé's arrival in 1972 changed the community. His personal enthusiasm for Islam gave him an insight into Muslim spirituality and a growing admiration for it. On arrival he found:

> A monastic community without a sense of purpose, six tempo-rary superiors had been appointed by Aiguebelle during the nine years following Algeria's independence. Eight monks, whose vow of stability was elsewhere, were on loan from France. . . . It had become like a "tossed salad," remembered Jean-Pierre, one of the monks from Timaduc, "flopping back and forth between traditional, cloistered contemplation and more openness to the surrounding population."[3]

A key element in de Chergé's commitment to Algeria dated from the time he was on national service. At one point, as officer charged with community relations at Tiaret, about two hundred kilometers to the southwest of Tibhirine, he befriended Moham-med, a family man and faithful Muslim.

> Christian had found in Algeria a freedom he did not experience in France. Muslims were infused with a sense of the divine. He could talk unselfconsciously with them about God. . . . [Mohammed] said, "You Christians don't know how to pray. We never see French soldiers praying. You say you believe in God. How can you not pray if you believe in God?" It was a question Christian had difficulty in answering.[4]

On one of their frequent walks, while in deep discussion, they were challenged by a rebel intent on killing de Chergé. Moham-med put himself between the gun and the intended victim. To the rebel he insisted this Frenchman was a friend of Muslims and a man of faith. Next day Mohammed was found dead near his

[3] Ibid., 39.
[4] Ibid., 9.

home, his throat cut, leaving a wife and ten children. De Chergé said, "He changed my life by liberating my faith in spite of the complexity of daily life and showed me how to live it simply as a response to what is natural and authentic in others."[5] A close friend wrote, "Mohammed was surely a saint. I don't think Christian ever felt guilty about Mohammed's sacrifice. I think he considered Mohammed's act a gift of love, freely given. But there is no question it profoundly marked his calling."[6]

In 1984 he was elected prior, for a renewable six-year term and was reelected in 1990 (another election was planned for the day after his abduction). Under his leadership the community had to surmount many difficulties simply to survive. Br. Luc, the doctor, was much in demand and offered his services without question to whoever came, even late at night. He wrote,

> I was rereading Pascal and came upon this, "Men never do evil as thoroughly or as joyfully as when they do it in the name of God." We are now "at risk" but our community stays on. Fear is the lack of faith. We follow the path of our Lord. He shows us the way—it is one of poverty, failure, and death. . . . I have no idea when it will end. Meanwhile I will do my work, receive the poor and the sick awaiting the day when I will close my eyes to enter into God's house, whose door is open to all who knock.[7]

Many visitors, local and more distant, came, including insurgents. All were treated. But no weapons entered the monastery.[8]

Ribat-es-salaam

In 1979, Christian founded a group for dialogue called *ribat-es-salaam* (Bond of Peace). Their meetings, at first only with Christians but later with Muslims, especially Sufis, were regular

[5] Ibid., 10.

[6] Ibid.

[7] Ibid., 192, quoting a letter from Luc to his friend Paul Grenot at the end of 1994.

[8] See John W. Kiser, *The Monks of Tibhirine*, 139.

participants. "The '*ribat*' dreams of another revolution, one that comes from within ourselves. God has allowed us to meet Muslim brothers who share the same dream. This keeps us from being locked into a view of Islam that does not do justice to how you live with us in the name of your faith."[9] On March 27, 1997, a meeting of Ribat was scheduled, the superior from Fez was present.

Martyrdom

In the early hours of March 27, 1996, seven of the monks were abducted, probably by a group of rebels.[10] The two survivors moved first to the little community at Fez, Morocco, and later moved to better accommodation in Midelt. On May 22 it was announced that all seven had been killed. That brought an end to the community in Tibhirine.[11] "On Sunday, May 26th, forty thousand churches throughout France tolled their bells for the monks."[12] De Chergé's testament, written some years before, contains these remarkable sentences:

[9] Ibid., 62.

[10] There is much speculation about this. The latest from *Christian de Chergé, A Theology of Hope* by Christian Salenson, page 1, footnote 2, states: "The Algerian military used Djamel Zitouni, a double agent and an infiltrated GIA (Groupe Islamiste Armé) cell to capture the monks. The idea was then to 'liberate' them and force them to leave the country for their own safety. But the plan backfired when another terrorist cell stole the monks from their original captors. The monks probably died as 'collateral damage' when the army strafed the second group from helicopters with bullets and napalm in a botched rescue attempt. Only the monks' severed heads were recovered and put in coffins to make it look like a terrorist execution: the bodies would have born the marks of military weaponry." The film of *Of Gods and Men* hints at this possibility by contrasting the heated discussion between the prior and the Algerian army officer, with a more friendly dialogue with the rebel leader.

[11] When I visited Tibhirine in 2008, I was taken by the priest for the day. Visiting once a week and staying overnight he is able to see the gardens continue, the workers paid, and produce sold.

[12] John W. Kiser, *The Monks of Tibhirine*, 234.

My death will satisfy my most burning curiosity. At last, I will be able—if God pleases—to see the children of Islam as He sees them, illuminated in the glory of Christ, sharing in the gift of God's Passion and of the Spirit, whose secret joy will always be to bring forth our common humanity amidst our differences. . . . And to you, too, my friend, of the last moment, who will not know what you are doing. Yes, for you, too, I wish this "thank-you," this "A-Dieu," whose image is in you also, that we may meet in heaven, like happy thieves, if it pleases God, our common Father.[13]

A Testimony from Archbishop Teissier, Archbishop of Algiers

The former community of Tibhirine provided an example of the role monastic life can play in a Muslim community. Mgr. Teissier[14] writes, "In a Muslim country like Algeria, it means that every Christian community sees its mission to be a sign of the Gospel in their relationship with each other and with Muslim society."[15] The monks achieved this by building friendship with their neighbors, through different areas of practical help (agricultural, commercial, and medical),[16] which is one reason why their deaths caused such deep pain. Gilles Nicholas[17] confirmed this: "If all the little people are sad today, if all the city of Médéa

---

[13] Ibid., 245–46.

[14] Mgr Teissier 1955 ordained priest for diocese of Algiers, 1972 bishop of Oran, 1980 Archbishop of Algiers, emeritus in 2008. One of few Catholic priests given Algerian nationality in 1965. A great friend of the Tibhirine community.

[15] The original French: "*Dans un pays musulman, comme l'Algérie, cela veut dire que chaque chrétienne et chaque communauté chrétienne reçoivent la mission d'être un signe d'Evangile dans leur relation à chaque musulman et à toute la société. Chaque groupe chrétien vit cette mission, selon son charisme propre,*" in Robert Masson, *Tibhirine, les veilleurs de l'Atlas* (Paris: Les Éditions du Cerf, 1997), 13.

[16] See Robert Masson, *Tibhirine : Les Veilleurs de l'Atlas*, 14.

[17] Fr. Gilles Nicholas (d. 2011) was parish priest of Medea, Algeria, the Catholic parish in which the monastery of Tibhirine was located. He was a great friend of the community.

is appalled, not only because the crime is a blow to the honor of their community, and their religion, but also because they know they have lost true friends and brothers,"[18] sure evidence that Christian monks can be appreciated in the Muslim world.

The Importance of the Community of Tibhirine

This Trappist community opened up a vision for a future community in dialogue with a local Muslim community, sharing the practical things of daily living, providing material support, attending family events, and sharing religious feasts. They had openness and respect for the poor, hardworking, loving, and loveable people, alongside respect for their faith in the God of Love and Mercy. Undoubtedly the dialogue would have deepened over time; today it offers fellow Christians an example of how fervent faith brings people of other faiths together; a dialogue of spirituality flows naturally from it.

[18] Robert Masson, *Tibhirine, les veilleurs de l'Atlas*, 223.

Chapter 30

Guidance for Those Approaching Dialogue

In his encyclical *Ecclesiam Suam*,[1] Pope Paul VI[2] defines dialogue as an "art of spiritual communication."[3] He offers four essential qualities that should be the foundation of a community dedicated to dialogue.

[1] Dated August 6, 1964.

[2] Pope Paul VI (1897–1978, pope 1963–78) b. in Lombardy; after ordination, 1920, moved to the Academia in Rome (Vatican diplomatic school). First assignment to Poland then for thirty years as the secretariat of state in Rome. In 1937 named "substitute" for ordinary affairs under Cardinal Pacelli. Responsible for the Vatican relief work during World War II. In 1952 turned down the invitation to become cardinal. In 1955 appointed archbishop of Milan, reformed the diocese, preaching the social gospel. In 1958 made cardinal. Elected pope in 1963. His image improves with time. First pope to visit five continents. Best known for his encyclical *Populorum Progressio* (1967) and apostolic exhortation *Evangelii nuntiandi*.

[3] Francesco Gioia, ed., *Interreligious Dialogue: The Official Teaching of the Catholic Church from the Second Vatican Council to John Paul II (1963–2005)*, *Ecclesiam Suam*, 76, para. 106.

First, clarity of expression to "review every angle of our language to guarantee that it be understandable, acceptable and well-chosen."[4]

Second, meekness, to ensure that dialogue is "not proud, it is not bitter, it is not offensive."[5]

Third, trust, which "binds hearts in mutual adherence to the good which excludes all self-seeking."[6]

Fourth, prudence, which "esteems highly the psychological and moral circumstances of the listener."[7]

Using these principles as a basis, a community can draw up its own guidelines. These recommendations provide guidance.

First, participants should be committed members of their own faith, knowledgeable enough to recognize echoes and counter-echoes in the other, while at the same time ready to learn more. Ian Markham[8] summarizes this as the need for "maturity and a strong sense of belonging."[9] Those uncertain about their own faith are likely to introduce instability that would threaten the building of mutual trust.

Second, participants should give priority to prayer, both personal and communal. All should be committed to their own spiritual tradition but are open to recognize the same commitment and enthusiasm alive in the spiritual lives of the other.

Third, the Christians should prepare well for the task by seeking advice from fellow believers with relevant experience of dialogue with Muslims. They should be inspired by a shared thirst

---

[4] Ibid.

[5] Ibid., 77, para. 106.

[6] Ibid.

[7] Ibid., 77, para. 107.

[8] Ian Markham (b. 1962); BD London University; M.Litt Philosophy, Cambridge University; PhD Christian ethics, Exeter University; preodained priest of the Episcopal Church 2007; dean and president of Virginia Theological Seminary, 2007.

[9] Ian S. Markham, *Engaging with Bediuzzaman Said Nursi: A Model of Interfaith Dialogue* (Farnham/Burlington: Ashgate, 2009), 132.

for God, satisfied only by drinking at the same divine well—an image that strengthens their sense of purpose.[10]

Fourth, the community will strengthen as it is open to divine inspiration. In prayer each prays that God will guide and sustain this vocation to dialogue. "Enjoying a focused silence together, is a much better starting point. Let God do some of the work. Words can come later"[11] is appropriate advice for this new community.

Fifth, this advice of Pope John Paul II should be given priority: "The differences are a less important element, when confronted with the unity which is radical, fundamental and decisive."[12] The shared humanity of every participant is a more powerful force for unity than anything that divides. No difference, theological, spiritual, or cultural, is so important as to deny another participant respect and affirmation. In this way it is possible "to engage the difficult questions. It is always interesting to learn how a 'holy' person in another tradition reflects on the difficult questions posed by his or her tradition."[13] In this way difference becomes more clearly understood and the atmosphere grows in mutual respect and affection. Sometimes in dialogue the teaching of one causes a strong counter-echo in the other, causing some tension. In dealing with this, each should be clear that the issue is accurately understood, then each should "accommodate what is true, resist that which is evil, and tolerate that which is tolerable."[14] Dialogue is about respecting *difference*, even when it seems wrong. In community each should, with charity, challenge those elements considered morally or theologically wrong as expressed by the other.

---

[10] See Christian de Chergé, *L'Invincible espérance* (Paris: Bayard, 1996), 74; also quoted in Christian Salenson, *Christian de Chergé, une théologie de l'espérance* (Paris: Bayard, 2009), 75. See chap. 2.

[11] Ian S. Markham, *Engaging with Bediuzzaman Said Nursi*, 133.

[12] John Paul II, "To the Roman Curia" (December 22, 1986), in *Interreligious Dialogue*, ed. Francesco Gioia, 400, para. 564.

[13] Ian S. Markham, *Engaging with Bediuzzaman Said Nursi*, 140.

[14] Ibid.

Sixth, a community committed to dialogue should be open, inclusive, and, by means of the dialogue, become ever more friendly. As hospitality becomes stronger, so "it should express itself in further opportunities for growth and understanding."[15]

In these ways a community creates its own dynamism, operating within its own agreed boundaries but free to put into practice the advice the Sufis offered Christian de Chergé: "In doctrine or theology, there are many barriers made by men. We feel we are called to unity. We want to allow God to create something new between us. This can only be done with prayer"[16]—advice particularly relevant for a Muslim-Christian group in a dialogue of spirituality.

---

[15] Ibid., 143.

[16] Christian Salenson, *Christian de Chergé: Une théologie de l'espérance*, 81, quoting *L'Invincible espérance*, 172.

31

The Role of Scriptural Reasoning in a Dialogue of Spirituality

Scriptural reasoning offers a proven framework for dialogue used for more than a decade.[1] The initiative of academics in Britain, the United States, and the Middle East, who "found that joint study across the Abrahamic traditions generates valuable new resources for meeting contemporary challenges."[2] Its achievement deserves detailed consideration as a method of respectful theological debate, which might be useful in a dialogue of spirituality.

Scriptural Reasoning as a Place of Meeting

Scriptural reasoning starts with texts focused on an agreed theme and proposed by each tradition, Jewish, Christian, and

[1] See David F. Ford and C. C. Pecknold, eds., *The Promise of Scriptural Reasoning* (Oxford: Blackwell, 2006).

[2] Ben Quash, "Deep Calls to Deep: The Practice of Scriptural Reasoning," *Cambridge Inter-Faith Programme* (2007), para. 8. Accessible at http://themathesontrust.org/library/deep-calls.

Muslim, enabling participants to "pursue an activity native to those traditions."[3] Participants comment on the selected texts provoking thought and discussion. As this progresses, "texts open up unexpected meanings for those whose sacred texts they are, even at the same time as participants from the other Abrahamic traditions learn more about a text that is not theirs."[4] This process fits naturally into the framework of a dialogue of the Word, stimulating discussion and offering new insights. This differs from *lectio divina* but offers a technique that might be useful in a dialogue of spirituality.

The Tent of Meeting

Scriptural reasoning requires a special place. Regular participants will meet in a *tent*, defined as "a virtual space created by the scriptures and their readers when engaged in the practice itself."[5] This image, taken from the tent used by Abraham, Moses, Jesus, and Muhammad, especially reminds participants of Abraham who welcomed his unexpected visitors (see Gen 18).

As a place for hospitality, this tent is ideally suited for discussion, reconciliation, and building friendship, undertaken in the presence of God.[6] It allows participants to occupy a space in which "their respective histories, traditions and languages do not provide strict boundaries, and are not sources of exclusion."[7] In such a space all recognize that its neutrality allows each to

---

[3] Ibid., para. 12.

[4] Ibid.

[5] Daniel W. Hardy, Peter Ochs, and David F. Ford, "The Tent of Meeting," para. 13, in Quash, "Deep Calls to Deep."

[6] Ibid. includes this comment on the web site that has some relevance: "One of the heads of a religious order at the study day I led confessed to a remarkable event. The near collapse of his community, for financial and other reasons, had led its members collectively to decide on a process of discernment to which scripture study—study as a community and not just as individuals—was made central. He said it affected the most extraordinary renewal of their common life and their sense of purpose."

[7] Ibid., para. 46.

focus on the Inspired Scriptures, seeing difference as a resource, not a problem.

The Values of Scriptural Reasoning

In scriptural reasoning, the question-and-answer method leads to new insights and encourages all participants to greater understanding and appreciation. With time and honesty, all realize they should "not be afraid of argument, as one intellectually honest way of responding to differences—part of mutual hospitality is learning to argue in courtesy and truth."[8]

Arrangements ensure that sessions have enough time for all to reflect and participate on the topic. Each session starts with participants focusing on the chosen texts, allowing time for the meanings to unfold, first within its own traditional interpretation and then by interpretations from other traditions. After each session there should be time for relaxation, and time to talk about other issues. In this way friendship will grow and become "the most tangible anticipation of future peace."[9]

The Deeper Meanings of the Inspired Scriptures

The longer participants are exposed to texts from the Inspired Scriptures of each other, the more profound meanings that emerge, called, in the language of scriptural reasoning, "deep sense reading."

This method resonates with the spiritual insights that emerge in *lectio divina* from the Inspired Scriptures.[10] In "deep sense reading" the participants "find themselves taking the plain sense seriously but going beyond it, linking it with other texts, asking new questions of it, extending the meaning, discovering

---

[8] David F. Ford and C. C. Pecknold, *The Promise of Scriptural Reasoning*, 5.

[9] Ibid., 6.

[10] See the work of Henri de Lubac, especially *History and Spirit* (San Francisco: Ignatius Press, 2007). First French edition (Paris: Éditions Montaigne, 1950).

depths, resonances and applications that have not been suggested before."[11] This opens up new understandings.

Scriptural Reasoning and a Dialogue of Spirituality

In sessions of scriptural reasoning, the differences are particularly important because they challenge participants to think, reflect, and pose questions. In this way, the dialogue moves forward and participants find their understanding enlarged. Major differences remind participants of the importance of tolerance and patience.

In scriptural reasoning, all participants have a working knowledge of theology, probably more than those dedicated to a dialogue of spirituality. Not all those involved in a dialogue of spirituality will find scriptural reasoning appropriate. For the more theologically minded, it would sit easily alongside *lectio divina*; they are complementary.

[11] Hardy, Ochs, and Ford, "The Tent of Meeting," para. 23.

Chapter 32

Spiritual Guidance: Muslim and Christian

An important resource for Muslim and Christian participants in such a community of dialogue is easy access to a spiritual guide from their own tradition. Such a person would not be a member of the community but available to those members who seek affirmation from one sympathetic to the dialogue.

Such a dialogue presumes the presence of God alive in the hearts of participants. The varied contributions might cause strong feelings of elation, confusion, or despair. Discussion with an expert from outside will bring affirmation and encouragement.

The Starting Point for Spiritual Guidance

Many Muslims realize that "purification of the soul is a prerequisite for closeness to God."[1] For this to happen, expert help

---

[1] Mohammad Ali Shomali, "Spiritual Direction: An Islamic Perspective on Self-purification," in *Spiritual Message of Islam*, ed. Mohammad Ali Shomali, vol. 4, Islamic Reference Series (London: Institute of Islamic Studies, Islamic Centre of England, 2010), 15–36, here at 16.

may be required. Only when the soul is purified can the believer "meet God, Who is the Most Pure."[2] Muslims recognize that the important struggle is against the personal desire for independence and autonomy: the spiritual journey begins with a determination to submit to the will of God in all things.

Christians seeking God do not find all the answers in theological manuals or reading books about spirituality. Cyprian Smith writes, "If we wish to know and explore the world of the spirit, we can only do this by exposing ourselves to it, opening ourselves to it, be 'possessed' by it. The proper mode for the mind which wishes to know God is not the scientist with his microscope, but rather the flower which opens to the light."[3] Put another way, it is discovering that sense of wonder, which is the way to the divine. One role of the spiritual guide is to affirm the uniqueness of the spirituality of each participant and affirm the gifts that could arise from membership of this community.

Mohammad Ali Shomali defines spiritual problems as "sicknesses" that can only be healed by special medicine. "The human soul is a patient in need of a cure in need of medicine. . . . Unfortunately the most difficult sort of illness is the suffering deep inside."[4] The healing is part of the journey beginning at birth. It requires constant attention. Signposts can be missed, and the journey can lead away from God. According to a hadith, "people are asleep and only wake when they die. When they die, they wake and never go to sleep again. But at that point it is too late."[5] A community of dialogue is orientated to fulfilling its particular vocation, but all recognize that its work links clearly with the deeper calling in faith well expressed by Mohammad Ali Shomali: "Eternal life is the thing for which they must really

[2] Ibid.

[3] Cyprian Smith, OSB, *The Path of Life*, 52.

[4] Mohammad Ali Shomali, "Spiritual Direction" in *Spiritual Message of Islam*, 18.

[5] Ibid., 20.

prepare."[6] To prepare successfully for that may require an experienced spiritual guide as well as wholehearted commitment.

Christians learn about the spiritual life as they grow and become more committed. Basil Hume encouraged his monks saying, "You have the opportunity to pray, read and reflect."[7] This is the way to get to know yourself and your fellow participants in this particular community of dialogue. He added this wise advice: "Remember, if someone else is getting on your nerves, you are almost certainly getting on his."[8] Underlying progress in the spiritual life is the desire to be freed from the slavery of self-seeking so as to become wholeheartedly committed to the God who is Love. The spiritual guide should offer encouragement and affirmation.

Stages in Growth

Ali Shomali from the Muslim perspective offers five elements in a regime designed to face the bad habits for which "it is necessary to struggle and find a cure."[9]

First, controlling speech: "The heart becomes ill from saying things that are unnecessary."[10] Each learns "there is no worship like silence,"[11] remembering the saying that "silence is the garden of contemplation,"[12] because when people are silent "their mind starts to enjoy the beauty of the spiritual world."[13]

[6] Ibid., 24.

[7] Basil Hume, *Searching for God* (1977; repr. London: Hodder and Stoughton, 1978), 30.

[8] Ibid., 31.

[9] Mohammad Ali Shomali, "Spiritual Direction," in *Spiritual Message of Islam*, 27.

[10] Ibid., 29.

[11] Ibid., 30, quoting from Ghuraal al-Hakam wa Durar al-Kalim, no. 10471.

[12] Ibid.

[13] Mohammad Ali Shomali, "Spiritual Direction," 31.

Second, to restrict eating: "Fasting is very important and useful where it is possible,"[14] but when it is not, there should be a reduction in the food eaten.

Third, to limit sleep: "More sleep than is necessary is harmful for both the body and the spirit,"[15] as it saps the energy for work and prayer.

Fourth, each should find private time every day, essential for prayer, reflection, and reading.

Fifth, the believer should keep the remembrance of God constantly in mind. This is the obligation that keeps the other four together, achieved by remembering the names of God. Here the believer finds "medicine and if the medicine is taken in order to remember God then it is possible to be healed."[16]

One Christian approach into spirituality is to start by recognizing one's state of spiritual poverty. This awakens, as Basil Hume puts it, "a sense of dependence, enabling us peacefully to commend ourselves to God's providence and see in the activity of daily life his guiding hand."[17] This is the daily direction finder, especially in moments of distraction, anxiety, or difficulty. In this way the Christian learns humility, total dependence on the will of God. The more the Christian penetrates the wonder of God, the greater the sense of unworthiness and the more important is fidelity to the discipline of silence; there each listens to the Divine Word, both affirming the struggle and, occasionally, tickling the pride.

These points confirm one important truth: for Muslims and Christians, there are no shortcuts to deeper union with God. Within a community dedicated to a dialogue of spirituality, there is an important role for spiritual guides, Christian and Muslim, with appropriate experience.

---

[14] Ibid.
[15] Ibid.
[16] Ibid., 34.
[17] Basil Hume, *Searching for God*, 35.

Chapter **33**

Community Prayer through the Day

Sanctifying the Day

Both Christians and Muslims are obliged to pray regularly at different times during the day and night. Said Nursi writes, "We are told to pray at those specific times to give more adoration and glory to the All-Powerful One of Majesty and to give more thanks for the bounties accumulated between any two periods."[1] Such prayer reveals both the remembrance and forgetfulness of God, and at the same time encouraging participants to renew their commitment to God, the source of healing.

By fulfilling the obligation to pray, the Muslim enacts a fundamental duty to God: "Holiness requires us to see our defects and seek His pardon."[2]

Cyprian Smith affirms that regular prayer helps the Christian to remember God and the central role played by that relationship

---

[1] Bediüzzaman Said Nursi, *Belief and Worship*, from the Risale-i Nur Collection, Humanity's Encounter with the Divine Series (2002; repr. Sommerset, NJ: The Light Inc., 2006), 65.

[2] Ibid., 66.

301

throughout life, proposing that "a great many, perhaps all, of our spiritual problems are due to our innate tendency to *forget* God, to simply allow him to be crowded out of our lives";[3] regular reminders are important.

Said Nursi goes one step further and suggests the "prayer times remind us of the Divine Power's miracles and the Divine Mercy's gifts regardless of time or place."[4] True joy comes from appreciating the miracles of God. Nursi continues, "Our mentality and sense inspire us towards glorious objective and eternal gains but we are unable, impatient, powerless, and have only a short lifetime."[5] Prayer helps us accept such weaknesses in faith and offers a way to peace of mind, assured by God's special promises recorded in the Inspired Scriptures and available especially to the powerless and exploited.

For both Muslim and Christian, prayer is a discipline. The more frequent the prayer, the less likely God is forgotten. At the same time, prayer is a support in times of pain, loneliness, and helplessness, feelings that may afflict participants in a community of spiritual dialogue.

Prayer at Sunrise/Lauds

The Muslim prayer at sunrise may be "likened to spring's birth, the moment when sperm takes refuge in the protective womb, or to the first of the six consecutive days during which Earth and the sky were created."[6] It is a prayer of thanksgiving for new life and the renewal of life that comes with daylight.

For Christians, Lauds or Morning Prayer sanctifies the morning. Basil the Great writes, "No other care should engage us before we

---

[3] Cyprian Smith, *The Path of Life*, 124; emphasis his.

[4] Ibid., 69.

[5] Ibid., 70.

[6] Bediüzzaman Said Nursi, *The Words* (Sommerset, NJ: The Light, Inc., 2005), 58, The Ninth Word.

have been moved with the thought of God."[7] This morning office, normally celebrated at the hinge of dawn and daylight, also recalls the resurrection of Jesus Christ, the True Light.

Prayer in the Middle of the Day / Little Hours

For Nursi, the prayer in the middle of the day is likened "to the completion of adolescence, the middle of summer, or the period of humanity's creation in the world's lifetime."[8] These are the moments when believers remember God's compassionate love and blessings, midday being an appropriate moment to give thanks. By linking adolescence to the summer, Nursi is able to see this prayer as particularly important for those with the greatest energy and enthusiasm.

The Christian Little Hours, Terce, Sext, and None, are celebrated at the third (9:00), sixth (12:00), and ninth (15:00) hours, respectively. These are the moments to remember: first, Jesus' suffering, then his preparation for execution, and finally his crucifixion on Calvary—poignant moments for those dedicated to him in faith.

Nursi adds that the afternoon prayer "resembles autumn, old age, and the time of the Last Prophet (the Era of Happiness). It also calls to mind the Divine acts and the All-Compassionate favors in them."[9] Autumn, the time of retirement, allows more time for prayer, during which there are moments to repent of sin and give thanks for gifts.

Prayer in the Evening / Vespers

The moment of sunset marks the end of light and entry into darkness, reminding all of their mortality and offering a moment to prepare for death. This prayer includes the hope that

[7] Vatican, *Apostolic Constitution Promulgating the Divine Office* (Vatican City, 1971), in *The Divine Office*, vol. 1 (London: Collins, 1974), p. xl, para. 38.

[8] Bediüzzaman Said Nursi, *The Words*, 58.

[9] Ibid., 59.

after the destruction of the world, the time of resurrection will begin. From this Muslims can learn "how to understand the manifestation of God's Majesty,"[10] causing us to wake "from a deep sleep of neglect."[11] While facing the process of dying, all should ponder the final judgment and its possible consequences.

For Christians, Vespers or Evening Prayer is celebrated as dusk gives way to darkness. At that moment they give thanks for the gifts of the day, recalling the redemption achieved by Jesus and encouraging all to offer their lives to God, saying, "Let my prayer be counted as incense before you and the lifting up of my hands as an evening sacrifice" (Ps 141:2). Vespers also recalls the evening sacrifice of the Old Covenant and Jesus' Last Supper. At this moment they pray not only that the sun will rise again but that Jesus Christ, risen from the dead, will lead all to share that risen life.

Muslims and Christians pray at the same moment. One gives thanks and is reminded of the divine initiative for all people, while the other points to the completion of earthly life and its evaluation in judgment. Both look forward to the risen life promised to the faithful and are united in giving thanks for this gift, but divided in the place of prayer and the rituals used.

Prayer after Dark / Compline

As the day gives way to night, prayer focuses on decay and the fragility of earthly life. For both Muslims and Christians, this is a reminder of the coming judgment when God is manifested.

This time after dark for Muslims "calls to mind the world of darkness, veiling all daytime objects with its black shroud, and winter covering the dead Earth's surface with its white shroud."[12] The darkness of the night proclaims the power of God.

Christian Compline or Night Prayer is celebrated before going to bed; a short prayer of thanksgiving for the day just completed,

---

[10] Ibid.
[11] Ibid.
[12] Ibid.

including an examination of conscience and a prayer for God's protection while asleep.

Prayer during the Night / Vigils or Matins

Nursi has two reflections on prayer after nightfall, the first recalling the season of darkness, when the cold puts plants and animals into hibernation, birds have flown to warmer climates, and human activity is restricted. It is a time for silence, bringing "to mind the remaining works of the dead being forgotten, and points to this testing arena's inevitable, complete decline."[13] It is a moment for peaceful reflection on human vulnerability; those with independent living are invited to give reverent praise.

Later in the night, the prayer "reminds us of winter, the grave, the Intermediate World and how much our spirit needs the All-Merciful One's Mercy. The late-night '*tahajjud*' prayer reminds and warns us of how necessary this prayer's light will be in the grave's darkness."[14] The grave is a form of exile, challenging all to prepare for resurrection, especially those whose prayer is weak or incomplete. There is plenty of time for this prayer during these silent hours.

In the Christian monastic tradition, prayer during the night is either called Vigils, celebrated before midnight, or Matins, after midnight. It is a service with psalms and readings, the latter taken from the Bible and commentaries from fathers of the church or recognized spiritual authors. The service is more meditative, lasts longer, and allows time for silence. On Sundays and feast days it will end with a prayer of thanksgiving.

These moments of prayer during the night focus more easily on the One God, in praise and petition, in repentance and thanksgiving, considered by many as more effective—an insight affirmed by Muslim and Christian.

---

[13] Ibid.
[14] Ibid.

An Overall View

Nursi locates the Muslim cycle of daily prayer within the cycle of nature—of seasons, of the life span of plants and animals, and of human life from birth to death to new life—to remind participants that God the Creator is responsible for all that exists. By following this cycle of prayer, participants will be affirmed in their commitment to the dialogue.

Christians recognize the primary function of this "Work of God" as giving thanks and praise to God. At the same time it encourages participants to sanctify every moment of the day, reminding all that their work is done in the presence of God, under the guidance of God. In addition, since all prayer has an intercessory function, the celebration of these "hours of prayer" is undertaken on behalf of those in greatest need, believer or not, who have no one else to pray for them.

This cycle of prayer is relevant in a dialogue of spirituality; arranged appropriately to mark sessions of dialogue. In this way, both seek the help of God and allow the reflections of participants to enrich the prayer.

Praying sacred words learned by heart and singing the praises of God together, all will be affirmed, their memory of God magnified, and their commitment strengthened.

Insights from the Lived Wisdom of the Rule of Benedict Relevant to a Community in Dialogue

A View from the Outside

A Muslim View. Muslims often say that they have no monastic life. It is not entirely accurate, for they have a contemplative, disciplined, and prayerful spirit: Frithjof Schuon[1] called Islam "a 'monastery-society' . . . that is to say that Islam aims to carry the contemplative life into the very framework of society as a

---

[1] Frithjof Schuon (1907–98), b. Basel, moved to France with mother, Frithjof became a French citizen. Interest in "metaphysical truth," read the Upanishads, Bhagavad Gita, René Guénon. After military service began to study Arabic. In 1932 visited Algeria, met Shaykh Ahmad al-Alawi, initiated into his order. To Morocco 1935, then 1938–39 Egypt, met Guénon, with whom he corresponded for twenty-seven years. WWII asylum in Switzerland, granted Swiss nationality, home for forty years. Married in 1949. Twice visited the native American Indians. In 1980, with his wife, emigrated to the US where he continued to write until his death in 1998.

whole. . . . The famous 'no monasticism in Islam' means . . . the world must not be withdrawn from contemplatives";[2] a view supported by the evidence of devoted Muslims round the world.

If that is the case the Rule of Benedict will have a particular affinity for Muslims and be a useful starting point for Christians engaged in a dialogue of spirituality. Significantly, Ian Markham suggests that Said Nursi saw the importance of creating communities to live the virtues, outlined not only in the Qur'an but also in the Rule of Benedict, adding that "a case could be made for Nursi to be called an Islamic St. Benedict."[3]

Spirituality

Inspired Scriptures. Muslims would echo the Benedictine desire for deeper union with God. They would find some Benedictine prayers echo their own, like "prayer and meditation on scripture so that the Word of God enters the silence of his or her humble heart each day, bringing its transformative power to re-form the person in the life of God."[4]

An example of the Benedictine Rule being lived by laypeople as much as by monastics is the Manquehue Movement, founded in Santiago, Chile, in the early 1980s. For them, *lectio divina* is central. They reflect in small groups on chosen texts, reading, pondering, and tracing echoes from other parts of the Word of God. The tracing is done by each. Later, the members share their insights with their *lectio* community. They cherish silence because it allows "room for listening and responding to God in prayer."[5] Their weekly meeting ends with refreshments to

---

[2] Frithjof Schuon, "The Universality of Monasticism and Its Relevance in the Modern World," in *Merton and Sufism: The Untold Story*, ed. Rob Baker and Gary Henry (Louisville: Fons Vitae, 2005), 319–34, here at 322.

[3] Ian S. Markham, *Engaging with Bediuzzaman Said Nursi*, 22.

[4] Donald W. Mitchell, "Christian Kenosis," *Pro Dialogo* 1, no. 100 (Vatican City, 1999), 146.

[5] *The Little Rule for Oblates of the Manquehue Apostolic Movement*, 2nd ed., 6, 8:5-6.

relax and build friendship. Each member attends an occasional retreat and a monthly *convivencia*, when, after reflection, review, and prayer, all in the *lectio* community will "share in a well-prepared meal and it is brought to a conclusion with the *Our Father* and an embrace or kiss of peace,"[6] resulting in stronger faith, deeper relationship with the Word, and tangible mutual support in community.

Praying Together: The Experience of Others and the Role of the Psalms. Various Benedictine threads come together to support the high profile of prayer in this community of dialogue. The Little Rule of Manquehue emphasizes that the role of the Divine Office is to develop "the oblates' sense of belonging to the Community."[7]

Similarly, Gilles Nicholas likens the prayer of the Tibhirine community (quoting Thomas Merton) to trees, whose silent existence purifies the atmosphere during the night, thus allowing others to breathe the following day.[8] When the monks heard the Muslim call to prayer, it reminded them that their neighbor was also sanctifying the day by praising God. Christian de Chergé specifically used it as a moment to pray with Muslims, being spiritually enriched by the prayer of Islam, keeping Jesus at the center. When the local Muslim community asked him if they could pray in the monastery grounds while their mosque was being built, he agreed without hesitation.[9]

At the heart of the monastic office are the psalms. They guard the health of the soul, as Rowan Williams writes, "a healthy inhabiting of the world of the Psalms . . . the world of praise, the world of lament, the world of bafflement, sometimes of protest and anger, a world of the naked . . . a pattern of speaking with one another to God that allows all the areas of our human life

---

[6] Ibid., 9, 12:3-4.

[7] Ibid., 8, 10:11.

[8] See Robert Masson, *Tibhirine: Les Veilleurs de l'Atlas*, 224.

[9] Ibid., 215. Testimony of Claude Rault.

and experience to be inhabited by God the Holy Spirit."[10] They build stronger faith in a heart filled with hope, becoming the word of the lover to the Beloved.

Human Qualities of a Community of Dialogue

Soundness of Living. Rowan Williams uses this phrase as a pointer to the "wholeness" of the life proposed in Benedict's Rule. It is, in his words, about "listening . . . that is about the Sabbath rhythm of work and recreation, the breathing out and the breathing in without which nobody lives sanely."[11] The community of dialogue should not be dominated by frenetic targets, nor be detached from the life of the world. Rather its life should be marked by quiet purpose: in short, a community oriented to the gift of holiness, or, in Rowan Williams' words, a "discipline for being where you are, rather than taking refuge in the infinite smallness of your own fantasies."[12] From this perspective, such a community should be balanced and open.

Community Life. Alongside its spiritual aims, the Manquehue Movement has a deeper intention: to build a stronger community for laypeople, of all ages, achieved through *lectio* groups and sharing a common work in education or formation. In this way friendship grows stronger. Inspired by Christ, they learn to open their hearts to "love that other person, to make space in one's thinking and listen to another among all the preoccupations

[10] Rowan Williams, "Sound in Spirit, Soul and Body" (Malling Abbey Sermon, September 12, 2006), para. 6, http://rowanwilliams .archbishopofcanterbury.org/articles.php/1592/sound-in-spirit-soul -and-body-malling-abbey-sermon.

[11] Ibid., para 10.

[12] Rowan Williams, "Shaping Holy Lives: A Conference on Benedictine Spirituality" (Trinity Wall Street, New York, April 29, 2003), para. 22, http://rowanwilliams.archbishopofcanterbury.org/articles .php/654/shaping-holy-lives-a-conference-on-benedictine-spirituality.

and tasks that absorb the mind"[13]—an ideal recognized by both Muslim and Christian.

This also happens through the mature charity of community, defined by Rowan Williams, as "an unselfconscious getting used to others,"[14] or is built on friendship, again in Rowan Williams's words, "as a tool worn smooth and grey in the hand."[15] Such qualities are found among people who have an accurate knowledge of themselves, are relaxed in the company of others, and have nothing to prove and plenty to offer.

Stability. This is a relationship founded on truthfulness and respect, expressed succinctly by Rowan Williams: "I promise that I will not hide from you—and that I will also, at times, help you not to hide from me or from yourself."[16] The Benedictine Rule requires a lifelong commitment; each is gift or trial to the other. In that context a community in a dialogue of spirituality will take time to truly fulfill its vocation.

Consultation and Decision Making. Communities living the Rule of Benedict know that each has a stake in its well-being, or, as Rowan Williams writes, a "commitment to the community is the ground upon which the right to be heard is based,"[17] and "in which a great deal of listening goes on."[18] The expectation is "always that the other carries to you a word of Christ."[19] Regular meetings and well-set-out agendas should provide all with an opportunity to contribute: an essential feature of a community in dialogue.

---

[13] *The Little Rule for Oblates*, 6, 7:8-10.

[14] Rowan Williams, "Shaping Holy Lives," para. 4.

[15] Ibid.

[16] Ibid., para. 17.

[17] Rowan Williams, "Benedict and the Future of Europe" (speech at San Anselmo, Rome, November 21, 2006), para. 12, http://rowanwilliams .archbishopofcanterbury.org/articles.php/1770/benedict-and-the-future -of-europe-speech-at-st-anselmo-in-rome.

[18] Rowan Williams, "Sound in Spirit, Soul and Body," para. 4.

[19] Ibid., para. 5.

Do They Encourage a Decision to Go Ahead?

There are many initiatives promoting Muslim-Christian dialogue in local communities and at national and international levels. This proposal for a community dedicated to a dialogue of spirituality is not so common—indeed quite rare. The advice offered here from the Christian and Muslim viewpoints is helpful: it starts to build bridges before any dialogue can start. This selected group of themes provides some guidance. At one level, it is the commitment of faith by the participants that will take the dialogue forward.

Part 7

*Seeking Inspiration and Encouragement:
Can Anyone Inspire?*

Chapter **35**

Christian de Chergé and Islam: Teaching That Points to the Future

Christian Salenson[1] has studied the theology and spirituality of de Chergé's writings; his book shows the novelty of de Chergé's thinking.[2]

Reflecting on his own journey into the spirituality of Islam, de Chergé wrote, "We believe we are called together, all of us, both to worship the One God and to share with all,"[3] affirming the overriding importance of this One God, "I have always known that the God of Islam and the God of Jesus Christ do not make two."[4]

---

[1] Christian Salenson, priest of the diocese of Nimes, France, onetime rector of the Seminary of Avignon, today director of the *Institut de science et de théologie des religions de Marseille*. He has published *Prier 15 Jours avec Christian de Chergé* (Nouvelle Cité), *Catéchèses mystagogiques pour aujourd'hui* (Bayard), and *Christian de Chergé: Une théologie de l'espérance* (Bayard, 2009).

[2] Christian Salenson, *Christian de Chergé: Une théologie de l'espérance* (Bayard: Publications Chemins de Dialogue, 2009), and in English, *Christian de Chergé: A Theology of Hope* (Collegeville, MN: Liturgical Press, 2012).

[3] Ibid., 38.

[4] Ibid., 42.

This reflection focusing on a theme of Muslim spirituality already discusses that God is merciful to the repentant sinner. For de Chergé this shows

> that the plan of God for Christianity and Islam remains constant: to invite us both to the table of sinners. The multiplied bread which is given to us to break together is bread of an absolute trust in the mercy of the All-Powerful. When we consent to meet in this sharing, doubly brothers and sisters because we are both prodigal and forgiven, it becomes possible for us. . . . to listen to and recognize one and the same word of God offering us its richness of life, one and the same Word offered to the multitude in the remission of sins.[5]

As convicted sinners, de Chergé continues, "The world would be less of a desert if we could recognize for ourselves a common vocation: to multiply the fountains of mercy along the way,"[6] and to remember that "our paths converge when one and the same thirst draws us to the same well."[7] The One Merciful, Compassionate, and Forgiving God is the One point where we meet God. Muslim and Christian stand in line, side by side, seeking that forgiveness of sins, so often impossible for us to seek from each other.

Another element of this Forgiving God is that our respective revelations cannot be reconciled because "it is always from beyond our reason that God comes to us, whatever our respective faiths may be."[8] By abandoning the stereotypes of centuries, Christians and Muslims need to be in a dialogue that allows God to "create something new between us. This cannot happen except in prayer."[9]

Both the Muslim and the Christian are called to prayer, whether by muezzin or bell. When the sound is heard, de Chergé

---

[5] Ibid., 45.
[6] Ibid.
[7] Ibid., 49.
[8] Ibid., 55.
[9] Ibid., 54.

recognizes he cannot remain indifferent: "On the contrary, they provoke me to engage in prayer. . . . No one but God can call to prayer";[10] for de Chergé "the calls to prayer establish between us [Muslims and Christian monks] a healthy reciprocal emulation."[11]

The call from God is answered by Muslims who show their commitment by "ablutions and preparations, a formulation of intention. . . . And then, there is the ritual psalmody. . . . And the Qurʾan is to be received and interpreted within this framework, exactly as the Word of God is the kernel of our *opus dei* in our liturgies."[12]

At Tibhirine, the monastic community was "able to join the experience of Muslims who pray and also to let ourselves be recognized by them [as ones who pray]."[13] The unique importance of this prayer to the One God is that it brings Muslim and Christian together before God as one in that belief. He writes, "We do not want to get involved in a theological dialogue with you, because this has often erected barriers which are of human handiwork. But we feel called by God to unity."[14] So the highest priority for his community is "to allow ourselves to be caught up, as deeply as possible, in the prayer of the other, if I want to be more than a Christian presence among Muslims. I have a vocation to unite myself to Christ through the one who lifts up every prayer and who offers to the Father, mysteriously, this prayer of Islam along with the prayer of every upright heart."[15]

From this perspective, he develops another theme: "Both Muslims and Christians are marked by the call of the Beyond,"[16] but that will require a commitment to build friendship and so "make

---

[10] Ibid., 181–82.
[11] Ibid., 182.
[12] Ibid., 183.
[13] Ibid.
[14] Ibid., 184.
[15] Ibid., 185.
[16] Ibid., 131.

things better between us, here and now,"[17] for God comes to us from "beyond the horizon of our reason . . . whatever our respective faiths, and we can truly expect something new each time we make the effort to decipher the signs of the Beyond at the horizons of worlds and of hearts."[18] This additional revelation from the other is perhaps one of the most important insights de Chergé offers. It comes as an experience of the divine, not as a result of theological discourse. At its heart it enables us "to recognize and welcome the portion of truth lodged in the heart of a brother."[19] Because we find that "our thirst and love for the Truth . . . exists only within God. Those who make an effort to grow in this way in mutual love cannot fail to progress together toward the Truth that surpasses them and unites them in infinity."[20] It is at this point that participants in a dialogue of spirituality will find themselves inspired by the insights of the other.

At the same time, de Chergé is realistic about dialogue. He warns that all should keep their "feet firmly planted on the ground (or even in the manure) but our head exploring the heavens."[21] He affirms that in dialogue all can expect "a new thing each time we make the effort to discern [humility's] 'signs' at the 'horizons' of worlds and hearts by becoming listeners and also students of the other."[22] He continues, "Believers of good faith should always begin with a joint recognition that God is calling us to humility. . . . We renounce any claim to be better or superior."[23] In this way "the faith of the other is a gift from God, albeit a mysterious one. Therefore it commands respect. . . . And this gift given to the other is also intended for me, to urge me in the direction of what I have to profess. To

[17] Ibid.
[18] Ibid.
[19] Ibid., 174.
[20] Ibid.
[21] Ibid., 56.
[22] Ibid., 58.
[23] Ibid., 57.

neglect it is to fail to contemplate the work of the Spirit and our share of this work."[24]

Christian de Chergé understands the Qurʾan to be "what the other has received as properly his own to cultivate within him the taste of God."[25] This leads logically to his view that "a genuine *lectio divina* of the Qurʾan is possible."[26] In response to the Sufi use of the gospels with their strong echo for Muslims, de Chergé asks, "Could we not let the Book of Islam resound, in the stillness of an interior listening, with the desire and the respect of these brothers who draw from it their taste for God?"[27] He relates that "quite often I have seen arising from the Qurʾan, in the course of an initially difficult and disconcerting reading, a shortcut of the Gospel, as it were, which then becomes a true path of communion with the other and with God."[28]

It follows that the Word of God, in de Chergé's eyes, is "present to Christians and Muslims as a viaticum, provisions for the crossing of the desert. The Scriptures are the treasure where the Christian loves to seek day and night for the new and the old"[29]—a confirmation of the spirituality of the Word outlined above.

On the role of Christ, de Chergé offers this approach: "The very meaning of the Incarnation is not primarily that the Word should become flesh, but that our flesh should be brought into the divine milieu of the Word";[30] its purpose is our conversion, for "I am sure that the Christ of the Qurʾan has something to do with the Christ of our faith."[31] Therefore, "in order to enter in truth into dialogue we will have to accept, in the name of Christ, that Islam has something to tell us on behalf

[24] Ibid., 58.
[25] Ibid., 67.
[26] Ibid., 65.
[27] Ibid., 68.
[28] Ibid., 72.
[29] Ibid., 71.
[30] Ibid., 88.
[31] Ibid., 92.

of Christ."[32] Salenson explains, "Given that salvific mediation operates within Islam, and given that Christians cannot claim to know everything about the Christ who transcends religious boundaries, Christians must receive also the Christ of Islam."[33] Christians conclude that "we let ourselves be moved, and the Spirit of Jesus remains free to do its work among us, making use of our differences, even those that shock us. We recognize the Spirit working. We receive from prolonged silent prayer, side by side, notably with our Sufi friends, a feeling of fulfillment all the more trustworthy for being known as deeply shared. God knows it much better than we do."[34]

In this way de Chergé keeps participants in dialogue focused on God's perspective. Inspired by the Holy Spirit, he continues:

> We are a people on the move between heaven and earth, astonished to discern this evolution of communion whose web the Holy Spirit is weaving among all people; for all, absolutely all, have been marked with the seal of sanctity in the image and likeness of thrice-holy God: this is our faith, but only the truly poor in spirit understand. . . . Since the Spirit began to circulate freely between heaven and earth, there is no longer any visible boundary among people.[35]

In the One God there can be no divisions, a logical conclusion from the path of prayer, *lectio divina / dhikr* and contemplation; the fulfillment of the path to God Who is Love. De Chergé continues, "It is up to us visibly to signify along with all the other mysteries of the Kingdom this *beyond* of the communion of saints, where Christians and Muslims share the same joy of sons and daughters."[36]

In that vision a community of dialogue is possible if all participants are "open to the contemplation of the wonders of God

[32] Ibid., 93.
[33] Ibid., 92.
[34] Ibid., 101.
[35] Ibid., 102, 104.
[36] Ibid., 105.

hidden in each person, signs of the One God written upon our faces as so many differences promised to the communion of saints, even if, necessarily for a little while these things are difficult for us to see."[37] For those perplexed he offers this clarification: "Seeing things differently does not mean that one is not seeing the same things,"[38] and "speaking otherwise of God is not speaking of another God,"[39] for "filled with the gift of the Spirit whose secret joy will always be to establish communion and restore the likeness, playing with differences,"[40] and "if differences really come from unity, they must logically tend to return to it,"[41] so "it is important that God be what each of us, from our respective faiths, say God is, and more than that for all";[42] God transcends human thought.

Three statements summarize de Chergé's spiritual theology:

1. "It is at the table of sinners that I learn best of all to become a sign . . . of the promised mystery of the communion of saints. The multiplied loaves that we Christians and Muslims are given to break together are the bread of absolute trust in the mercy of God alone. When we accept to discover each anew in this sharing, doubly brother, both prodigal and pardoned, there can be a celebration among us something of the feast ordained from all eternity to gather us together into his House."[43]

2. "To wish to see or imagine the future is to make a fiction out of hope, and this seems to me to be doing violence to hope. . . . Obviously, since we do not have God's imagination, when we think of the future, we think of it in terms of the past. . . . When we are in a tunnel, we see nothing,

[37] Ibid., 108–9.
[38] Ibid., 115.
[39] Ibid.
[40] Ibid., 116.
[41] Ibid., 117.
[42] Ibid., 129.
[43] Ibid., 129–30.

but it is absurd to want the landscape when we come out to be the same as when we went in. . . . Let us let the Holy Spirit do its work. . . . It is the Spirit's business: this is what I call poverty."[44]

3. "I will decipher it [that is, the answer to the question concerning the place of Islam in the plan of God] in the dazzling Easter light of Him who presents himself to me as the only possible Muslim, because he is all Yes to the will of the Father."[45]

In these paragraphs we find a unified framework for dialogue beginning with a joint commitment to trust the mercy of God. This opens up a path for dialogue, relying on prayer rather than theology. In this way both have access to the life *beyond*, a future in God. To achieve this, the dialogue should be conducted with humility, recognizing that inspiration comes from both sides. To help this he encourages Christians to engage in *lectio divina* with their Muslim partners, using both Inspired Scriptures.

Affirming the role of Christ underlines difference but opens up a path for the Spirit to work, providing strength and insight to deal with the challenge of difference. Only in the resurrection will participants fully understand the true significance of their shared insights. Until then, both have access to the endless mercy of the One God.

It is clear from the above that Christian de Chergé offers an encouragement to Christians seeking a closer dialogue of spirituality with Islam, based on prayerful reflection on the Word of God revealed to each.

Christians and Muslims living and working alongside each other will find time and are encouraged to share their Inspired Scriptures and in that sense build a culture of mutual respect, each becoming more aware of the Revelation of the One God of Mercy and Compassion.

---

[44] Ibid., 195.
[45] Ibid., 39.

Can Anyone Inspire?

For anyone who has seen the film *Of Gods and Men*, these lines from the Tibhirine community need no further explanation. The film shows the Christian community of Trappist monks engaged closely with the lives of their local Muslim community. The extent of the friendship was shown by the deeply felt loss at their deaths and the subsequent closure of the monastery.

It was their decision to live simply alongside a fervent Muslim community in rural Algeria. They honored that commitment by refusing to leave when encouraged to do so. The result is that they have become a special inspiration for a dialogue of spirituality.

There, Muslims and Christians formed a single community of faith in the One God, divided in prayer but united in their support for each other, divided in their religious festivals but united in respecting those of the other.

They have offered witness to what could be developed in other places with people of similar commitment to the One God of Love and Mercy, passionate to lead all to the union of eternal life in the resurrection. They are an inspiration. To go forward still needs strong faith and courage. If it is God's will, it will happen.

36

No Peace without Prayer: Encouraging Muslims and Christians to Pray Together; A Twelve-Point Summary

Point One: There can be no peace in our world without peace between Muslims and Christians, the two largest religions.

Point Two: There can be no peace between Muslims and Christians without a dialogue of spirituality, enabling each to grow in respect of the other's faith.

Point Three: A dialogue of spirituality between Muslims and Christians can only be based on the Inspired Word, revealed to each in a unique way.

Point Four: There can be no dialogue with the Inspired Word without recognition that both confess their faith in the One God.

Point Five: There can be no recognition of the One God unless each accepts that this God is Omnipotent, Creator, Revealer through Word, a Word of Love, offering mercy and forgiveness to the repentant sinner and promising a vision of risen life after death.

Point Six: This dialogue of spirituality should take place in an atmosphere of prayer, during which Muslims and Christians can share their insights into the Inspired Word.

Point Seven: This dialogue of spirituality is not primarily intended for religious authorities and theologians, Muslim and Christian. Their legitimate vocations are to define their respective boundaries, separating Truth from error and establishing *difference*.

Point Eight: This dialogue of spirituality is proposed for the local level, where Muslims and Christians live alongside each other as neighbors, colleagues at work, or sources of support for those in need, irrespective of faith.

Point Nine: Those taking part in this dialogue of spirituality stand confidently within their own belief, confess their faith in the One God, acknowledging that their Inspired Scriptures show God to be passionately interested in every person, with or without faith. An appropriate way to start this dialogue of spirituality is to form small groups.

Point Ten: This is one approach to a dialogue of spirituality. There is room for others. The more secular and materialistic the world becomes, the more likely difference will grow stronger and communication break down: violence and war are possible results.

Point Eleven: I have met many Muslims and Christians in my travels who are keen to see such encouragement and leadership do just this. They realize there can be no lasting peace without believers sharing their Inspired Scriptures and praying together.

Point Twelve: Some people may ask if this proposal excludes those of the Jewish faith. The answer is of course not. Just as scriptural reasoning, as discussed earlier, includes Jews, so could these dialogues if they were willing to take part. It is very encouraging to note that Pope Francis is already thinking along these lines.

These twelve points provide an outline of something new. Such an initiative, blessed by God, raises the possibility of lasting peace founded on ever-greater mutual respect. Christians, Muslims, and if appropriate, Jews could become partners in bringing greater mutual appreciation and respect of each other in the context of this dialogue of spirituality. As partners, each offers a life of faith in a revealing God who promises an eternity of love fulfilled.

Appendix
How Might We Start?

There may be some readers who would like advice on how to proceed in seeking to build a relationship with their local community, Christian or Muslim, in a dialogue of spirituality.

I offer these suggestions, recognizing that dialogue is not a difficult skill.

Here are some preliminary questions:

First, ask yourself whether you are committed to your own faith, Islam or Christianity, and have the time and commitment to learn the skills of this form of dialogue.

Second, I suggest you identify friends of your faith and of the other faith. These may be family friends, colleagues at work, or friends who share common interests. From these, your first community will be formed. An essential skill is that all participants should be willing to share their own Scriptures and listen to others sharing theirs. In this sharing all are encouraged to speak from their own experience in daily life and in prayer.

Third, after the group has formed and the numbers are balanced, all meet to arrange a place and a time for the first meeting. Then, determine the length of the meetings, the texts to be used, and themes to be covered. Those more knowledgeable in their faiths may be consulted as necessary.

Fourth, arrange the first meeting. This structure is offered as a guide:

1. Choose a time and a place for meeting that all can attend.

2. Choose a topic, agreed on by all.

3. For the chosen topic, find one relevant text in each of the Inspired Scriptures (Bible and Qurʾan).

4. At the first meeting outline the format:

   a. Recall the agreed theme.

   b. Read the chosen text from the Inspired Scriptures.

   c. A period of silence, as agreed (five to ten minutes), to ponder and reflect.

   d. The one who chose the text offers a reflection on it (not more than five minutes). A short period of silence follows, and then members of the group each offer his/her own reflections on the text (each not more than five minutes). This can be done spontaneously or the group may decide a specific order. All participants are encouraged to say something. (Some may want to make notes of what has been said as a reminder—the group would agree how such notes might be used subsequently as a record of the dialogue.)

   e. After the last response, a further period of silence allows all to reflect on what has been said. The one who opened that meeting brings the session to a close. There follows a period for relaxation, discussion, and, if appropriate, refreshments.

   f. The process is repeated for the second text.

   g. At the end, over refreshments, participants may share further thoughts and ideas. Plans would be made for the next meeting, at a date, time, and place convenient for all.

5. Once the group is happy with its way of working, it can reflect on how the insights of each can be recorded to provide that evidence of a new shared spiritual memory, mentioned earlier. This, in the first instance, is a private record for participants; only later will it be available to others.

Bibliography

Benedictine

Baker, Augustine. *Holy Wisdom Directions for the Prayer of Contemplation*. Wheathampstead: Anthony Clarke Books, 1972.

Barry, Patrick, trans. *Saint Benedict's Rule*. York: Ampleforth Abbey Press (Gracewing), 1997.

Bianchi, Enzo. *Praying the Word*. Cistercian Studies Series 182. Kalamazoo: Cistercian Publications, 1998 (1992).

Burrows, Ruth. *Interior Castle Explored*: *St Teresa's Teaching on the Life of Deep Union with God*. London: Sheed and Ward, 1981.

Cary-Elwes, Columba, and Catherine Wybourne. *Work and Prayer: The Rule of St Benedict for Lay People*. Tunbridge: Wells, Burns & Oates, 1992.

Casey, Michael. *Sacred Reading: The Ancient Art of Lectio Divina*. Liguori: Liguori/Triumph, 1996.

———. *The Undivided Heart: The Western Approach to Contemplation*. Petersham: St Bede's Publications, 1994.

Clément, Olivier. *The Roots of Christian Mysticism*. London: New City, 1993 (French original, 1982).

De Lubac, Henri. *History and Spirit: The Understanding of Scripture according to Origen*. San Francisco: Ignatius Press, 2007 (French original, 1950).

Driot, Marcel. *Fathers of the Desert: Life and Spirituality*. Slough: St Paul's Publications, 1992 (1991).

Ford, David F., and C. C. Pecknold. *The Promise of Scriptural Reasoning.* Oxford: Blackwell Publishing, 2006.

Fry, Timothy, ed. *The Rule of St. Benedict in English, RB80.* Collegeville, MN: Liturgical Press, 1982.

Hart, Patrick, ed. *Survival or Prophecy?: The Correspondence of Jean Leclercq and Thomas Merton.* Monastic Wisdom Series 17. Collegeville, MN: Liturgical Press, 2008.

Hume, Basil. *Searching for God.* London: Hodder and Stoughton, 1978 (1977).

Illich, Ivan. *In the Vineyard of the Text: A Commentary to Hugh's Didascalicon.* Chicago: University of Chicago Press, 1996 (1993).

Kiser, John W. *The Monks of Tibhirine.* New York: St. Martin's Press, 2003.

Leclercq, Jean. *The Love of Learning and the Desire for God: A Study of Monastic Culture.* London: SPCK, 1978 (1961).

———. *Alone with God.* Bloomingdale: Ercam Editions, 2008 (1961).

Magrassi, Mariano. *Praying the Bible: An Introduction to Lectio Divina.* Collegeville, MN: Liturgical Press, 1998 (1990).

Salenson, Christian. *Christian de Chergé: A Theology of Hope.* Translated by Nada Conic. Collegeville, MN: Liturgical Press, 2012.

Smith, Cyprian. *The Path of Life.* York: Ampleforth Abbey Press (Gracewing), 1995.

Stewart, Columba. *Prayer and Community: The Benedictine Tradition, Traditions of Christianity Series.* London: Darton, Longman & Todd, 1998.

Ward, Benedicta, trans. *The Desert Fathers: Saying of the Early Christian Monks.* London: Penguin, 2003.

General, Including Dialogue

Baker, Rob, and Gray Henry, ed. *Merton and Sufism: The Untold Story.* Louisville: Fons Vitae, 2005 (1999).

Bulliet, Richard W. *The Case for Islamo-Christian Civilization.* New York: Columbia University Press, 2004.

Cornille, Catherine, ed. *Criteria of Discernment in Interreligious Dialogue*. Eugene, OR: Cascade Books, 2009.

Cutsinger, James S., ed. *Paths to the Heart: Sufism and the Christian East*. Bloomington, World Wisdom, 2004 (Kindle edition).

de Chergé, Christian. *L'Invincible espérance*. Paris: Bayard, 1997.

Elliott, Charles. *Memory and Salvation*. London: Darton, Longman & Todd, 1995.

Gioia, Francesco, ed. *Interreligious Dialogue: The Official Teaching of the Catholic Church 1963–2005*. Boston: Pauline Books & Media, 2006.

Griffith, Sidney H. *The Church in the Shadow of the Mosque: Christians and Muslims in the World of Islam*. Princeton: Princeton University Press, 2008.

Gude, Mary Louise. *Louis Massignon: The Crucible of Compassion*. Notre Dame: University of Notre Dame Press, 1996.

Ipgrave, Michael, ed. *Scriptures in Dialogue: Christians and Muslims Studying the Bible and the Qurʾan Together*. London: Church House Publishing, 2007 (2004).

May, Gerald G. *Addiction and Grace*. HarperCollins e-books (Kindle edition).

Netton, Ian Richard. *Islam: Christianity and Tradition, a Comparative Exploration*. Edinburgh: Edinburgh University Press, 2006.

———. *Islam, Christianity and the Mystic Journey: A Comparative Exploration*. Edinburgh: Edinburgh University Press, 2011.

O'Mahony, A., Wulstan Peterburs, and Mohammad Ali Shomali, eds. *Catholic and Shi'a in Dialogue: Studies in Theology and Spirituality*. London: Melisende, 2004.

———. *A Catholic-Shi'a Engagement: Faith and Reason in Theory and Practice*. London: Melisende, 2006.

O'Mahony, A., Timothy Wright, and Mohammad Ali Shomali, eds. *Catholic-Shi'a Dialogue: Ethics in Today's Society*. London: Melisende, 2008.

Ong, Walter J. *Orality and Literacy: The Technologizing of the Word*. London: Routledge, 2010 (1982).

Ratzinger, Joseph Cardinal. *Truth and Tolerance*. San Francisco: Ignatius Press, 2004 (German original, 2003).

Volf, Miroslav. *The End of Memory: Remembering Rightly in a Violent World*. Grand Rapids, MI: Eerdmans, 2006.

———. *Allah: A Christian Response*. HarperCollins e-books (Kindle edition).

Islam

ʿAbbād of Ronda, Ibn. *Letters on the Sūfī Path*. New York: Paulist Press, 1986.

Afsaruddin, Asma. *The First Muslims: History and Memory*. Oxford: Oneworld, 2008.

Ali, Maulana Muhammad. *The Holy Qurʾān*. Columbus, OH: Ahmadiyya Anjuman Isha'at Islam Lahore, 2002 (1917).

Al-ʿArabī, Ibn. *The Ringstones of Wisdom*. Chicago: Great Books of the Islamic World, 2004.

Armstrong, Karen. *Muhammad: A Biography of the Prophet*. London: Phoenix, 2001 (1991).

Asad, Muhammad. *The Message of the Qurʾān*. Bristol: Book Foundation, 2003.

Bulliet, Richard W. *Islam: A View from the Edge*. New York: Columbia University Press, 1994.

Chittick, William C., trans. *The Psalms of Islam*. Qom: Bargozedah Publications. No date given.

———, ed. *The Essential Seyyed Hossein Nasr*. Bloomington: World Wisdom, 2007.

Dehlvi, Sadia. *Sufism: the Heart of Islam*. New Delhi: Harper Collins Publishers India / The India Today Group, 2010.

Eaton, Charles Le Gai. *Remembering God: Reflections on Islam*. Chicago: ABC International Group, 2000.

Al-Ghazālī, Muhammad. *The Ninety-Nine Beautiful Names of God*. Cambridge: Islamic Texts Society, 2009 (1992).

———. *Remembrance and Prayer: The Way of Prophet Muhammad*. Markfield: Islamic Foundation, 2000 (1992).

Haleem, M. A. S. Abdel, trans. *The Qurʾan: English Translation and Parallel Arabic Text*. Oxford: Oxford University Press, 2004 (Kindle edition).

Haleem, M. A. S. Abdel. *Understanding the Qurʾan: Themes and Style*. London: IB Taurus, 2011 (1999).

Jafari, Allameh MT. *The Mystery of Life: A Secret inside Secrets*. Tehran: Allameh Jafari Institute, 2005.

Johns, A. H. *Jonah in the Qurʾan: An Essay on Thematic Counterpoint in The Journal of Qurʾanic Studies*. Vol. 5. London: School of Oriental and African Studies, London University, 2003.

Kung, Hans. *Islam: Past, Present and Future*. Oxford: Oneworld, 2007.

Maneri, Sharafuddin. *The Hundred Letters*. New York: Paulist Press, 1980.

———. *In Quest of God: Maneri's Second Collection of 150 Letters*. Gujarat: Gujarat Sahitya Prakash, 2004.

———. *A Mine of Meaning*. Louisville, KY: Fons Vitae, 2012.

Markham, Ian S. *Engaging with Bediuzzaman Said Nursi: A Model of Interfaith Dialogue*. Farnham: Ashgate Publishing, 2009.

Nasr, Seyyed Hossein. *The Garden of Truth: The Vision and Promise of Sufism, Islam's Mystical Tradition*. New York: HarperOne, 2007.

———. *Ideals and Realities of Islam*. London: George Allen & Unwin, 1971 (1966).

———. *Knowledge and the Sacred*. New York: State University of New York Press, 1989.

———. *The Heart of Islam: Enduring Values for Humanity*. San Francisco: HarperSanFrancisco, 2004 (2002).

Nicholson, R. A. (Ali bin Uthaman al-Hujwiri), trans. *The Kashf Al-Mahjub*. New Delhi: Adam Publishers and Distributors, 2009.

Nursi, Bediüzzaman Said. *The Reasonings: A Key to Understanding the Qurʾanʾs Eloquence (Risale-I Nur Collection)*. Sommerset, NJ: Tughra Books, 2008.

———. *The Words: The Reconstruction of Islamic Belief and Thought, from the Risale-I Nur Collection*. Clifton, NJ: The Light, 2005.

Padwick, Constance E. *Muslim Devotions*. London: SPCK, 1961.

Ruthven, Malise. *Islam in the World*. London: Granta Books, 2006 (1984).

———. *Islam: A Very Short Introduction*. Oxford: Oxford University Press, 2000 (1997).

Schuon, Frithjof. *Sufism: Veil and Quintessence*. Edited by James S. Cutsinger. Bloomington: World Wisdom, 2006 (Kindle edition).

Shakir, Muhammed S. *The Glorious Quran*. Qum: Ansariyan Publications, 2001.

Shomali, Mohammad Ali. *Mary, Jesus, and Christianity: An Islamic Perspective*. London: Institute of Islamic Studies, 2007.

———. *Apostle of God, Islamic Reference Series*. Vol 3. London: Institute of Islamic Studies, 2009.

———. *ShiʾI Islam: Origins, Faith and Practices*. London: Islamic College for Advanced Studies Press, 2003.

———, ed. *Spiritual Message of Islam: Islamic Reference Series 4*. London: Institute of Islamic Studies, 2010.

Siddiqui, Mona. *How to Read the Qurʾan*. London: Granta Books, 2007.

Smith, Margaret. *Readings from the Mystics of Islām*. London: Luzac & Co., 1972 (1950).

———. *Rābiʾa the Mystic and Her Fellow Saints*. Lampeter: Llanerch Publishers, 1994 (1928).

Sultan, Sohaib. *The Koran for Dummies*. Indianapolis: Wiley Publishing, 2004.

Tabarsi, Hassan Ibn Fazl Ibn Hassan. *The Lamp Niche for the Best Traditions*. Qum: Ansariyan Publications, 2007.

Wheeler, Brannon M. *Prophets in the Quran: An Introduction to the Quran and Muslim Exegesis*. London: Continuum, 2002.

Reference

The Catechism of the Catholic Church. London: Geoffrey Chapman, 1994.

Abbott, Walter M., ed. *The Documents of Vatican II*. London: Geoffrey Chapman, 1966.

Brown, Raymond, Joseph A. Fitzmyer, and Roland E. Murphy, eds. *The New Jerome Biblical Commentary*. London: Geoffrey Chapman, 1990 (1968).

Esposito, John L. *The Oxford Dictionary of Islam*. Oxford: Oxford University Press, 2003.

Geoghegan, Jeffrey, and Michael Homan. *The Bible for Dummies*. Hoboken, NJ: Wiley Publishing, 2003.

Glassé, Cyril. *The New Encyclopedia of Islam*. Walnut Creek, CA: Altamira Press, 2002 (1989).

Greaves, Ron. *Key Words in Islam*. London: Continuum International Publishing Group, 2006.

Kassis, Hanna E. *A Concordance of the Qur'an*. Berkeley: University of California Press, 1983.

Léon-Dufour, Xavier, ed. *Dictionary of Biblical Theology*. London: Geoffrey Chapman, 1967 (1962).

McKenzie, John L. *Dictionary of the Bible*. London: Geoffrey Chapman, 1965.

Netton, Ian Richard. *A Popular Dictionary of Islam*. Richmond: Surrey, Curzon Press, 1992.

Electronic and CD-ROM

BibleWorks, LLC. *BibleWorks 8*. Norfolk, VA, 2008.

Encyclopedia of Islam Vols. 1–12. Leiden: Brill Academic Publishers, 2004.

Encyclopedia of the Qur'ān. Edited by Jane Dammen McAuliffe. Leiden: Brill Academic Publishers, 2008.

Fathers of the Church: Christian Classic Ethereal Library, Grand Rapids: Calvin College, 2007. http://www.ccel.org/.

Hadith Collections: See www.sahih-bukhari.com or www.msawest .net/islam.

Kronemer, Alexander, and Michael Wolfe. *Muhammad: Legacy of a Prophet*. Kikim Media and Unity Productions Foundation, 2002.

Liguori Faithware. *The Bible Library for Catholics*. Liguori, MO: Liguori, 1996.

Rains, Scott, ed. *Rule of Benedict Library: Primary and Secondary Sources*. Order of Saint Benedict, 1999.

The Friends of New Norcia. *The Abbot and the Sheikh: Abbot Placid Spear-ritt and Sheikh Mohammad Agherdien*. Three-disk audio set. 2007.

Index of Biographies